THE SCIENTIFIC STUDY & TEACHING OF ANGUAGES

D1882504

Owing to the antiquity and rarity of this book, certain pages are regrettably absent, and readability is compromised due to the blurring of the original text. If you possess any insights regarding the availability of these missing sections, kindly inform us. Your assistance is crucial in ensuring the completion of this significant work for the benefit of future generations.

THE SCIENTIFIC STUDY & TEACHING OF ANGUAGES

A REVIEW OF THE FACTORS AND PROBLEMS CONNECTED WITH THE LEARNING AND TEACHING OF MODERN LANGUAGES WITH AN ANALYSIS OF THE VARIOUS METHODS WHICH MAY BE ADOPTED IN ORDER TO ATTAIN SATISFACTORY RESULTS

HAROLD E. PALMER

GYAN

Published by

Gyan Publishing House
5, Ansari Road
Daryaganj, New Delhi-110002
Phone: 011-47034999, 9811692060
E-mail: books@gyanbooks.com

Distribution Network
gyanbooks.com
India, USA, Canada, UK, Australia

© Publisher

All rights reserved. No part of this work may be reproduced, stored, adapted, or transmitted in any form or by any means, electronic, mechanical, photocopying, micro-filming, recording or otherwise, or translated in any language, without the prior written permission of the copyright owner and the publisher.

ISBN: 978-93-7447-095-4 (PB)

First Published, 1917

2nd Impression 2026

Printed at: Gyan Press, Delhi.

The book is sold subject to the condition that it shall not, by way of trade or otherwise, be lent, resold, hired out, or otherwise circulated without the prior publisher's written consent.

THE SCIENTIFIC STUDY & TEACHING OF LANGUAGES
Author: HAROLD E. PALMER

THE SCIENTIFIC STUDY & TEACHING OF LANGUAGES

THE SCIENTIFIC STUDY & TEACHING OF LANGUAGES

A REVIEW OF THE FACTORS AND PROBLEMS CONNECTED WITH THE LEARNING AND TEACHING OF MODERN LANGUAGES WITH AN ANALYSIS OF THE VARIOUS METHODS WHICH MAY BE ADOPTED IN ORDER TO ATTAIN SATISFACTORY RESULTS

By

HAROLD E. PALMER

LATE ASSISTANT IN THE PHONETICS DEPARTMENT
UNIVERSITY COLLEGE LONDON

LINGUISTIC ADVISER ATTACHED TO THE JAPANESE
DEPARTMENT OF EDUCATION

AUTHOR OF "THE PRINCIPLES OF LANGUAGE STUDY"
ETC.

GEORGE G. HARRAP & COMPANY LTD.

LONDON TORONTO BOMBAY SYDNEY

DEDICATORY PREFACE

LONDON: *January*, 1917

To MONSIEUR EDOUARD MATHIEU

MY DEAR MATHIEU,

There was once a time, in a past now very remote, when you, Georges Bevernage, and I came together in conference. All three attracted by the same subject and moved by the same impulse, we passed our leisure in examining a particular aspect of what we came to call ' the Linguistic Problem.'

During the course of our long walks in the Hertogenwald Forest and of our wanderings on the Great Moor we would talk of many things: of language and its nature, of the dialects spoken around us, of sounds and spellings, of teaching and learning, of teachers and pupils, of methods good, bad, and indifferent.

They were heart-searching talks, for we were terribly in earnest; we judged and tested many theories, and found them good or found them wanting.

Our association in matters linguistic continued and developed. At the Société Polyglotte or at the Mutuelle we would preach reforms and carry glad tidings of phonetics, of ergonics, or of semantics.

We would read Sweet, Jespersen, and Bréal, and comment on what we read, we would discuss the latest articles in *Le Maître Phonétique* and *Modern Language Teaching*. So free from prejudice were we, and so open were our minds, that we would accept and reject the doctrine of the Direct Method at least once a year.

You will remember our search for the one true standard and universal method, the goal that ever seemed so near, and yet which ever proved just beyond our grasp. You will also remember the day when we formulated our conclusion: *Ce n'est pas la méthode qui nous manque ; ce qui nous manque c'est la base même de la méthode.* Out of this arose the question, *Does the Science of Linguistic Pedagogy exist?* We regretfully concluded that it did not.

You it was who exhorted me to go seriously to work with a view to laying the foundations on which the science of language-teaching might some day repose. You reminded me of the exceptional facilities that I possessed for research work. You pointed out that I had an unlimited number of all sorts and conditions of pupils upon whom to practise and experiment, that my position gave me full scope and liberty to innovate, to amend, to modify, and to reform, and that I enjoyed a special immunity from inspectors, directors, and objectors in general.

Your advice was good ; I started on an organized series of researches, submitting all sorts of methods to all sorts of tests under experimental conditions. The normal 'preventive' course was differentiated from the special 'corrective' course ; the ergonic method gradually developed, although then without a name ; the replacing of the traditional orthography by the phonetic transcription produced the splendid results that we had foreseen ; three distinct methods of 'conversation drill' resulted in fluency with accuracy ; the respective principles of the 'Microcosm,' of 'Catenizing,' and of 'Substitution' began to stand out clearly, and various types of exercises were designed, each one having its appropriate and distinct function to perform.

Eight or nine years have passed since then ; several times I have been on the point of making known the results of these experiments, but on each occasion I have realized that this would have been a premature step. There were, as you know, gaps in the chain of reasoning, there was a lack of co-ordination between the various parts, there were 'previous questions' still unanswered, and my data were voluminous but not well proportioned.

During all this time your new career deprived me to a large extent of your help and collaboration, but you would still at times listen with a patient ear while I outlined the latest developments of these many systems of teaching and the results of the latest phase of each. Your shrewd comments served to crystallize into concrete form what had hitherto been nebulous, and your suggestions would inspire me to new activities.

More recently I have been successful in isolating the several factors of which the sum constitutes what we used to call *le désespoir du débutant*. This has resulted in the respective principles of 'Segregation,' 'Passive Work,' and 'Subconscious Comprehension.'

In the meantime, however, the tragic events of August 1914, commencing by the sudden and unexpected irruption of the invaders in the streets of our town, put an end to our association, and, incidentally, deprived me of the documents that I had so laboriously collected. Some months passed before I was able to pick up the threads of the work so dramatically interrupted.

When I did so, it was in another place and with another environment. The conditions were not unfavourable, and I was enabled to gain a first-hand knowledge of linguistic methods as practised in England. What struck me most here was to find such abundant signs of a new spirit in the language-teaching world. The whole atmosphere seems charged with new and healthy ideas; these are spreading sporadically from I do not know how many centres; there is an unmistakable movement toward what we have termed *scientific* and what others term *organized* methods. For the first time in my experience I have the satisfaction and relief to find myself in agreement with a large and increasing number of my contemporaries.

A few months ago I had the pleasure of reviewing a book entitled *How to Learn a Language.*[1] In this the author states and explains those principles to which we gave the names of 'Catenizing,' 'Immediate Fluency,' and 'Substitution.'

In the current number of *Modern Language Teaching*[2] appears the review of a recent publication. In this most inspiring article (every word of which I enthusiastically endorse) the writer sets forth some of my most cherished ideas. The book

[1] By Thomas F. Cummings, D.D., New York.

[2] December, 1916. By S. A. Richards.

which is the object of his review[1] enunciates principles in favour of which I have long striven, and exposes some of the identical fallacies which it has been my joy to pillory.

In short, I am confident that we are not far from the day when our aspirations will be realized, and when we shall see, not the one universal standard method of our earlier dreams, but one universal set of principles from which will be derived a number of methods, each perfectly adapted to the particular end which it is designed to serve.

In a recent letter you ask me for the latest news concerning the work in which you were so interested. You ask whether I have succeeded in correlating the various aspects of the problem in one homogeneous system of linguistic pedagogy. My answer takes the form of the present book. I have been able to reconstruct the body of it from memory, and to augment the original documents by a large quantity of new material, and have finally ventured to submit it as my contribution to the literature of linguistic pedagogy.

I have not been entirely without assistance during this last stage; two friends of mine, Mr A. B. Winnifrith, M.A. (Principal of Clapham Grammar School), and Mr Thomas Beach (Kilburn Grammar School), to whom my most cordial thanks are due for their timely help, have given me some valuable hints and have helped me in many ways. Mr J. E. Mansion (Educational Adviser to the publishers of this book) and others have very kindly helped me considerably in what is to me the intolerable burden of the revision and reading of proofs.

In conclusion, my dear Mathieu, I dedicate to you this volume, in remembrance of the happy period of our first collaboration, as a token of our common interest in an engrossing subject, and as a mark of that sympathy which has always subsisted between us.

HAROLD E. PALMER

[1] *The Teaching of Modern Foreign Languages by the Organised Method*, by Hardress O'Grady.

CONTENTS

SYNOPSIS

In order to facilitate reference, the consecutive numbered paragraphs of this synopsis serve as headings to the consecutive thirty-nine Sections of this book.

PART I: INTRODUCTORY

Section 1.—Does the science of language-study exist? (*P.* 19.)

Section 2.—Evidence of various kinds shows that this subject has not yet attained the scientific stage, but is so far in the experimental or empirical stage. (*P.* 19.)

Section 3.—It is time that language-study should be placed on a scientific foundation, and to that effect it would be well to institute a general inquiry into the whole question. (*P.* 21.)

Section 4.—The results of our inquiry must necessarily be of interest to method-writers, to teachers, and to students. (*P.* 24.)

PART II: THE NATURE OF LANGUAGE

Section 5.—Language is a series of natural phenomena. (*P.* 29.)

Section 6.—Language is distinct from the art of literature. (*P.* 30.)

Section 7.—Language consists essentially of lexicological units popularly supposed to be *words*, but the term *word* is vague and impossible of definition. (*P.* 32.)

Section 8.—What is called a word generally proves to be but an accident of graphic continuity. (*P.* 37.)

Section 9.—Let us rather speak of Lexicological Units, and note that they may be Monologs, Polylogs, Miologs, or Alogisms. (*P*. 39.)

Section 10.—Let us classify these units according to the respective principles of Morphology (with its subdivisions), Semantics, and Ergonics. (*P*. 42.)

PART III: PRELIMINARY FACTORS OF LINGUISTIC PEDAGOGY

Section 11.—A complete and ideal language method has a fourfold object, and this is *to enable the student, in the shortest possible time and with the least effort, so to assimilate the materials of which the foreign language is composed that he is thereby enabled to understand what he hears and reads, and also to express himself correctly both by the oral and written mediums*. (*P*. 47.)

Section 12.—In order to determine the best programme for a given student, we must take into consideration four subjective factors: (*a*) The student; (*b*) his previous study of the language; (*c*) his preliminary equipment; (*d*) his incentive. (*P*. 48.)

Section 13.—We must also take into consideration five objective factors: (*a*) The language to be studied; (*b*) the orientation of the study; (*c*) the extent of the study; (*d*) the degree of the study; (*e*) the manner of the study. (*P*. 58.)

PART IV: THE PRINCIPLES OF LINGUISTIC PEDAGOGY

When we are in possession of full information concerning the student and his aim we may prescribe for him an appropriate programme of study. This programme will be drawn up more or less in accordance with a series of principles which we may term *the Principles of Linguistic Pedagogy*. (*P*. 71.)

Section 14.—*The Fourfold Aim of the Student*. In all but special cases the ultimate aim of the student is presumed to be fourfold—namely,

(*a*) The understanding of the language as spoken by natives.

(*b*) The understanding of the language as written by natives.
(*c*) The speaking of the language as spoken by natives.
(*d*) The writing of the language as written by natives. (*P*. 71.)

Section 15.—*Segregation.* In order to exclude confusion and misunderstanding, during the initial period of conscious study the phonetic, orthographic, etymological, semantic, and ergonic aspects of language must be segregated from each other and taught independently. In the process of subconscious study, and in the later periods of conscious study, such segregation is neither possible nor desirable. (*P*. 72.)

Section 16.—*Active* v. *Passive Work.* Study may be active or passive. The young child only comes to speak his native language after an 'incubation period,' during which he has passively received and stored up in his mind a considerable quantity of linguistic material. The same process may profitably be employed by the adult person in the study of foreign languages. (*P*. 75.)

Section 17.—*Semanticizing* (*i.e.* the conveying of meanings). There are four different manners or modes of conveying to the pupil the meaning of a given unit.

(*A*) By material association—*i.e.* associating the unit with that which is designated by it.
(*B*) By translation—*i.e.* associating the unit with the equivalent native unit.
(*C*) By definition—*i.e.* associating the unit with its definition or paraphrase (*i.e.* its polylogical equivalent).
(*D*) By context—*i.e.* giving examples of its use. (*P*. 77.)

Section 18.—*Learning by Heart* (*i.e.* memorizing or catenizing). Learning by heart is the basis of all linguistic study, for every sentence ever uttered or written by anybody has either been learnt by heart in its entirety or else has been composed (consciously or subconsciously) from smaller units, each of which must at one time have been learnt by heart. We may term *primary matter* all units learnt by heart integrally, and *secondary matter* all units built up or derived by the pupil from *primary matter*. (*P*. 103.)

Section 19.—*Gradation*. In order that the pupil may proceed by the line of least resistance, he should pass from the known to the unknown by easy stages, each of which will serve as a preparation for the one immediately following. (*P*. 119.)

Section 20.—*The Microcosm*. In order that the pupil may reach the 'point of transition' with the least delay, the vocabulary must be selected with the greatest care and perspicacity; it should include none but the commonest and most characteristic units, representing the most important ergonic classes. A vocabulary of this nature may be termed the Quintessence or the Microcosm of the language. This Microcosm should be formed and organized systematically in accordance with and as a compromise between the principles of Frequency, Ergonic Combination, Concreteness, Proportion, and General Expediency. (*P*. 122.)

Section 21.—*Subconscious Comprehension*. The pupil's powers of subconscious (or immediate) comprehension will be developed concurrently with his conscious study of the microcosm, and quite independently of the matter contained therein. (*P*. 131.)

PART V: AN IDEAL STANDARD PROGRAMME

Having reviewed the main principles of Linguistic Pedagogy, we will now endeavour to draw up a working programme embodying the conclusions suggested by our inquiry. We will consider as a standard programme that which will prove to be the most suitable for school-children. It will comprise the study of the foreign language (which we will assume to be French) in its oral and written aspects with a view to active and passive use. The whole period of study will be divided into three stages. (*P*. 138.)

Section 22.—The first or elementary stage, of the duration of at least one term, will consist of:

(*a*) Easy exercises in subconscious comprehension.
(*b*) Imperative drill.
(*c*) Easy articulation exercises.
(*d*) Easy exercises in the use of phonetic symbols.
(*e*) Simple talks on the five lexicological theories. (*P*. 138.)

Section 23.—The second or intermediate stage, of the duration of from one to three years (according to the radius of the microcosm), will consist of:

(*a*) More advanced exercises in subconscious comprehension.
(*b*) Articulation and fluency exercises.
(*c*) The assimilation of primary matter by means of various catenizing devices.
(*d*) The production of secondary matter by means of a large number of varied exercises based on etymology, semantics, and ergonics.

During this stage the traditional spelling will be introduced and taught by means of various types of orthoepic exercises. (*P*. 168.)

Section 24.—The third or advanced stage, of the duration of from one to three years, will complete the scholastic training of the pupil. It will consist of:

(*a*) Subconscious work (rapid reading, mental and oral; listening to talks, stories, and lectures).
(*b*) Free composition (descriptions of objects, pictures, and events).
(*c*) Free translation (French into English and English into French).
(*d*) Conversation.
(*e*) Systematic study of texts. (*P*. 198.)

Section 25.—We may append here a comprehensive and descriptive list of most of the types of exercises which will be found of use during the three stages. While many of them are suitable for work in the class-room, they will generally be utilized as material for homework and for private study. (*P.* 207.)

PART VI: SPECIAL PROGRAMMES

Section 26.—In that part of this book devoted to the Preliminary Factors of Linguistic Pedagogy, we have seen that no one programme can possibly be ideally suitable for all classes of students; hence, in addition to the Standard Programme that we have just described, we must be prepared to draw up Special Programmes. *Limited Programmes* of various types are designed to meet the special requirements of those whose aim is less than the four aspects of a given language. (*P.* 225.)

Section 27.—*A Documentary Programme* is designed to meet the special requirements of those whose aim is not the assimilation of a language in any or all of its aspects, but a documentary knowledge only. (*P.* 228.)

Section 28.—*Corrective Programmes* are designed to meet the special requirements of those who have previously studied the language in so disproportionate a manner that one or more of the four aspects has, or have been, totally or partially neglected, or of those who have previously studied the language in so defective a manner that the unsound knowledge so acquired will have to be converted into sound knowledge. (*P.* 230.)

PART VII: THE FUNCTIONS OF THE TEACHER

Section 29.—The first qualifications of the expert teacher are a knowledge of the foreign language and of the student's native tongue, and the ability to organize the programme, to choose the appropriate material and the most appropriate means of conveying and of inculcating it. (*P.* 238.)

Section 30.—Another function of the teacher is to furnish explanations. (*P.* 243.)

Section 31.—The vehicular language for all explanatory matter should be that which is best known by the student. (*P.* 249.)

Section 32.—The teacher should foster and encourage the

pupils' capacities of visualization by adopting for explanatory purposes the principle of visual correlation. (*P.* 251.)

Section 33.—Further functions of the teacher are :

(*a*) To cause or to stimulate the pupil to work.
(*b*) To give the pupil opportunities of hearing the language spoken, and to act the part of second person in a conversation.
(*c*) To act as examiner, to award marks, and to correct errors. (*P.* 261.)

Section 34.—A very important function of the teacher is to react against the six vicious tendencies to which all students are more or less subject. (*P.* 263.)

Section 35.—In order to perform effective work, the teacher (or student) should have at his disposal an adequate number of the right sort of instruments in the form of a practical library for reference and other purposes. (*P.* 265.)

PART VIII : THE STUDENT

Section 36.—There are two categories of students who are necessarily the architects of their own programme or method :

(*a*) Those who are unable to command the services of any teacher whatever.
(*b*) Those to whom the services of casual or non-expert teachers are alone available. (*P.* 268.)

Section 37.—The relations between teacher and student in point of authority can only be determined in accordance with certain delicate factors, among which are the relative degree of expertness possessed or claimed by either, the particular end that the student has in view, and the inducement which the pupil is prepared to offer in order to secure the unconditional and unqualified services of a docile teacher. (*P.* 272.)

Section 38.—The least satisfactory type of student is the one who has neither confidence in the programme suggested by the teacher nor the capacity for working out one of his own. He is the source of constant trouble, and we should do well to advise him to seek another teacher. (*P.* 274.)

PART IX: CONCLUSION

Section 39.—May all those who have followed us in our inquiry so unite and co-ordinate their efforts that language-teaching and language-study shall be placed once for all on a stable and scientific basis. (*P.* 281.)

THE SCIENTIFIC STUDY & TEACHING OF LANGUAGES

PART I

INTRODUCTORY

Section 1.—Does the science of language-study exist?

Does the science of language-study exist? "Of course it exists!" some readers may answer. "Was it not initiated, created, discussed, fought for, and finally established by the leaders of the Reform Movement years ago? Is not the principle of the Direct Method an accomplished fact? Have we not witnessed the introduction, growth, and triumph of the Phonetic principle? Do we not find the text-books of the science of language-study in every teacher's library? Has it not been proved that grammar should be taught inductively, that translation is a delusion, that the dictionary is a snare? Has not "the aunt of the Dutchman in the garden of the baker's brother" been consigned to the limbo of forgotten things? Are we not living in the age of object-lessons, pictures, and the total exclusion of the mother tongue? Are we not . . . ?" Just so, just so; all these things have come to pass, and many others also; reforms have been effected, many bad things (and some good things) have been swept away, many good things (and some bad things) have apparently come to stay.

Section 2.—Evidence of various kinds shows that this subject has not yet attained the scientific stage, but is so far in the experimental or empirical stage.

If the science of language-study exists and is generally recognized in the same way that other sciences are recognized, then the majority of trained teachers will be found to be working on the same lines, differing only in minor details. But the most superficial inquiry tends to show that the methods of teaching adopted in any one country are almost as numerous as the teachers themselves; that each conscientious teacher has his own particular views on the subject and is prepared to maintain them against all comers; that the divergences of views are not on questions of detail, but are based on totally different conceptions of the whole problem.

If the science of language-study exists, it must have been founded in accordance with the scientific method, which is:

(*a*) To collect isolated facts and factors in such numbers as to cover the whole field of inquiry.

(*b*) To classify, examine, and correlate them.

(*c*) To draw from them certain conclusions upon which the fundamental principles may be established and stated in categoric terms.

(*d*) To confirm and justify these principles by putting them to the test of actual and continual practice.

Has this been done ?

If the study of language is a science, countless isolated facts covering the whole field of inquiry must have been collected, sifted, and correlated; valid conclusions must have been drawn in such a manner that the principles of the science have stood forth, each clear, unequivocal, and unassailable.

If the study of language is a science, a scientific terminology must have been formed and must exist, consisting of an adequate number of terms both old and new, all accurately defined by the creators of such terms and perfectly understood by all who use them.

If the study of language is a science, then definite and complete answers must exist to a vast number of vexed questions of which the following are specimens:

What is the function of the teacher ?—of the pupil ?—of the book ?—of the exercise ? What do you understand by Translation ?—by Grammar ?—by Semantics ?—by Function ?—by Words ?—by Direct Method ? How many types of exercise exist, and how may they be classified? What are the main differences between a 'preventive' and a 'curative' language course? What are the various vicious tendencies toward which all language-learners are more or less inclined, and which are the most efficacious means of reacting against each? Under what conditions is the use of the mother tongue permissible?—reprehensible? On what principles should the author of a language method choose the material to be presented and taught? To what extent should the reference-book and language method be combined? Problem-solving *v.* Memorizing the solutions to problems: when should the pupils do either, and why? Upon what axiom must we base all considerations of language-study?

If the study of language is a science, then where is the textbook which will give us the answers, the true answers, the logically reasoned answers to these and to hundreds of similar questions of equal importance?

If we follow out this train of reasoning and reflect seriously on the varied aspects suggested by the above questions, we must inevitably come to the conclusion that the study of language learning has not yet emerged from the empirical stage, that we are still groping our way in a labyrinth of factors the extent and nature of which we are only just dimly beginning to realize, that our progress is hindered at every step by undefined and ambiguous terms, that our way is beset by side issues, down which we wander and lose ourselves anew.

The science of language-study does not exist, but it is high time that it *should* exist.

Section 3.—It is time that language-study should be placed on a scientific foundation, and to that effect it would be well to institute a general inquiry into the whole question.

The main object of this book is to sketch out the lines upon which research work might well be undertaken, to suggest a suitable terminology, to set forth the data which the writer has collected over a period of sixteen years' work, both as teacher and as student, and to state the conclusions which he has drawn from them.

To lay the foundations of the science of language-study it will not be necessary to make new discoveries; it will be quite sufficient to collect factors which are perfectly well known and to co-ordinate them into one comprehensive system. Of data we have a sufficiency; philologists tell us what language is, phoneticians can give us the most accurate information concerning sounds and the methods of teaching them, most of the essential facts of grammar can be explained clearly by grammarians, and the nature of words, including their etymological, morphological, semantic, and ergonic aspects, is already known to the lexicologist. Modern pedagogy has shown us the value of concretization, and psychologists can supply us with all the data we require concerning the laws of memory. Our new science will consist of a compilation of facts culled from these several domains, but placed in such order and with such observance of proportion that the inevitable conclusions will suggest themselves. If our facts are right, and if no essential fact is missing, our conclusions must be valid. Most of our facts will so bear the imprint of obviousness that their citation will border on the trivial, and yet it is only by insisting on the perfectly obvious that we can arrive not merely at dogmatisms, but at valid conclusions.

Our survey of the problems must be on a most comprehensive basis; we must not be content with stating formulæ for the teaching of French to English children; our outlook must embrace the study of any aspect of any foreign language by students of all ages and nationalities. We shall certainly not discover any one royal road to success, but we may in all probability determine a number of paths, each being the shortest and easiest route to the particular end toward which it is intended to lead us.

In comparing various processes of study or tricks of pedagogy we must be careful not always to apply them to problems that we have already overcome, but to test them by problems in languages which are strange to us. A difficulty once overcome appears in its new perspective of so simple a nature that we wonder however it could have seemed so formidable. Those who use French verbs or German adjectives with that complete unconsciousness that can only result from a perfect mastery fail to realize the months of patient effort devoted to their study. Most of us have the illusion that these and other things came to us naturally and automatically. That is why the language that we are learning always seems far more difficult than any of those which we have already learnt. It has often been stated quite seriously that some of the more modern forms of artificial language (in reality the quintessence of logic and simplicity) are more difficult of acquisition than German or Russian. The fancied facility of difficulties overcome by us can only be compared with the fancied difficulties of problems in store for us.

A teacher is impatient because a pupil cannot memorize a French sentence in five minutes; let that same teacher endeavour in five minutes to memorize a sentence of corresponding length in Arabic or Chinese, and he will discover that his impatience was ill warranted.

The familiar must necessarily give an impression of facility, just as the unfamiliar conveys an impression of extreme difficulty.

For this reason the reader should not consider as superfluous the various devices and exercises suggested as methods of overcoming certain difficulties in French or any other language perfectly known to him; before pronouncing them efforts to *enfoncer des portes ouvertes*, let him apply them to the mastery of problems pertaining to Finnish or Swahili.

Our inquiry might take the form of a comprehensive account of all the language methods in use in all countries and in all ages; it might include detailed reports gathered from an analytic examination of the various linguistic programmes followed in schools both in England and abroad. But in view of the extremely divergent character of all methods of language-study, and of the seeming absence of any really fundamental principles, it will probably be more to the point if we first endeavour to ascertain the basic principles upon which an ideal method should be founded.

Section 4.—The results of our inquiry must necessarily be of interest to method-writers, to teachers, and to students.

The science of language-study must necessarily be of the highest interest to all engaged in the teaching or the learning of foreign languages.

These fall under three headings: (1) Writers of methods; (2) teachers; (3) students.

In most methods or text-books destined to convey the material of a language to the student we find a preface in which the author implies that his particular work is superior to all others.

If we submit to a critical analysis the various arguments employed and the various reasons adduced, we must come to the conclusion that every one of these works is well meant and that the intentions of each author are admirable.

Each claims to follow the line of least resistance, and each asserts or more modestly hints that his way is the one true way.

One will show that his method is based on Grammar and must therefore be sound.

Another will call attention to his system of imitated pronunciation, or 'phonetics,' as he miscalls it.

Others will confess that no written characters can possibly convey any notion of the true pronunciation of a language and therefore abandon all idea of making them do so.

In another case the author is proud to announce that as translation is an untrustworthy process, the meanings of the words are given by definition and the use of the mother tongue entirely avoided.

In the contrary case stress is laid on the fact that every word is accompanied by its translation.

Some of these books are based on literary and etymological considerations.

Others give such a full treatment to the phonetic aspect that all the other aspects seem to have been forgotten.

Others claim to teach the most difficult language within a stated period; six months it may be, or six weeks. These seem to be based on the assumption that the pupil will be prepared to work twelve hours a day and is incapable of forgetting a single fact once read.

We find guides and manuals, companions and helps, all implicitly claiming to be based on common-sense principles.

This provokes the obvious question: What are common-sense principles? Is it sufficient for an author to compile a list of some few thousand words and their 'translations,' supply a few dozens of fragmentary 'rules,' and garnish with a hundred or so 'exercises'?

Has the method-maker done his duty by taking some text more or less literary, adorning it with comments and 'notes,' and appending a vocabulary? Is it sufficient to furnish the rules of grammar and syntax and to call these the 'directions for use' of the language in question?

A favourite proceeding seems to be to work out a number of formulæ (unknown to the native users of the language themselves) and to invite the students to convert these into living speech. A few examples are thrown in as a makeweight; not many, for fear of dulling the intellectual faculties of the pupil and tempting him to memorize instead of to think!

Is it a common-sense principle to treat the student as though he were a child about to embark on the study of his mother tongue?

Many of these methods are not at all badly composed; some of them are excellent. As far as they go, some of them succeed in their aims. Some people *do* succeed in learning foreign languages by their aid.

But a careful analysis will bring to our minds one evident conclusion: that there exist no generally accepted principles at all. There appears to be no distinct notion in the minds of the authors as to what the function of a language method is, no conception of the real work it is destined to perform and at what point the student is presumed to fly with his own wings. We gain an impression of praiseworthy efforts clashing one with another and of a general haziness and lack of co-ordinated system.

It is not astonishing, after all, that this should be so. The qualifications of a method-writer are often no more than a knowledge of two languages and the desire to make a book.

A missionary goes to some distant land and spends some years there in the exercise of his calling. Incidentally he learns the native language, an unwritten idiom, little known, one of those dialects which, in the absence of any dictionary or other written documentation, has to be 'picked up.' Linguistic work is not his profession; he is no phonetician and his knowledge of linguistics is based on recollections of his Latin and Greek grammars. With laudable endeavour and patience he will write a book for the benefit of those who come after him.

What can be expected of such a book? In other professions many years of intensive training are required, training in theory and practice based on accepted and incontrovertible facts; in the profession of method-writing no training at all would appear necessary.

When the author is not a phonetician, and is ignorant of the simplest laws of lexicology, when he has no clear idea of the functions of a method, when he is no psychologist and ignores the laws of memory, when he is even ignorant of the true nature of language, is it surprising that the result of his labours should savour more of rule of thumb than of science, and should bear on every page the mark of the amateur?

And yet it certainly must be possible to write a language method on scientific principles; it must be possible to discover beyond any doubt what really is the line of least resistance; it should surely be feasible to codify the hundreds of complex factors in the problem and to arrive at certain conclusions concerning them.

The reformation and standardization of language-study must be effected primarily through the writer of methods, for a rational book, properly conceived and efficiently worked out, will show the teacher what to do, and when and how to do it, and the teacher in his turn will convey the results to the pupils.

For those reasons, for the sake of progress in a little-understood subject, for the sake of 'unified knowledge,' it is important that method-makers should come to an understanding; that the 'ploughing of lonely furrows' should be replaced by co-ordinated efforts to discover the best means and to adapt these means to the right end.

The teacher is often himself a method-writer; if he is not, he is generally a method-criticizer, for it is comparatively rare to find a teacher in complete agreement with the views of the author of the book he uses. The function of a teacher, however, differs from that of a method-writer. The difference bears an analogy to that existing between the tactician and the strategist.

The method-maker may work at his writing-desk or in his arm-chair; the teacher works in front of his class. It is the latter who is the personal link between the chooser of material and those who are destined to assimilate it.

Many factors in language teaching concern the teacher alone; the question of speed, the problems of cohesion, of stimulus, and of articulation are more particularly his. It is he also who has to carry out in actual practice the principles of concretization, of memorizing, of catenizing, and a host of other essential pedagogic processes. And he, like the method-writer, seems to work according to no fixed principles. He chooses the text-book, works out a programme, presents matter, provides exercises and tests, corrects mistakes, blames, congratulates or encourages, often without any clear notion of any determined starting-point or of any precise idea as to the particular end toward which he is supposed to be working. He cannot well do otherwise: if he works unsystematically it is because there exist few or no principles in system. If he suffers from a lack of training, it is because there exists no school or institution for the training of teachers.

Much has been written on the need of training; indeed it is obvious that a teacher without training in practical linguistics is in the same position as a doctor without clinical experience or a solicitor unversed in legal procedure.

Many congresses have been held, many reports have been written, the subject can boast a literature, and yet apart from that branch connected with phonetics we may search in vain for any text-book treating the subject comprehensively from starting-point to finish.

To the adult student of language the conclusions to be drawn from our inquiry must also be of the highest importance. If it is shown that fully three-quarters of the efforts that he devotes to study are not only ineffectual but are positively mischievous in their effects, if it can be proved that with less work a better result may be obtained, and if we can show how best he may utilize his effort by directing it into right channels, it will obviously be to his interest to become acquainted with the data we shall have collected, and the conclusions to which they point.

PART II

THE NATURE OF LANGUAGE

Section 5.—Language is a series of natural phenomena.

Language is the medium by which thoughts are conveyed from one person to another, consequently all words or combinations of words used orally or by writing must be considered as coming within the scope of language. It matters little to the student of linguistics whether any particular word or expression is sanctioned by classical authority; slang and pedantism, vulgarism and flower of speech, elegant expression and coarse metaphor, all these from the moment that they serve as effective mediums of thought are elements of language.

Language is the mirror of thought (if only the distorting mirror), and both reflector and reflected are conventional. In spite of the efforts of Pascal and Descartes, neither language nor thought is philosophical. Were it so, the units of thought would be fixed quantities, Roget's *Thesaurus* would be the universal text-book, and each operation of the mind would be a valid syllogism.

And there would be no more wrangling.

Thought is irregular, its concepts or units are irregular, there are redundancies and lacunæ, in all terms but the mathematical there is ambiguity, the declarative and the emotional are hopelessly involved, and misunderstanding is the rule and not the exception.

We are probably not yet civilized enough to have learnt to think.

Language is the dim reflection of thought, and, paradoxically enough, it is at the same time the instrument of thought.

To fit the word to the thought in our own native language is at times a thankless task, but when we compare our English concepts with those manufactured abroad, doing so perforce with the medium of those impossible national units called words, it is a marvel that the machinery of thought does not break down under the strain.

Each language possesses a set of terms called words; these may be combined and recombined into propositions and thereby thought becomes manifest to all who have learnt to play with the same set of counters. But when we go to the foreign country, or when the foreigner comes to ours, we find that we are playing with counters that have no currency. Hence the language problem.

Universal language would replace the diverse national counters or coinages by one international system of general currency. International language would produce a convenient auxiliary coinage easily convertible into the various national systems.

At present, however, language stands in the domain of natural phenomena, its development and evolution generally depend, not on the artifice of man but upon the dictates of fashion. We speak, not according to abstract laws of logic; we simply speak as others speak. It is the exception rather than the rule for man to make the words he uses; he is content to use the words that have already obtained currency in that particular part of the globe in which he finds himself.

The only aspect of language in which the conscious will of man can manifest itself is that concerned with its graphic representation. The alphabetic aspect alone is artificial; the literary aspect is artistic, the rest is natural science.

Section 6.—Language is distinct from the art of literature.

There must necessarily be a fundamental difference between *language* and *literature*. In spite of this difference the two terms have become almost inextricably mixed in the minds of the uninitiated; when we discuss questions connected with language, most people immediately turn the subject into the channel of literature.

How many people really study pure philology, *language*? How many really know anything about it? And yet everybody who has been to college imagines himself qualified to pronounce the most definite opinion on the subject. What people generally learn is the literary aspect of language, either their own or foreign.

Literature is an *application* of the linguistic science, but it is not the science itself. Literature is the history and practice of the written form of a language which has become classical. It is even maintained by many that a language which has no written form is not a language! It has often been stated that language does not exist apart from the written characters of orthographic tradition!

The linguistic science known as philology is a comparatively recent one; it is as yet barely a century old. It began when it was discovered that languages are subject to evolution in sound, in form, and in meaning, it began when it was discovered that each language possessed a parent language from which it had come by slow evolutionary change. For, one day, the truth began to dawn on the minds of the thinkers that not only had French been gradually evolved from the popular Latin of Gaul, and that Italian and other Romance languages were modern offshoots of Latin, but that every language possessed at least one parent, that Latin itself, instead of being a god-given speech, was simply the daughter of some unknown mother, that Greek was not fatherless, that there are children languages and ancestral languages, that there are sister languages, and that languages possess uncles and cousins!

And so the pure science of language was founded (founded on phonetics, by the way, although phonetics was in a rudimentary state at the time). Literature was found to be, not language itself, but an *aspect* of language, intimately connected with it but still merely an application, the *decorative* side of language.

Let us remember, however, that literature has always been *par excellence* a pedagogic study, that this subject has centuries of tradition behind it, whereas philology is modern, only studied by the few, and is not yet a current or obligatory subject. At school or at college we only study the literary aspect of language. We study the classical authors, we justify our forms and phrases by the literary models. We learn grammar, but the grammar we study is only the collection of classical models of the written language. The French Academy reigns over the French language considered as literature; it is a *literary* and not a *philological* authority. We might even say literature is the artificial aspect of language; those who make use of literary forms when speaking are said to 'speak like a book'; we feel these forms to be unreal? Beautiful? Yes, beautiful, but not the normal colloquial speech of everyday life.

Now, as we would not consult a sculptor on a question of geology and as we would not quote an artist as an authority on colour chemistry nor maintain that the best singer is at the same time the best throat specialist, we must not quote the opinions of *littérateurs*, of professors of literature, nor even of grammarians, and produce these opinions as proofs of philological truths or untruths. We must not claim or proclaim Academicians as philological experts, because they are not, and they do not pretend to be. They know (or they ought to know, if they have received an elementary scientific education) that literature is not language, nor language literature.

The learning of foreign languages must proceed on a philological basis and not on a literary one, because before we can learn the foreign literature we must be acquainted with the language itself, just as when we started learning the literary form of our own tongue we were already acquainted with the language itself.

Section 7.—Language consists essentially of lexicological units popularly supposed to be 'words,' but the term 'word' is vague and impossible of definition.

Considered from the point of view of the student, the study of language is synonymous with the study of the elements or units of which it is composed. These units are popularly assumed to be *words*.

A general and vague idea exists that the study of a given language should proceed on a double basis: lexicology, or the study of words, and grammar, or the study of their mutations and combinations. A little reflection, however, will convince us that this is far from being a true and logical conception of the problem. It will be found that the two subjects are bound up with each other and interdependent, and that they can only be differentiated by doing violence to each. The words themselves and their attendant phenomena cannot be separated except by invoking the arbitrary.

And after all, what is a word? What possible definition can we frame which will be adequate to describe what we understand by this term? In what cases must we assert that two given words are independent entities, and under what conditions are we entitled to consider as one word any two or more units intimately connected either in form, function, or meaning?

This is a fundamental question of identity and must be understood clearly before we can proceed to any form of classification.

Is the word *go* identical with the word *goes*? The answer is either affirmative or negative. Let it be affirmative. Let us say that *goes* is merely the inflected form of *go*, just as *trees* is the inflected form of *tree*.

Then if inflected forms are identical with the root word or etymon, *go* and *went* are one word. No; *went* is the inflected form of *wend*, now obsolete. But *went* is not obsolete, therefore one and the same word may be alive and dead at the same moment! But *went* is used as the preterite of *go* and for all purposes except etymological ones may be considered as the preterite of *go*.

If we concede this identity we are thrusting the thin edge of the wedge dangerously far.

There is a tendency to avoid the plural noun *corpses* and to substitute for it the term *dead bodies*; this term might conceivably become the effective plural of *corpse*. Shall we then be justified in saying that *dead bodies* is the inflected form of, and therefore identical with, *corpse*?

The word *ought* is, or was, the preterite of the verb *owe*. Are we to adopt the principle of "once a preterite always a preterite"? Let us concede the point and claim identity for *owe* and *ought*. But *owe* having lost its preterite formed a new one, and the preterite *owed* exists and is presumably identical with its etymon *owe*.

Puzzle: Find the relation between *ought* and *owed*, and

consider the absurdity of the situation when some time in the distant future *ought* has succeeded in forming a new infinitive of its own (He didn't ought to !).

Having got into an inextricable muddle, let us modify our first answer and declare that the inflected form of a given word has a separate existence, that *go* and *goes* are separate words. We can justify our new answer on perfectly rational grounds. From the foreign student's point of view *buy* and *bought*, *hold* and *held*, *tell* and *told* are almost as much separate words as *bell* and *bold* in that he may have learnt one and still be in ignorance of the other.

We are moreover justified when we consider that, after all, *hardly* is the inflected form of *hard* and they are obviously two different words, and that *sing*, *singer*, and *song* are obviously etymological cognates and equally obviously possess separate identities. Were this not so *drinker* and *drunkard* would be the same word !

But if this theory is true, it means that every French verb is a group of forty-seven words, that each Latin adjective is a group of thirty-six. And we shrink from the contemplation of such multiplicative statistics!

A middle course would appear to suggest that *regular* inflected forms must be considered as identical with their primitives, but *irregular* inflected forms as separate words. Hence *go* and *goes* are identical, as are also *tree* and *trees*, *long* and *longer*, but *give* and *gave*, *child* and *children*, *good* and *better* are separate words.

Even if it were possible to draw a sharp line of demarcation between regular and irregular inflexions, our compromise would be like all other compromises, unsatisfactory to all interests; but few of us would be bold enough to attempt the tracing of such a line. Moreover, which is to be the test of *irregularity*, the orthographic or the phonetic aspect of the word? for an inflexion may be regular in one but not in the other.

This is, however, not all. We have yet to consider the problems of semantic cognates—that is to say, significative varieties of one and the same word.

Bear (animal) and *bear* (support) are two distinct words with an entirely separate history; so also are *can* (be able) and *can* (metal box), *box* (case) and *box* (to fight with fists), *see* (perceive) and *see* (bishopric).

It does not need etymology to tell us that; our semantic instincts suffice to apprise us of such facts.

But *like* (similar to) and *like* (be fond of) are not chance resemblances, but true cognates; etymology tells us that these are not two different words, but two semantically differentiated varieties of one and the same word.

Have, in *I have it done*, is the same individual as *have* in *I have done it*. Can we then say that in *Je le donne à mon ami* and *Je le prends à mon ami* the preposition *à* remains the same individual although of directly opposite semantic value in the respective cases?

Two words then may be identical or entirely different individuals when considered respectively from the standpoint of etymology or of semantics. To the language-learner the significative distinction is everything and the historical identity nothing.

What does it matter to the English student that *devoir* (to have to), *devoir* (to owe) and *devoir* (duty) are historically identical? What does it matter to the foreign student that *like* (be fond of) and *like* (similar to) are cognates? The student of language (as opposed to the student of linguistic history) is concerned with the present-day semantic values, identities, and differences.

The only sane method of learning the English verb *get* would appear to be to separate it into its nine or ten semantic varieties and to teach each as a separate word.

Verbs such as *mind* (I don't mind minding the children, but they'll have to mind what I tell them, mind!) or *wear* (a cloth that will wear well = a cloth that will not wear. This hat is very much worn!) *must* be taught as if there were no historical identity between their significative varieties.

All these factors and considerations make our problem very complex, and well may we hesitate when asked to specify the number of words it is necessary to learn in order to make oneself understood in the foreign language.

In Chinese there is one hard and fast rule: every syllable is a unit and to each syllable is assigned a definite ideogram which serves to identify it.

Viewed in the light of European perspective, most of these units appear to have no semantic value until juxtaposed with others.

In many agglutinative languages, sentences and strings of significative syllables and 'words' are loosely grouped bunches of syllables as susceptible of cleavage and of combination as the figures in an arithmetical statement or the bits of glass in a kaleidoscope.

To sum up, we find ourselves in the presence of three separate factors, each of which precludes us from assigning any precise connotation to the term *word* and from determining even arbitrarily a convenient unit of speech without involving ourselves in a maze of contradictions, inconsistencies, and absurdities.

The first of these factors, which we may term the factor of *graphic continuity*, is manifested by our inability to demarcate on rational grounds affixes (as *-ness*, *-able*, *-less*, *-ful*, *-ly*), simple indecomposable vocables (as *dog*, *take*, *good*), compounds (as *sunlight*, *understand*, *lovely*), and intimate word-groups (as *of course*, *at last*, *leave off*, *last week*).

The second factor is that of *Inflexional Identity*. We cannot decide whether *tree* and *trees* constitute one word or two, nor whether *go—went—gone* is (or are) an entity or a trinity.

The third factor, which may aptly be termed the *Differentiation of Semantic Cognates*, tends to prove that one and the same vocable constitutes as many separate words as there are meanings contained in it, that *like* (similar to) and *like* (be fond of) are separate words, and that there is no more reason for unifying *keep* (retain) and *keep* (persist) than the two vocables *retain* and *persist*.

The object of the foregoing remarks is neither explanatory nor creative, but purely destructive. It may serve to bring about a certain desirable confusion of mind without which the necessity of a new terminology, or even of a new science, is not always apparent. It is only when we are convinced of the inadequacy of our present instruments that we aspire toward more perfect ones.

Section 8.—What is called a word generally proves to be but an accident of graphic continuity.

The factor which confuses the issue at the outset is that of Graphic Continuity. In theory this factor has little or no importance; it is a side issue, a mere orthographic accident, but as all our linguistic habits happen to be based on this convention it will require some little effort on our part to view it in its true light and proportion, to assign to it no more than the importance it deserves.

Is the entity or oneness of a word to be determined by the fact that it is or is not *written* without a break? If so, then *matchbox* is one word and *gas fire* is not; then *cannot* is one word and *may not* is two; then French *quoique* is one word and *bien que* is two; then German *gehen aus* is two words and the infinitive *ausgehen* is one, as is also *auszugehen.*

In almost every written language (except perhaps Chinese) we find abundant proof that there is no consistent rule as to what shall and what shall not constitute a word. We know that all syllables were once independent words, that *lovely* used to be *love like,* that *understand* is a compound of which the units are *under* and *stand.* We know also that many, if not most monosyllabic English words were once compounds, that affixes have dropped off that were themselves words long before; we know that the Early English, Latin, and Greek forms of many of our dead syllables were living words, and that they in their turn were the clipped remnants of prehistoric words the form and meaning of which can be guessed but not guaranteed.

We know that the word of one century may have been a loose compound of the century before, and that before that it was two or more words, that in some future century it may become compounded anew and at a more distant future period may become a dead syllable and finally disappear.

We find that two or more words frequently juxtaposed have

a tendency to become joined graphically, and imagination, stimulated by our visual sense, considers them as one word. There is often a hyphened transition. Before *motor car* came to be written *motorcar* it appeared as *motor-car.* When we reflect upon the number of hyphened words in English we may form an idea of the number of compounds that will go down to our descendants.

A board upon which cups were placed was called a *cup board,* this passed through the hyphenated stage into *cupboard*; phonetic and semantic changes set in, and to-day the foreigner learns it phonetically as [kʌbəd] and semantically as "a piece of furniture or a recess with shelves and door suitable for containing or storing whatever can be put into it."

All this is fairly comprehensible and clear, and one might assume an orthographic law which enacts that "when a pair of juxtaposed words have another pronunciation than when not so juxtaposed, they shall be written not as two words but as one." Or we might assume alternatively or simultaneously that "when a pair of juxtaposed words acquire by such juxtaposition a special meaning not to be found in either word used separately, such words shall be written as one."

But no such laws would appear to exist. It is true that many isolated examples may be found which seem to justify our supposition (*cupboard, waistcoat, forehead, gentleman, Sunday, halfpenny, cardboard, sixpence, altogether, understand, workbox,* etc., etc.), but still more numerous examples will show us that if such laws exist the executive is apparently very lax in enforcing them. Witness *long way, leave off, blow up, pick up, hardly ever, scarcely any, of course,* etc., etc., all of which ought to be compounded as words. Witness also the unjustified compounding of *bedroom, gaslight, sunlight, teacup, teaspoon,* etc., etc.

Can this inconsistency be explained? Why *matchbox* but not *letterbox*? Why *teaspoon* but not *soupspoon*? Why *teapot* but not *coffeepot*? Why *gaslight* but not *gasfire*? Why *cannot* but not *mustnot*? Why *highways* but not *highseas*?

Is there any reason why *yesterday* should be one word, *last week* two words, and *to-day* or *to-morrow* doubtful compounds?

Why, in French, should *quoique* have the right of wordship but not *bien que*; *aujourd'hui* (*à+le+jour+de+hui*) is a five-barrelled word, *puisque* is one word, *parce que* is two!

The Germans make one word of *zweihundertfünfundzwanzig* and may therefore claim that their vocabulary is as unlimited as mathematical conception.

The English word *hopeless* is represented in French by *sans espoir*; *typewriter* by *machine à écrire*; *cherry tree* by *cerisier*. In English we write as three words *to go out*, in German we find *auszugehen*; *High Street* corresponds to *Hochstrasse*; *on my account* is represented by *meinerhalb*. The Spaniard considers and writes as one word *cójalo* where in English we insist on two words: *take it*.

Although these facts are, or should be, fully recognized by everybody, so patent and numerous are their manifestations, we often find students marvelling that *good evening* should figure in French as *bonsoir* and generally adopting an attitude either of passive resistance or of aggressive criticism when confronted with such phenomena.

Section 9.—Let us rather speak of Lexicological Units, and note that they may be Monologs, Polylogs, Miologs, or Alogisms.

The only way to avoid misunderstanding and self-contradiction is to make up our minds to replace the elusive term *word* by the three fixed terms *monolog*, *polylog*, and *miolog* whenever we wish to differentiate. If we observe this principle it will matter little what are the mutual relations and affinities between the three. We may leave it to hairsplitters (or hair-splitters, or hair splitters) to wrangle and to argue round and round the question of when a word is and is not a word.

It is sufficient for us that all miologs were once monologs and that monologs were once polylogs, that the polylog of to-day may become the monolog of to-morrow and the miolog of the day after and finish by disappearing altogether leaving nothing behind it but an *alogism*.

Monologs are words considered merely as conventional orthographic units of vocabulary in virtue of their being—

(*a*) Written all in one piece without any interrupting break or space;

(*b*) Separated by a break or space from the words with which they may happen to be juxtaposed.

EXAMPLES: *dog, mankind, good, beautiful, go, understand, of, slow, slowly, up, upstairs, instead, daresay, cannot.*

Polylogs are units composed of two or more *monologs* in juxtaposition but functionally and semantically equal to a *monolog.*

EXAMPLES: *garden city, in case, of course, in spite of, leave off, on Sunday, during the winter, every year, for a long time, in view of the fact that, as a matter of fact, hardly ever.*

Polylogs are often called *phrases, group-words*, or *word-groups.* The distinction between polylogs and monologs is purely arbitrary. A polylog may have a monolog as a translation (bilingual equivalence) or as a synonym (unilingual equivalence). Thus the polylog *leave off* equals in signification the English and French monologs *cease* and *cesser.*

Miologs are significative or functional units such as affixes and the more concrete inflexions. They are generally considered (but for no consistent reason) to be less than words, or as fractions of words.

EXAMPLES: *-ly, -ment, -less, -ful, -ed, -ing, -graph, -gram, -phone, -log* (or *-logue*), *-ism, -logy, -graphy, -ist, -er, -est. Mono-, bi-, multi-, poly-, uni-, con-, ortho-, in-, ex-, de-, re-, a-, 's, o'.*

The miolog is to the monolog what the monolog is to the polylog, or conversely the monolog is to the miolog what the polylog is to the monolog. There is the same problem as to what should and what should not be written monologically or miologically.

We may say that the French monological *parlera* equals the English polylogical *will speak*, or conversely that the English monological *will* equals the French miological *-era.* Or we may say that *did want* is the polylogical form of the monological *wanted*, or conversely that the miological *-ed* equals the monological *did.*

All of which considerations lead us to the conclusion that the accidental and transitory conditions of monologicism, polylogicism, and miologicism have no logical importance whatever in practical linguistics. The three forms of graphic continuity are interchangeable and interconvertible; monolog may be translated by polylog and by miolog.

The non-recognition of this principle constitutes what we may term the linguistic *fallacy of the monolog,* which consists in assuming that monologs alone have the right to be considered as words, that they alone have the privilege of a place in the dictionary, that they alone possess the quality of translatability and even of identity.

A most typical example of this fallacy is to declare that the word *longer* does not exist in French, that we have to say *more long.* All that this amounts to is that a certain idea is expressed in English monologically and in French polylogically, or conversely that French monologic *plus* becomes in certain cases English miologic *-er.*

Alogisms is the term we may use in order to designate those cases in which a given concept is expressed without the use of any concrete lexicological unit. Alogisms fall into three chief categories: (1) Position; (2) Stress and intonation; (3) *Sous-entendus.*

Instead of saying *tree which bears fruit* we may say *fruit tree,* placing stress accompanied by a certain intonation on the word *fruit*; in the former case we express the idea *which bears* by two monologs, in the latter case the idea is expressed alogistically.

In some languages, including English, this particular alogistic form of expression is common; in other languages it is not available. In English we say *coffee-cup, letter-box, post-office*; in French we must say *tasse à café, boîte aux lettres, bureau de poste*; the English alogisms are replaced by monologs.

I am going to my friend's contains an alogistic concept equivalent to the monolog *house* (curiously enough, in the French equivalent expression, *Je vais chez mon ami,* the concept corresponding to the monolog *to* is alogistic). *I gave the money to the man* may be expressed with an alogism as *I gave the man the money.* In English and other languages the interrogative idea is generally expressed, not by means of an appropriate monolog (such as the Polish *ći* or the Japanese *ka*), nor by means of a polylog (such as the French *est-ce que*), but alogically by inversion.

Dubitative questions are expressed in English by means of a rising intonation on the last syllable or syllables of the sentence:

The rising intonation is equivalent to the polylog *or not* and effectively replaces it. Interesting examples of this type of alogism are given and explained in an article in *Miscellanea Phonetica* (1914) by Mr H. O. Coleman, entitled "Intonation and Emphasis." A perusal of this article will show to what extent concrete lexicological units may be replaced by alogisms.

The lexicological units, then, may be considered in point of graphic continuity as *monologs*, *polylogs*, and *miologs*, and may also be manifested as disincarnate *alogisms*; of these four elements the matter of the written language is made up.

Section 10.—Let us classify these units according to the respective principles of Morphology (with its subdivisions), Semantics, and Ergonics.

The essential principle of *classification* consists of forming groups of individual units all possessing some common attributes. By using these groups we are enabled to teach and to learn facts on a wholesale scale; without such groups our acquisition of knowledge must necessarily proceed on 'retail' lines and such knowledge is of the 'ununified' order. It is only when we realize the nature of the agreements and differences shown by the scheme of classification that we may be said to understand the subject of our study. One of the first duties to be performed in our efforts to lay the foundations of the scientific study of language is therefore to proceed to a scientific classification of the units of which language is composed.

The lexicological units of a language, like all other entities conceivable by the human mind, may be classified in many different ways; each scheme of division constitutes what is known as a *basis of classification*.

The chief of these fall under the headings of *Form*, of *Meaning*, and of *Function*.

Morphology or Form (including Phonetics, Phonology, Orthography, and Etymology)

From the point of view of *phonetics* the unit of language is the *sound*. The phonetician is concerned chiefly with the classification of sounds according to the manner in which each is articulated.

From the point of view of *phonology* the unit of language is the *phoneme*. Each language possesses a set of phonemes; most of these generally coincide with the phonetic unit (*i.e.* the *sound*); others are or may be intimate sound-combinations, such as English [ei] (as in the word *day*) or German [ts] (as in the word *zehn*).

One of the differences between the *phoneme* and the *sound* lies in the fact that the sound is *absolute*, a thing-in-itself, a fixed quantity of a physiological and acoustic nature, whereas the phoneme is *relative*, not a fixed entity, but the result of a long historical development varying and variable in its nature. Thus the vowel element in the English unit *bone* may be considered phonetically as consisting (in the South of England) of the vowel-sounds [o] and [u], each of which is produced in a particular way by a particular position of the organs of speech. This same element considered phonologically is a phoneme of which one of the ancestral forms (Early English) was probably pronounced [ɑː], and of which the present-day pronunciation varies between two extremes [əu] and [oː].

From the point of view of *orthography* the ultimate unit of language is the *letter*; one or more of these may form a syllable, and one or more syllables may form that which is the general conception of a *word*.

From the point of view of *etymology*, the unit of language is the *etymon*. We may perhaps venture to define an etymon as "any group of significative speech-units cognate with each other and with their common ancestral form or forms." Thus English *dish* and German *Tisch* are etymologically cognate with each other and with a common ancestral (Latin) form *discus*. Similarly English *dry* is etymologically cognate with *drier, driest, dries, dried, drying, dryness, dryish*, and also with foreign and ancestral cognates, the whole group and succession constituting one *etymon*.

Most phenomena of *inflexion* in general (including conjugation proper and declension proper), and of *derivation*, come into the province of *etymology*, using the term in its more ancient and broader sense.

Semantics or Meaning

From the point of view of *semantics* the unit of language is what we may term the *semanticon*, or unit of signification. These units of meaning (or of thought) sometimes coincide with monologs, but may often be equally well expressed by means of polylogs or miologs; the monolog *again*, the polylog *a second time* and the miolog *re-* all serve to express the same idea.

Any group of linguistic units expressing the same or nearly the same idea may be called a *semantic group*, each member of which will be a *synonym* of the others. The three words *hardly, scarcely*, and *barely* are identical in meaning; they form a semantic group and are synonyms. It does not need an etymologist to tell us that the three words are of entirely different origin and history; they are distinct etymons. Except for the suffix *-ly* they differ from each other both phonetically and orthographically; their sole affinity lies in the fact that they all express precisely the same meaning.

A synonym however need not express precisely the same meaning as one of its fellow-members of the same group. In some cases we do indeed find pairs or groups of units so closely related in meaning that any one member may be used for another in any conceivable context. From these, however, we may pass almost imperceptibly to other pairs and groups less similar in meaning, until we finally reach examples in which only by a considerable stretch of imagination can the members be called synonyms.

A *definition* is nothing other than a polylogical synonym of what is generally a shorter unit (a monolog, for instance).

The admission into a semantic group of members from two or more different languages constitutes the basis of all *translation*, for a translation is simply a foreign synonym of a native unit or *vice versa*.

Ergonics or Function

Considered from the point of view of *grammatical function* or *analysis*, the unit of language can only be what we shall term the *ergon* (*i.e.* the unit of work). The ergon, like the semanticon, may be a monolog, a polylog, a miolog, or even an alogism.

Ergons may be classified according to their degree of completeness, ranging from those complete units called *sentences* down to ultimate units which we may term *insecables*.

Sentences are complete units of thought; they are decomposable into component parts (each of which may be still further decomposed) and may (as clauses) constitute parts of other sentences.

Insecables constitute fractions of greater ergons, but cannot themselves be decomposed into lesser ergons. Between these two extremes there are ergons of an indefinite number of degrees of integrity.

Were the number of sentences in a given language limited to a few hundreds, or even a few thousands, a student might reasonably be expected to learn them off by heart, and by so doing to become master of the language. The number of sentences, however, being infinite, recourse must be had to the study of their mechanism in order that from the relatively limited number of lesser ergons an infinite number of sentences may be composed at will.

It must not be thought, however, that the key to language-study is to be found by taking the insecable as a starting-point. Were the insecables of a given language of the same character as the ultimate units of mathematics, the building-up of sentences would be a mathematical operation. This, however, is not the case; insecables, like all other ergons, are purely arbitrary, they are not scientific units but conventional units, the insecable of one language may equal ergonically the compound of another.

Ergons may also be classified according to the precise function they perform in the sentence. Auxiliaries, finites, infinites, prepositions, modifiers, adjuncts in all their varieties, and the modifiers and adjuncts of these, all have their functional values and definite relations one toward another.

Strange to say, the science the object of which is to determine the relations between such groups, and to specify the manner in which greater may be built up from lesser ergons, is so far without a name. The terms generally used to designate this branch of linguistic science are *syntax*, *syntactic analysis*, *logical analysis*, *sentence analysis*, or *metaphysical analysis*. None of these terms, however, appears to meet the case. *Analysis* denotes but half the scope of this science, which is both *analytic* and *synthetic*. *Syntax* is more suitable, but unfortunately this term (as generally accepted) only considers classes of ergons such as *subject*, *predicate*, and *complements*, leaving to *etymology* the examination of their respective components.

To cover all the phenomena and operations connected with analysis and synthesis, from the sentence down to the insecable, and *vice versa*, we suggest and shall henceforth use the comprehensive term *Ergonics*.

Let us, then, sum up our conclusions by stating that language is made up of units considered variously as—

Sounds (the units of phonetics)
Phonemes (the units of phonology)
Letters (the units of orthography)
Etymons (the units of etymology)
Semanticons (the units of semantics)
Ergons (the units of ergonics)

PART III

PRELIMINARY FACTORS OF LINGUISTIC PEDAGOGY

Section 11.—A complete and ideal language method has a fourfold object, and this is to enable the student, in the shortest possible time and with the least effort, so to assimilate the materials of which the foreign language is composed that he is thereby enabled to understand what he hears and reads, and also to express himself correctly both by the oral and written mediums.

If somebody asked us point-blank, "What shall I do to become rich?" we should consider it a strange question and be tempted to give a flippant reply. If our questioner persisted in all seriousness in his inquiry, we should be obliged to reply in vague terms by advising him to adapt the right means to the desired end.

Were he then to inquire what are the right means, we should have to ask him to specify quite a number of points. We should want to know something about the seeker after riches, who and what he was, his age, what capital he already possessed, what was his trade or calling, to what extent nature and art had endowed his brain with money-making faculties, whether he had so far been a successful financier or a successful bankrupt.

When in possession of this information, we should have to ask the most pertinent question: "What do you understand by the term rich? For what is riches to one is poverty to another. Are you thinking of £500, £5000, or £50,000 a year?"

Only when we had received a full reply to our questions could we attempt to answer his, and even then we should find ourselves reduced to generalities and negative advice in the shape of a few dozen *don'ts*.

We find ourselves in a similar position when confronted with the question: "What is the best method of learning a foreign language?" We can only answer by the general formula quoted above as a heading to this section.

When pressed for details as to how this counsel of perfection is to be put into actual practice, we in our turn must submit our interrogator to a series of questions. Until we receive complete answers to these, it is impossible for us to suggest any precise lines on which to apply the general formula.

It is manifestly absurd to attempt to solve a problem the factors of which are unknown. These initial factors may be grouped under two headings, *subjective* and *objective*. The subjective factors concern the student himself; they constitute the personal equation. The objective factors relate to the end in view, the object to be attained; they constitute the linguistic aspect of the problem.

Section 12.—In order to determine the best programme for a given student we must take into consideration four subjective factors: (*a*) The student; (*b*) his previous study of the language; (*c*) his preliminary equipment; (*d*) his incentive.

(*a*) The Student

Our first three questions deal with the personality of the student, his age, temperament, and nationality.

Obviously the whole question of study is profoundly affected by the age of the student. The treatment which would suit a child ten years old will be most unsuitable for an adult student, and *vice versa*. The reasoning faculties of the adult will help him to overcome with ease many problems of an intellectual nature, and at the same time, according to the dictum that a little learning is a dangerous thing, will create for him all sorts of artificial difficulties and false analogies.

The adult will perceive dangerous analogies which will lead him astray. The child, whose reasoning faculties are comparatively undeveloped, will not fall into these traps. Two French pupils, one aged ten and the other twenty, make the acquaintance of the English verb *let* in the sentence *let me come*. The adult will associate *let* with his native *laisser*, and ere long will create artificial and un-English sentences such as

I wish to let my parcel here. The child with his restricted capacities of analogy has not associated *let* and *laisser*, and consequently will not misuse the verb in question.

As a matter of fact, the young child may be perfectly bilingual and yet unable to establish any bilingual equations. When the writer's daughter was six years old she could speak English and French with almost equal facility, but was never able to give the English equivalents of the simplest French words, or *vice versa*. If asked to point to the window, she would point to it; or if asked, "Montre-moi la fenêtre" she would do so. But when asked, "How do you say *window* when you are speaking in French?" there would be no other answer than a bewildered look. Then "Comment dis-tu *fenêtre* quand tu parles en anglais?" The same puzzled expression was the only answer. The child had formed no associations whatever between pairs of words which we are accustomed to consider as almost perfect translations. Things which were equal to the same thing were not yet equal to one another.

Thanks to the non-development of what we shall call *bilingual consciousness* there is little danger of the child's importing into one language the characteristics of another.

An adult Englishman hears the French word *peu*. He associates it immediately with the English sound in *purr*, and until corrected by an energetic application of practical phonetics will persist in pronouncing the two words identically. There is no danger that a young child will do this. In short, the younger the student the less will be his proneness to the six 'vicious tendencies' (each of which is described in Section 34).

The teacher must utilize and take full advantage of the precious factor of ignorance or the undeveloped powers of analogy, false or otherwise.

It is true that in the vast majority of cases the student will already have arrived at the age of reason and of false analogy. The factor of natural ignorance not being there to help us, it will be necessary to introduce tactics the object of which will be to induce an artificial ignorance so that the adult may not be unduly handicapped by his faculties of reasoning. With this we shall deal when we come to consider the functions of the teacher.

The temperament of the student is a factor which must be taken into consideration. The tactics that will suit the plodding, patient, and unimaginative will not be efficacious when applied to the nervous, energetic, and imaginative type. Those who work by fits and starts with strenuous activity are capable of efforts unknown to the dull but patient plodder. An impatient genius will tire of a programme worked out for the use of a steady worker ; the tricks and devices invented to circumvent the vagaries of the bad learner will be a source of useless irritation to the student who has no need of them. The expert assimilator, clamouring for new words to conquer, is in a different position from the sluggish learner, to whom a dozen new words will give a severe attack of linguistic indigestion.

In class-work, of course, this factor and many others besides will have to be partially or totally neglected. No two members of a class possess the same temperament, but the exigencies of such teaching will necessitate a general treatment calculated to suit the average case.

The nationality of the student is sometimes of importance. Certain races seem to possess the faculties of language-study in a greater degree than others. The Latin races, it would appear, are generally less adaptable than the Germanic. Scandinavians, Flemings, Hungarians, and others whose mother-tongues are not in universal currency would seem to be better favoured with the innate gift of linguistic study. These, however, are problems of comparatively little importance in our present quest.

(*b*) The Previous Study of the Pupil

There is a world of difference between the raw beginner and the pupil who already has a nodding acquaintance with the language. The former may to a certain extent be compared with the child; his perceptive faculties have a fair start, he is less likely to fall into the traps of defective analogy. Ask an Englishman to pronounce the French word *bon*. If he has no knowledge whatever of the language it is more than likely that his reproduction will be tolerably exact. If, on the other hand, he is already familiar with the word (more especially in its orthographic form), his performance will probably be unsatisfactory. It is very interesting to note what takes place when a class of beginners includes a member who has already acquired a few superficial notions of the language. Unspoiled by defective cross-association, the beginners will tend to attach the right pronunciation to the words they learn and to give them their true semantic value, whereas the more 'advanced' member will rely on his old associations and amuse his fellow-students by his blunders.

If such previous study has been extensive, our student will fall either into the category of the advanced worker (in which case he must be transferred to an advanced class), or into that of the spoiled learner (in which case he must be transferred to a special class and be given special corrective treatment).

Which of the two alternatives will best suit his case must be determined by a series of tests—in other terms, an examination. If his former teacher worked according to sound principles, his efforts seconded by a rationally composed book, it will be possible to place the student in the first category. But if his former training has been defective such a course will probably not be expedient. He may have studied under a teacher who himself had an inadequate knowledge of the language, in which case he will have inherited his teacher's defects. His book may have been one of those monstrosities which pass off a caricature of the language as the real article. In this case he will have the exceedingly difficult task of unlearning everything and effacing from his mind all the false associations that he has acquired. His degree of knowledge must be expressed by a minus instead of by a plus, and to be strictly logical we should give him a course of memory-obliteration (if such a process were possible) until he has attained the state of ignorance already enjoyed by his fellow-students.

(c) The Preliminary Equipment of the Student

Calligraphy.—If our student is illiterate he will be unduly handicapped in his efforts to learn the language. If he has never learnt to use a pen or a pencil it will be impossible for him to take notes or to write exercises; if he has never learnt to read he will be unable to make use of a book. Although conceivable, it is hardly possible that we shall ever be confronted in this country by students lacking this essential preliminary. In remote lands, however, this may be the rule rather than the exception. The missionary giving a course of English to adult Polynesians must come face to face with this factor. A somewhat similar situation is necessarily present when the student has no notion of the script forms of the language he is setting out to learn. The study of literary Chinese may necessitate a preliminary course in which we learn to hold and to use the native writing-brush and to rub our 'Indian ink.' The converse is certainly the case. The European may be permitted to trace his Chinese characters with a European pen, but the Chinaman will not find it convenient to write English and French with a native brush!

The English boy or girl of ten years of age may be so badly endowed with the art of using a pen, that the writing of legible matter is an impossibility. Nor are adults always perfect penmen. It is difficult to correct the exercises of a student whose writing is so bad that he himself is unable to decipher it!

The art of using a pen or a Chinese brush forms no part of language-study proper, but is certainly an essential preliminary to it.

This is such a patent fact that it would hardly seem necessary to call attention to it; indeed, we only do so in order to specify clearly what we are to understand by an *essentially preliminary study.*

Oral Imitation.—This is another essential preliminary to the study proper of language. For general purposes it is more important to possess the faculty of imitating speech than to be an expert penman, for while we recognize the arbitrary or artificial nature of writing, the imitation of a speaker is a natural gift which although possessed by every one in his infancy has become wholly or partially atrophied in the case of adults. The very young child learns a most extensive vocabulary in the form of useful sentences purely by the method of imitation. Listen to the babblings of a child of eighteen months; note how he listens and with what fidelity he reproduces, in spite of his rudimentary articulation, all he hears; vowels, stress, and intonation, all are reproduced with accuracy; consonants and diphthongs are yet a little above his articulatory powers, but these will come a little later. To the English child of eighteen months it matters little whether the sentence to be reproduced is a native or foreign one. Uninfluenced by any written forms, with no cross-associations to confuse the issue, the child goes on day by day imitating the speech of his elders, until he becomes a speaking machine of which the parts have each learnt their respective functions.

When his innate powers of oral imitation have played their part, as soon as he becomes a fully articulate creature with a vocabulary sufficient for everyday use, these powers of reproduction by ear seem to weaken, and at an age varying between five and ten they have become dormant. If at the age of ten the child begins to learn a second language it is no longer with the precious aid of his imitative faculties. What he does is to liken the foreign sounds to his own, to hear his English *ay* (in *pay*) where he should hear the French *é*, to reproduce French *eau* (in *l'eau*) in the guise of his English *ow* (in *low*).

This is not true for all cases. A minority, a very small minority, of children retain this power of imitation; others who have lost it may regain it with some facility; hence among language students we find a certain number who are able to imitate foreign speech, just as they imitated in their infancy those who spoke what has become their native language.

In addition to the two extreme types, those who can imitate anything and those who can imitate nothing, there would appear to be a rather curious intermediate type. The writer has known many cases in which Belgians with a marked Walloon pronunciation go to Paris and after a stay varying between a few months and a few years return to their own country perfectly able to speak Parisian. But although these people were able merely by exercising their latent faculties of imitation to acquire the pronunciation of a cognate dialect, they were unable to utilize them in order to acquire a passable pronunciation of English. The writer would note here the curious case of an Englishman who was able to produce perfect imitations of any English dialect and could reproduce to the exact tone the various street cries of the French town in which he lived, but who, during the course of his French lessons, was unable to produce any but the most Britannic sounds.

It is more than probable that the inability to use these latent powers of imitation is due more to shyness and to unconscious restraint than to any physical obstacle. If it were possible to react against this sense of restraint, if it were possible to produce a state of natural *abandon* with a supreme disregard of self-ridicule, each of us might become an imitator with the same success as in our infancy.

If the student with whom we are dealing is one who can imitate, the muscles of whose vocal organs are 'tuned' to his auditive perceptions, then he will already have overcome the greatest obstacle to the acquisition of a foreign language. An ideal imitator is an ideal language-learner, for correct auditive perception and correct oral production are the natural bases of all true language-study.

Those who have lost their early faculties of oral reproduction must be prepared to reacquire them, else will their progress be as that of the snail, or at best as that of a crab or a waltzing mouse.

The faculty of correct reproduction is not only of phonetic importance, but it has a most direct bearing upon the whole process of study, which, as we shall see later, reposes on a groundwork of perfectly memorized sentences. Without these there is no real progress whatever, and without the faculty of correct reproduction, memorizing is a slow and almost impossible process.

A Knowledge of the Theory of Language.—A valuable asset in studying the structure of a foreign language is a rough but working knowledge of the nature of language itself. Its value, it is true, is more of a negative than of a positive nature, for if this knowledge does not go very far in the direction of furthering the student's progress, it will at least show him many of the pitfalls which beset his way and will expose most of the linguistic fallacies. The more the student is the victim of the six 'vicious tendencies' the more necessary it is for him to possess the knowledge which proves them to be vicious. Those who imagine words to be homogeneous units, each with a fixed semantic value determined by its etymology; those who consider the phonetic aspect as a mere offshoot of the written; those who mistake literature for language, whose knowledge of semantics and ergonics is confined to a pocket dictionary and classical grammar, such students are in sore need of a course of language theory, including precise (even if concise) notions as to the nature of words, sounds, functions, and meanings.

A Knowledge of the Theory of Study is closely allied to the point treated above and is complementary to it. In the same way that a knowledge of linguistics disposes of the fallacies of language, so may a knowledge of the processes of study dispel the illusions connected with the pedagogic side of the problem. Those who learn isolated lists of words will cease wasting their time in so doing when they realize the futility of such proceedings; those who learn grammatical rules by heart and imagine this to be the royal road to success will stop this practice when they clearly see this road to be a *cul de sac.* Few adult pupils will give themselves the trouble of memorizing sentences until they are convinced that this is the most direct road to the end they wish to attain, and of this they will certainly not be convinced unless they devote a few hours to the understanding of such pedagogic principles as do exist in the linguistic world.

A Knowledge of the Theory of Memory.—The last of the five subjects suggested as useful or even indispensable preliminaries is that connected with the laws of memory. Many students realize intuitively and with a perfect consciousness what it is necessary to do in order to remember the isolated facts the aggregate of which make up the sum of the required knowledge. For such persons no special memory course is needful, but for those who, despite their best efforts, are unable to assimilate knowledge it is a very useful thing to have a first-hand acquaintance with those laws which fall under the headings of localization, visualization, association, separation, analogy, concentration, catenizing, semanticizing, and assimilation.

Most people confess to a bad memory. Doubtless there do

exist cases in which the faculty of remembering is neither apparent nor latent, but in the great majority of persons there are wonderful, if latent, powers of memory. A short and simple course of training in most cases produces results which the uninitiated would be tempted to call miraculous.

The five factors *Calligraphy*, *Oral Imitation*, *Theory of Language*, *Theory of Study*, *Theory of Memory* make up the sum of what we may call the Preliminaries to Language-study. As we have already noted, none of these forms an essential part of the study of any particular language. A text-book of French for the use of English students will not include any one of them. Our inquiry, however, will plainly show that if these preliminaries form no part of language-study, they are very valuable outside auxiliaries and capable of rendering the greatest possible help to the student.

That is why, on examining in advance the mental faculties of our student, we wish particularly to know whether and in what degree he is conversant with these pertinent factors.

In that section of our inquiry which will treat exclusively of the Programme of Study we shall conclude that it will be a real economy of time and of effort for the student to acquire at least the outline of the leading features of these five subjects. It may be noted here that such acquisition is in the nature of a permanent investment, good for a lifetime, and a sound preparation for any number of languages. It is work which may be accomplished once for all, and it will prove to be of constant utility.

(*d*) Incentive

Before passing to the objective factors it would be well to know what is the incentive of our student. Is he going to learn in order to please himself, or for some exterior reason? The incentive is the mainspring of his mechanism of study; if he realizes that the successful attaining of the end in view is essential to his well-being, this alone will quicken his mental faculties and encourage him to supreme efforts.

In a very small number of cases the language itself constitutes the interest and the end in view; in the vast majority of cases the study of the language is looked upon as a necessary evil, only endurable on account of the reward which will attend its successful termination.

A decides to learn French because a knowledge of that language will further his interests by making him a more efficient clerk or salesman.

B comes to the same decision because it will give him greater comfort in his journeys abroad.

C will learn because the exigencies of competitive examination compel him to do so.

D has no choice; he goes to school and he must obey his teacher.

E determines to become a French scholar because it will enable him to read certain scientific works of which no English translation exists.

F is anxious to know French in order that he may enjoy the masterpieces of French fiction.

G intends to learn French because he is interested in philology and the structure of language.

So many men, so many motives.

Some of these will prove to be powerful mainsprings; others will be such poor incentives that artificial stimulants will have to be applied continuously by the teacher in order to make the machine go at all. To maintain that the sum of all these diverse incentives represents the total number of different treatments required to fit each individual case would be a manifest exaggeration. Since, however, we have set out to inquire into the nature of all the factors connected with language-study in order that the essential may be distinguished from the unessential, we must recognize, if only in abstract theory, the possibility of a vast number of courses open to us in accordance with the purely subjective factors in the problem. We must acknowledge that the student of even temperament, an expert penman, an artist in mimicry, an expert in the linguistic, pedagogic, and mnemonic sciences, unspoiled by previous defective study and possessing a powerful incentive, is more likely to study a foreign language with success than one who is his antithesis in every particular. We may even go so far as to say that such an ideal subject requires no teaching at all; place him in France and within three months he will speak like a native. We may venture to predict that his contrary counterpart will do nothing but waste his time and that of his teacher if he tries to learn a foreign language, and that his best course would be to relinquish whatever linguistic ambition he possesses.

On broad lines we may say that some pupils will need very careful handling and require us to take all possible precautions, whereas others may be left largely to their own devices without much fear of their contracting bad linguistic habits.

Section 13.—We must also take into consideration five objective factors: (*a*) The language to be studied; (*b*) the orientation of the study; (*c*) the extent of the study; (*d*) the degree of the study; (*e*) the manner of the study.

The following group of five factors concerns the object of study; we will therefore speak of them as the objective factors, as distinct from the four factors just examined, which concern the student himself and his capacities.

(*a*) The Language

The problem to be faced by a Frenchman about to learn Italian has a very different character from that encountered by an Englishman setting out to learn Hungarian. French and Italian are cognate or sister languages; English and Hungarian are not even distant relatives: the two tongues have nothing at all in common. The resemblances between two cognate languages constitute both a facility and a source of danger. French and Italian are very similar in structure, and by far the greater part of their vocabularies may be arranged in homo-etymonic pairs. That is to say, most French words have their etymological equivalent in Italian, which may generally be recognized at sight. When a Frenchman can take a long passage in Italian and decipher its meaning by converting each word into its French morphological equivalent, he may be excused for assuming that etymological and semantic identity are one and the same thing. To a certain extent also he may be justified in concluding that it is possible to speak and understand Italian while thinking in French. It will be difficult, perhaps impossible, for him to resist putting his theory into practice, and by so doing to become the victim of all the fallacies which militate against success in language-study; he will become a 'bad learner.'

An Englishman studying Hungarian will have no such temptation. On the face of it there is no possible etymological or morphological identity between Hungarian words and English ones. The superficial difficulty of the language will tend to force him to adopt a right line of study, just as the superficial facility of Italian will tempt the Frenchman into the wrong path. A paradox-loving Belgian pupil of the writer's once declared English to be far more difficult of acquisition than German. Written English, he said, looked so absurdly easy that it was impossible not to believe that it was a word-for-word transcription of French; its apparent facility discouraged serious study. German, on the contrary, was so different from French in every respect that all efforts at a similar method of translation were doomed to failure.

This shrewd observation concretizes the essential difference between a pair of cognate languages and a pair which are non-cognate. The former constitute a direct temptation to a vicious system of mechanical conversion; in the latter case the absence of morphological resemblance tends to a sounder system of study.

A pupil will be more docile and require fewer disciplinary measures when learning a language of a totally strange nature.

(*b*) Orientation

It is not enough for a student to state that he wishes to learn a certain language. Unless the teacher knows in what aspect he wishes to learn it, he and the pupil will soon be at cross-purposes. Each language may be said to embrace three groups of dialects. In addition to this, each language may be viewed from the point of view of its graphic or oral manifestation. Furthermore, an acquaintance with the language may be of a passive or an active nature. These three considerations, dialect, manifestation, and state, may be grouped under the common heading of *Orientation*.

Dialect.—Three sorts of dialects may be distinguished: regional, temporal, and social.

It must be clearly recognized that no language possesses an intrinsically standard form. That each language possesses an ideal 'correct' form from which all divergencies constitute 'impurities' or 'mistakes' is not only a popular superstition, but also one which is shared by the majority of academicians and literary experts. Nearly all Frenchmen are imbued with the doctrine that French is great, there is but one French and Littré is his prophet! As a matter of fact, French, like all other languages, is a mass of regional, temporal, and social dialects. Of these, one variety has become classic and artificialized under the auspices of the French Academy.

There are many English dialects. In point of space we have Southern English, North Country, Scottish, Irish, American, and Australian dialects, each of which contains numerous subdivisions.

Let it be understood that we use the term 'dialect' in the sense of a variety of a given language, the sum of which varieties constitutes the language itself.

Dialectal varieties include not only divergencies of pronunciation, but also differences in general lexicological aspects; we find in one dialect sounds, etymons, semanticons, and ergons unknown in the sister dialects. In short, the dialects of a given language bear the same relation to each other as do the sister languages of a given cognate group. As the Walloon dialect of French is to the Provençal dialect of French, so is Portuguese to Italian. There is but a difference in degree.

When we speak of the Spanish language we generally mean that one of the Iberian dialects known as Castilian. By German we mean that variety of Modern High German which its literature has caused to become classical. When we speak of the Chinese, Flemish, or Norwegian languages, we have no precise notion at all of what we mean.

Although no one dialect of a language is in itself intrinsically more 'correct' or 'purer' than its sister dialects, it is generally convenient to specify a so-called standard dialect and to consider it as the one most worthy of our attention. This standard dialect is generally defined as being the one which is spoken by educated persons in and within a certain radius of the capital or the centre of intellectual activity.

When the scene is placed in London the majority of the characters in a play by Shaw, Jones, or Pinero speak educated Cockney, and the books in which such plays are presented to the public in printed form are written in educated Cockney. Let us add that this will be the *colloquial* variety as distinguished from the *literary* variety of a leading article in *The Times.*

As modern literary English is based on the London or educated-Cockney dialect, we may consider this to be a convenient standard type suitable to be the object of study for a foreigner.

Similarly it is expedient to study Northern or Parisian French; the more discriminating will claim that even this dialect should be differentiated according to its subdivisions. As to those who claim a special 'purity' for the French of Tours, Blois, Lyons, or Liège, let us dismiss their talk as mere literary babblings having no weight in a serious linguistic inquiry.

No sounder precept can be given to the student than to assimilate the vocabulary (and all that term implies) of educated people speaking what is generally considered to be the standard dialect of the language.

Apart from *regional*, we are faced with *temporal* varieties of a given language. A Frenchman wishes to learn English. We may give him a number of lessons in modern educated Cockney and then discover that he wanted to follow the shortest path to Shakespeare! His requirements were concerned, not with the twentieth-century, but with the sixteenth-century dialect. He should have specified his requirements instead of assuming that in England to-day we speak the language of Shakespeare. To read the comedies of Molière or the fables of La Fontaine with a view to acquiring a knowledge of modern French is an example of misdirected energy arising from ignorance of the nature of the language. A case is known of a conscientious but short-sighted student who set out to learn modern French *via* Latin and the *Chanson de Roland.*

We may perhaps distinguish varieties of a given language neither of a purely regional nor of a purely temporal character. The difference between an article in *The English Review* and the speech of a Hyde Park politician is great. While the former tends toward elegant archaisms, the latter is garnished by homely allusions and vigorous metaphor of a most unclassical nature. "The old bloke didn't ought to say nuffink," compared with "The elderly gentleman ought not to say anything," "You ain't got no call to [bad word] off," compared with "There is no need for you to go," represent two varieties of speech of which the differences, being neither regional nor temporal, must be designated by a third term; we might call them *social* differences.

The Literary Style.—That style which is used in *written composition* and in public speaking.

It may be divided into 'strata' (to use the term of the late Henry Sweet), the highest of which is represented by the archaic language of poetry, the lowest approximating to everyday speech.

The study of the literary style is essential for students of literature and of written language.

Colloquial Style.—That style which is used in everyday conversation, in familiar letters, and in the reproduction of conversations.

The colloquial style may also be subdivided into various strata, the highest being the speech of educated persons when speaking to strangers, and the lowest being represented by the most vulgar forms of speech.

These social dialects may be classified according to the following scale: poetical and (practically identical with archaic) high literary prose; normal literary prose (the style of leading articles); high colloquial (as when speaking to strangers); normal colloquial (as when speaking to intimate friends); vulgar colloquial (as used by vulgar persons).

There is, of course, a gradual transition from one stage to another; they are not separated by hard and fast lines. Normal colloquial may become more and more slangy and less and less attention may be paid to its conformity with literary usage until it becomes vulgar. All five degrees may be both written and spoken: we may recite poetry, and in novels we may write vulgar talk.

The social dialects of most interest to the average student are those we have designated as *normal literary prose* and *normal colloquial.*

It must be perfectly understood by all students that no one of these styles is ever used by natives to serve both for literary and colloquial purposes. The French in general (and their *professeurs* in particular) maintain with sad insistence that good colloquial French and good literary French are synonymous terms. If this were true we should be forced to the inevitable conclusion that every Frenchman (including the members of their Academy) invariably speaks bad French except when in the pulpit and on the platform.

Similar superstitions exist in England. It is often stated that expressions such as "Have you got it?" "I don't know," "Who did you give it to?" are bad English, because they are not used in the literary dialect. We must conclude again that all Englishmen use bad English.

It matters little after all whether *bad French* and *colloquial French* are synonymous terms. What is important is clearly to realize that the general form of language used in everyday speech is a variety distinct from the literary, differing from it in all the aspects of lexicology from phonetics to semantics.

When the European sets out to learn Japanese he is told frankly at the outset that he must fix his choice either on the classical literary language or on the colloquial language, and is shown that the two differ as much as any two cognate languages.

If all students were informed that similar differences (although not in so marked a degree) exist between literary and colloquial French, English, Spanish, etc., there would be less time wasted in misdirected effort and we should no longer see pupils labouring at the acquisition of the *passé défini* and the *imparfait du subjonctif* as stepping stones to everyday spoken French.

In addition to the three groups of dialects to which we have given the respective names of regional, temporal, and social, we may perhaps also mention *artificial* dialects.

These are the varieties of a language as used by the majority of foreigners, various forms of 'pidgin' less known but just as real as the 'pidgin' English of the Chinese coasts. We mean by pidgin dialects such perversions as Franco-English (example: aï mék mi véri ouelle eunderstand hwenne aï gau inne enneglcunde"; or Anglo-French: "Zher swee commonsong der parlay Frongsay tray biang nayce par?").

Readers of that delightful book of Du Maurier's *Peter Ibbetson* will recall the quaint artificial dialects of English and French invented and spoken by 'Gogo' and 'Tarapatapoum.'

Strange as it may seem, the highest aspiration of many students on both sides of the Channel is toward monstrous dialects of this sort. How often have we heard apologies for these commencing "Voyons, c'est déjà quelque chose de pouvoir se faire un petit peu comprendre en anglais; on fait ce qu'on peut et, ma foi, on ne peut pas s'attendre à la perfection, quoi?; ce que j'estime, c'est . . ." and so on!

Obviously our inquiry and conclusions include no serious consideration of such views, nor countenance any such practices. Such students must be left to the mercies of the quack, and he alone will profit by their doctrine.

Manifestations.—Our thoughts may be made manifest through the spoken or through the written word. It is not necessary for us to compare the relative importance of each nor to insist upon their mutual independence (no, not *interdependence*!). What does concern us is the fact that for most students a knowledge of both manifestations is ultimately required, and that in special cases it may be expedient to learn one and not the other.

A correspondence clerk who receives orders from his employer to make himself acquainted with the contents of letters in the French department finds it imperative to make a special study of written French as used in modern business correspondence. If these orders are to be carried out in the shortest possible time, if his promotion and prospects depend upon such acquisition with the least delay, it is difficult to see why he should trouble himself with the phonetic aspect of colloquial French.

If, on the other hand, it becomes necessary for him to travel in France, to make himself understood at stations, hotels, and in offices, then it is equally difficult to see why he should confuse his understanding, spoil his pronunciation, and misuse his energy in learning the French orthographic tradition as applied to the classical or literary aspect of the language.

For those to whom both manifestations are to have their importance we shall probably discover on pedagogical grounds that it will be more expedient first to master the oral and later on to study the graphic aspects, and only in the advanced stages to progress simultaneously in both.

Active and Passive Use of Language.—Apart from all question of dialect, apart also from the question of manifestation, we have to consider two aspects of language which from their very nature require absolutely different treatment.

The use of a language, in the fullest acceptation of the term, implies the faculty of transforming thoughts into speech (both oral and graphic), and also that of transforming oral and graphic speech into thoughts. The former of these two operations constitutes the *active* and the latter the *passive* states of language. When we speak and write we use language actively; when we listen and read we are making a passive use of it.

Many persons are able to use language in one state and not in the other; their respective capacities depend entirely on the manner of their study and training. One who has read extensively and written little may have a passive command of the written language little inferior to that of his mother tongue; one who has listened much, who has frequented lecture-halls and theatres in the foreign country, will have so sharpened his auditive faculties that nothing of importance escapes his comprehension. But neither of these may be able to express his thoughts in the foreign tongue with any degree of facility or accuracy. If the language is a near relative of our own, we may at first sight make out the gist of an article written in it, but fail to reproduce a single word of it.

Conversely, a contrary line of study or experience may enable us to express our most urgent needs, and yet leave us unable to comprehend what is said or written to us in reply. It is possible to memorize a hundred or so of the most useful sentences and to use them successfully, but we have no guarantee that the natives will confine themselves to this limited repertory when answering us.

Although special cases may arise in which either of these aspects may be of far greater importance or utility than the other, we shall generally find that both are essential and are inseparably bound up one with the other. The correspondence clerk of whom we spoke may have received instructions to learn to understand the foreign letters received, and to answer them in English. But on the whole, let us repeat, the use of the language normally comprises the active and the passive aspects.

For certain pedagogic reasons we shall conclude at a later stage in our inquiry that passive work should precede active work; this was the case in our infantile study of the mother tongue.

(c) Extent of Study

The student who contemplates the acquisition of a small working vocabulary in order not to be entirely helpless when abroad is in a different position from the one whose aim it is to be able to use the foreign language like a native. Under the headings of *Incentive* and *Orientation* we have examined cases in which a partial knowledge of one aspect of a given language alone is aimed at. Many other examples can be framed, in which a very limited programme will cover all the requirements of a given student.

On the other hand, a large number of people set out to acquire the language in its entirety. The French wife of an Englishman comes to settle with her husband in England; she must almost necessarily become anglicized, and this process includes a continual progressive study of the language, so that in the end her knowledge of it will hardly be inferior to that of her own tongue. For those whose desires or interests induce them to become naturalized subjects of another country, the almost perfect acquisition of the foreign tongue is a necessity.

For such people time is not a pressing factor; they have years before them in which to pursue their aim. Although it is natural that they should wish to attain the desired end with as little delay as possible, a few weeks or a few months will not have the same importance as it has in cases where speed is the one essential.

When, on the other hand, some tangible results are required within a given period, when the successful issue of a business enterprise depends on the practical acquisition of a limited programme, every hour is of value; it is simply impossible to devote the same number of days, hours, weeks, or months to the formation of those sound linguistic habits which alone will afford ultimate perfection.

"Quelques notions d'anglais suffisantes pour permettre à quelqu'un de se tirer d'embarras" is a very different proposition from "Une connaissance approfondie de la langue anglaise sous tous ses rapports." To submit to one and the same programme two students the difference between whose respective aims is expressed above is to misunderstand or to ignore the golden principle of adapting the right means to the required end.

(*d*) Degree of Study

Apart from considerations of *extent*, we are faced with the problem of *degree*. While the former term is an expression of *quantity*, the latter expresses the *species* or *quality* of the desired knowledge.

Some students wish merely to learn about a language, others wish to assimilate the material of it. We may call these respectively the documentary and assimilative aspects of study. A philologist often finds it necessary to become acquainted with the peculiarities of the structure of a given language; he wishes to know which are the sounds it possesses, to understand its ergonic or semantic machinery. This information is necessary in order to support a theory, or to furnish examples of some linguistic principle. Just as one's native language can only be properly appreciated after one has viewed it from the foreigner's standpoint, so also the nature of inflected languages can only be understood by the aid of some acquaintance with non-inflexional languages.

The student of comparative phonetics, ergonics, or semantics will find it of inestimable value to have a rough theoretical knowledge of a large number of languages, as will also the teacher whose aim it is to give lessons to foreigners. For these and other reasons it often becomes necessary to obtain a first-hand documentation of certain languages without troubling to assimilate the matter contained in their vocabularies.

Here again we must be prepared to differentiate between two classes of students, and to provide programmes drawn up on entirely different bases in order to suit their divergent requirements.

A book setting forth the characteristics and peculiarities of the language in logical and grammatical order, treating exhaustively each point in its proper place, is an ideal reference work for all who are seeking a documentary knowledge. But such a book gives little or no help to those whose primary object is to assimilate the material of the language itself. For them the matter must be sorted and selected in order of frequency and utility, with due regard to the principles of proportion, ergonic combination, etc.

(*e*) Manner of Study

The last of the factors serving as the basis of our inquiry is that which concerns the means of tuition. The vast majority of language-learners work with a teacher; indeed, the teacher is generally considered so essential an instrument that it occurs to few that his presence is not absolutely indispensable. But in language-study, as in the case of other studies, self-instruction is not only possible, but in certain cases imperative. How, except by self-instruction, is the student whose home is a small English town or village to become acquainted with Arabic, Urdu, or Chinese?

There is, however, no hard and fast limit separating those who study with from those who study without a teacher. There are many degrees of self-instruction, varying from the case in which the student is wrestling with the mysteries of, let us say, Finnish, from a German-Finnish dictionary which he has picked up at a second-hand bookshop, to that in which he has subscribed to a correspondence course in French and receives his lessons and phonograph record weekly by post. The only difference between the subscriber to the correspondence course and the pupil who visits his teacher twice a week lies in the fact that in one case his instructions are conveyed orally and in the other by the written medium.

We may sum up our conclusions in the form of the two following axioms :

1. *Let the student determine in advance what is his aim.*
2. *Let the work of the student be directed in accordance with his aim.*

1. *Let us determine in advance what is our aim.*

When we take our ticket at the railway booking office we cannot always determine whether our journey will be long or short, easy or difficult, nor is it necessarily essential for us to know by what line or series of branch lines we shall arrive at our destination.

Our fortune on the road is more or less in the hands of the railway company. But one point we are absolutely forced to fix in advance, and that is the destination itself.

Before embarking on any enterprise, before undertaking any work, whatever difficulties may occur and whatever the nature of the obstacles that lie before us, the end we have in view, the purpose of our work, is perfectly clear to us.

So should it be when we embark on the study of the foreign language. It is not sufficient for us to say that we wish to learn French or Chinese or English ; we must determine what variety we wish to acquire, of what branch we mean to become the master.

Why do we want to learn the language ? As a manner of passing the time ? For reasons of curiosity ? Because we are impelled to do so for business reasons ? Because the literature of that language interests us ? In order to have direct access to scientific or technical books written in that language ? Because we wish to travel in the country where it is spoken ?

Do we wish to qualify for the post of interpreter ? Do we wish to be able to understand business letters ? Do we wish to write business letters ? Do we wish to make a speciality of the phonetics of the language? or of its grammar? or of its history?

Do we wish to become teachers of that language? Is it to enable us to pass an examination? Or do we wish to acquire a general knowledge of the language in its four aspects, speaking, understanding, writing, and reading?

Is our object the rapid acquisition of the most important elements, or have we the time for a leisurely survey of the whole of the language? We must determine our aim, for much depends on it.

2. *Our work must be directed in accordance with our aim.*

If we wish to make a study of the literary language, let us study the literary form and avoid the purely colloquial. If the ancient literature is our aim, let us study the ancient literary language. If the commercial language interests us, let us work in such a way that we shall be able to write and to understand business letters in the shortest possible time.

If the speaking and the understanding of the spoken language is not our aim, let us not waste time on this aspect. If, on the contrary, it is our sole aim, then let us not waste our efforts on the acquisition of the written form.

If we wish both to speak and to read, then let us study the two branches proportionately.

When the essential preliminaries have been mastered, let us aim directly at what we wish to accomplish. Let us master the elementary preliminaries, and then proceed directly toward the accomplishment of our object.

PART IV

THE PRINCIPLES OF LINGUISTIC PEDAGOGY

When we are in possession of full information concerning the student and his aim we may prescribe for him an appropriate programme of study. This programme will be drawn up more or less in accordance with a series of principles which we may term *the Principles of Linguistic Pedagogy.*

Section 14.—The Fourfold Aim of the Student. In all but special cases the ultimate aim of the student is presumed to be fourfold—namely,

(*a*) The understanding of the language as spoken by natives.
(*b*) The understanding of the language as written by natives.
(*c*) The speaking of the language as spoken by natives.
(*d*) The writing of the language as written by natives.

To many this principle will appear so obvious as to border on the trivial; to others it may appear a novel and revolutionary thesis. At first sight we might conclude that the partisans of the Direct Method will agree and that those of the Translation Method will disagree with this principle, but on further reflection we shall find that this is not necessarily the case.

In the opening pages of this book we suggested that most of the friction between the adherents of the various types of method is due to the fact that the first principles of linguistic pedagogy are so far undefined. Were it possible to determine sharply two opposing camps occupied respectively by the partisans of the Direct (or Reform) Method and those of the Translation (or Old) Method, we should probably find that the former tend to favour the principle as we have set it forth, and that the latter consider it either as a pernicious doctrine or as a Utopian counsel of perfection.

The old-fashioned (and now generally discredited) school of

linguistic pedagogy proceeded more or less in accordance with the following formula:

(*a*) Learn to decipher isolated sentences or texts by identifying *each etymon* with its supposed equivalent in the mother tongue.

(*b*) Reverse the process and convert isolated native sentences into foreign sentences on the same etymological basis.

Proficiency in this bilingual consciousness was considered to be the essential basis of all language-study, and was tacitly assumed to result ultimately in the power of reading, writing, speaking, and understanding the foreign language.

The modern school has done much to expose the fallacy of this conception; it proceeds on diametrically opposite lines, and assumes that foreign languages are to be acquired in much the same way as we have acquired our mother tongue. The various means suggested and adopted in furtherance of this plan are generally spoken of collectively as the Direct Method.

Although this modern school of linguistic pedagogy commands the respect of the bulk of modern language teachers, there is a growing feeling that the means generally adopted do *not* conduce to the ends which its founders had in view.

In many cases, indeed, the Direct Method, as used by the average teacher, resolves itself into the negative precept: *There must be no translation.* We may perhaps be justified in suggesting that the greatest reform is yet to come, and that the basis of this reform will be the formula that stands at the head of this section, including the all-important qualifying clauses "as spoken by natives" and "as written by natives."

Section 15.—Segregation. In order to exclude confusion and misunderstanding, during the initial period of conscious study the phonetic, orthographic, etymological, semantic, and ergonic aspects of language must be segregated from each other and taught independently. In the process of subconscious study, and in the later periods of conscious study, such segregation is neither possible nor desirable.

The principle of Segregation is the logical consequence of the fact that the student of language is pursuing simultaneously four entirely different ends, each of which may conceivably be subdivided. The types of work which are best calculated to ensure proficiency in the understanding of rapid speech are inoperative when used as a means of constructing correct written sentences; exercises devised to give the student command over his organs of speech will not further his power of understanding what he reads; ergonics cannot be taught on etymological lines, nor has orthoepy anything in common with phonetics; the art of making oneself understood is to be attained by processes appropriate for this end, but manifestly inappropriate for any other end.

Whenever we devote a determined period (be it one minute, half an hour, or six months) to the exclusive study of a given aspect of a language we are observing the principle of segregation. Whenever we teach two or more aspects simultaneously by means of one and the same form of exercise we are replacing *segregative* by *aggregative* study.

The phonetician requires his pupils to devote their entire attention to the recognition and to the production of sounds, excluding all considerations of their representation in the conventional spelling. By so doing he is insisting on the principle of segregation as applied to phonetics.

When we are demonstrating the precise *meaning* of a given unit we do not allow irrelevant inquiries as to its pronunciation or its ergonic powers. By so doing we are acting in accordance with the principle of semantic segregation.

Generally speaking, subconscious study is aggregative, and conscious study segregative. The former implies *diffusion* and the latter *concentration* of thought. The young child engaged at an early age in the development of his faculties of speech is doing so with perfect unconsciousness and without any regard to the principle of segregation. The adult student, grappling with problems of the etymological order, concentrates the whole of his attention to that which is the immediate object of his study, and by so doing observes this principle of segregation.

What is generally called *difficulty* often turns out to be

perplexity, *bewilderment*, or *confusion of thought*, a state of mind which precludes any possibility of effective progress. The remedy for this is to segregate the factors of confusion, and to direct successively the attention of the pupil to each of them in turn.

Just as subconscious study from its very nature requires the diffusion of the pupil's attention, so in conscious study should the pupil focus his entire attention on any phenomenon or group of phenomena to the exclusion of all extraneous factors.

In order to carry out the principle of segregation in an ideal programme the seven following precepts will be observed:

(1) *The phonetic aspect* will be taught by means of a series of appropriate exercises, the first of which will deal with isolated sounds, followed successively by those dealing with syllables, groups of syllables, and fluent sentences.

(2) *The orthographic aspect* will be taught by means of graduated exercises in reading, transcription, and dictation.

(3) *The etymological aspect* will be taught by means of graduated tables and exercises designed in such a manner as to demonstrate the mechanism of inflexions and derivatives.

(4) *The semantic aspect* will be taught by means of systematic exercises of various types based on material association, translation, definition, and context.

(5) *The ergonic aspect* will be taught by means of graduated and systematic exercises based on the ergonic chart.

(6) *Immediate expression* will be taught by means of systematic catenizing and substitution exercises.

(7) *Immediate comprehension* will be taught by developing the pupil's powers of subconscious assimilation in a regular and graduated series of passive exercises.

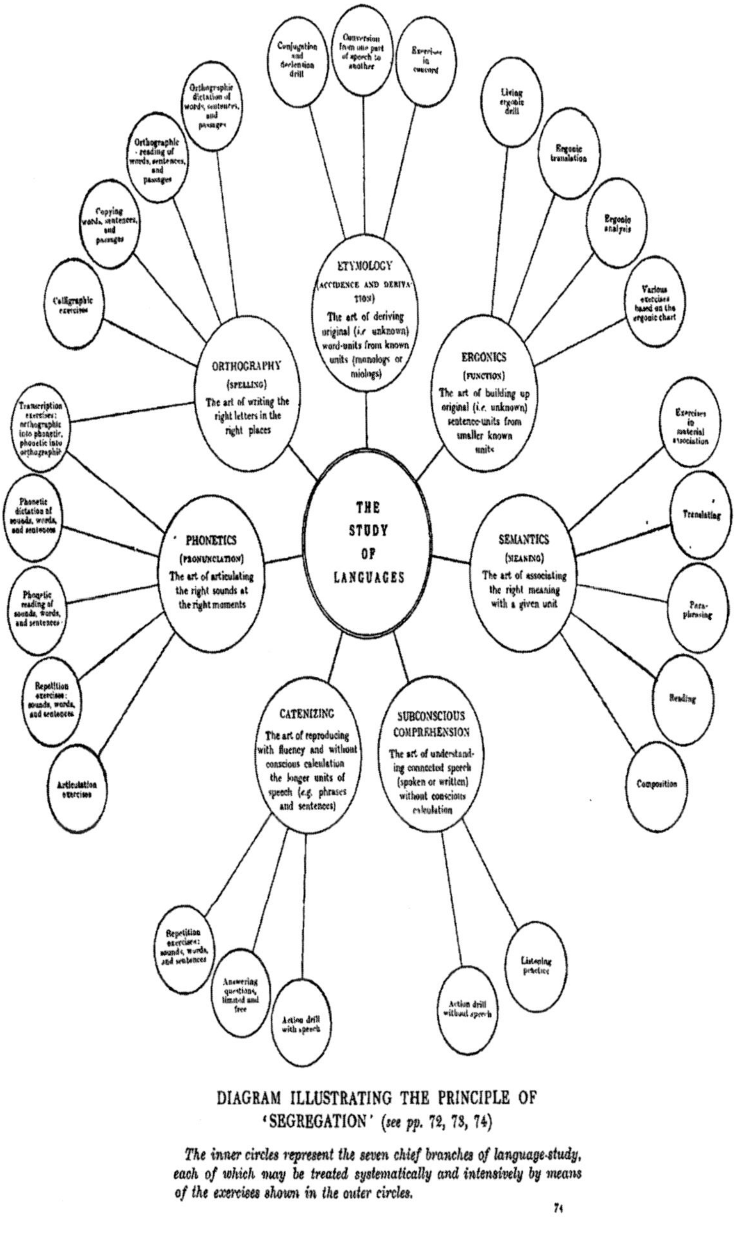

DIAGRAM ILLUSTRATING THE PRINCIPLE OF 'SEGREGATION' (*see pp.* 72, 73, 74)

The inner circles represent the seven chief branches of language-study, each of which may be treated systematically and intensively by means of the exercises shown in the outer circles.

Section 16.—Active *v.* Passive Work. Study may be active or passive. The young child only comes to speak his native language after an 'incubation period,' during which he has passively received and stored up in his mind a considerable quantity of linguistic material. The same process may profitably be employed by the more adult person in the study of foreign languages.

During the course of the last twenty or thirty years many systems of language-teaching have been designed, the object of which is to cause the language to be assimilated by processes similar to those by which each of us has learnt his mother tongue. In setting forth the manifest advantages of this over the purely artificial type of method, it has been rightly observed that the degree of success attained by adults in their efforts to acquire a foreign language is always in direct ratio to the degree in which they observe the natural laws of language-study. It has been pointed out repeatedly that most persons taking up their residence abroad acquire with remarkable rapidity and fidelity the speech of those by whom they are surrounded, *provided that they observe certain conditions*. These conditions are generally assumed to consist of the exercising of their powers of observation and imitation, unaided by such artificial processes as translation, etymological analysis and synthesis, or the mental conversion of written into spoken forms.

In support of this theory it has been pointed out that the illiterate often seem to succeed where the educated fail; that, other things being equal, the scholar will be handicapped by his developed intellect and the peasant will profit by his ignorance and unformed mental capacities.

A family of French people takes up its residence in England. A year later the younger children may be speaking to each other in idiomatic and fluent English; the older children also speak, but less in conformity with English habits of thought and articulation; the parents, if they speak at all, produce the usual French variety of broken English.

In view of the vast amount of cumulative evidence tending to prove this thesis, the compilers of methods appear to be justified in their efforts to organize programmes of study in accordance with it. One factor, however, seems to have been overlooked, a factor which in the opinion of the writer is the most essential of all, and the neglect of which constitutes an omission of the most serious kind. It is the undoubted fact that the *active* use of speech under natural conditions is invariably preceded by a period during which a certain proficiency is attained in its *passive* aspect. The faculty of recognizing and of understanding the units of speech is probably always developed by the child long before he ever reproduces them in order to make himself understood.

From a most illuminating work by M. Jules Ronjat, entitled *Le Développement du Langage observé chez un Enfant bilingue*,[1] we may note the following passage:

"Il se produit chez les enfants, tant qu'ils ne peuvent pas articuler, un emmagasinement et une sorte d'incubation. Ils s'assimilent le vocabulaire et la prononciation. Si bien que lorsqu'ils peuvent parler, ils ont dès le premier jour un vocabulaire de vingt, trente, ou quarante mots. Une petite fille française ayant eu une nourrice italienne qui parlait français avec un fort accent italien, s'étant mise à parler un mois après le départ de cette nourrice, a parlé français avec un vocabulaire dû presque entièrement à ses parents et une phonétique due à sa nourrice, la personne qu'elle avait le plus entendu parler dans la première année de sa vie. . . . Une petite fille allemande passe les dix-huit premiers mois de son existence en Silésie; elle n'y acquiert qu'un vocabulaire d'une extrême indigence. Elle est alors amenée à Berlin, où elle acquiert vers l'âge de trois ans un vocabulaire normal. Là, à l'âge de cinq ans, elle produit tout à coup des tournures silésiennes qu'elle n'avait plus eu l'occasion d'entendre depuis trois ans et demi; il est impossible d'expliquer leur présence autrement que par la persistance des impressions latentes *emmagasinées* pendant une période très reculée et où, chose remarquable, l'enfant ne savait pour ainsi dire pas parler."

During this *incubation period* it would seem that a vast number of units are 'cognized' in all their aspects: sounds, combinations, and successions of sounds, metamorphism, and the semantic values represented by all of these. We suggest

[1] Published by Champion, Paris (1913).

that success in the production on a wholesale scale of linguistic matter (either in its spoken or in its written form) can only be attained as the result of the previous inculcation of such matter by way of passive impressions received repeatedly over a period the length of which has been adequate to ensure its gradual and effective assimilation.

Passive work is not necessarily subconscious work, any more than active work is necessarily conscious. Passive work means listening and reading; active work is speaking and writing. We may listen and read consciously and subconsciously; we may speak and write consciously and subconsciously. In the case of our mother tongue the probability is that there is a vast preponderance of subconscious work, both active and passive; when the average person studies a foreign language the contrary is usually the case.

We would suggest that one of the essential principles of all methods designed on the 'natural' basis should be never to encourage nor expect the active production of any linguistic material until the pupil has had many opportunities of cognizing it passively. If this principle is valid, then most of the teaching of the present day violates a natural law!

Section 17.—Semanticizing (*i.e.* the conveying of meanings). There are four different manners or modes of conveying to the pupil the meaning of a given unit.

- (*A*) **By material association—*i.e.* associating the unit with that which is designated by it.**
- (*B*) **By translation—*i.e.* associating the unit with the equivalent native unit.**
- (*C*) **By definition—*i.e.* associating the unit with its definition or paraphrase (*i.e.* its polylogical equivalent).**
- (*D*) **By context—*i.e.* giving examples of its use.**

In view of the endless controversies which have raged and are still raging around the subject, it will be well for us to examine in detail the several confusing factors of that vexed question, *Under what circumstances and in what conditions is translation salutary or pernicious?*

To many the difference between the older methods and those

which are known collectively as the Direct or Reform Method is equivalent to the acceptance or rejection of translation as a means of teaching the signification of the units which are the object of study.

In order not to miss the point at issue, we must note that in this respect alone translation may perform two functions. The first of these is to *inform the pupil what a given unit means*, and the second is to *cause the pupil (by means of repeated exercises) to form a perfect association between the unit and its meaning.*

While some exponents of the Direct Method are fully prepared to admit or even to counsel the use of translation for the first of these purposes, others are not disposed to tolerate the presence of translation in any circumstances whatever. It has often been stated that the inclusion in any text-book of, let us say, a French-English vocabulary debars us from applying to such a text-book the term 'Direct Method.'

Let us proceed to examine the data upon which we must base our conclusions.

(*A*) Semantic Demonstration by Material Association

When the word or word-group designates concrete objects, qualities, or actions, the most direct manner of demonstrating its meaning is to pronounce the *word* while pointing to, touching, or handling the *object*, pointing to or otherwise suggesting the *quality*, and performing the *action* to which it corresponds.

We wish to teach the meaning of the words *la boîte*, *la clef*, *le crayon*, *la fenêtre*, *le tableau noir*. The most concrete and direct way of doing so is to point to, touch, or handle the objects in question: "Voilà la boîte; voici la clef; je prends le crayon; j'ouvre la fenêtre; je touche le tableau noir." To teach the colours, we may point to coloured objects, saying: "Ceci est noir; Cela aussi est noir; Cela n'est pas noir—c'est blanc. Voilà quelque chose de rouge; Voilà du bleu; ça c'est vert. Regardez le livre; il est vert. Regardez la boîte; elle est verte." To teach words designating dimensions we may hold up a long and a short pencil: "Ce crayon-ci est long, celui-là est court"; we may compare the size of two books and of two boxes: "Ce livre-ci est grand, l'autre est petit. Voici une grande boîte et en voici une petite," etc., etc. To teach verbs designating concrete actions we have only to perform the actions with a running commentary, such as: "Je prends le livre, je l'ouvre, je le ferme, je le mets sur la table; je marche, je m'arrête, je me lève, je m'assieds; je laisse tomber la craie, je la ramasse, je la mets dans ma poche," etc., etc.

"What does *s'appuyer* mean?" asks a pupil. We answer by leaning against the wall and saying: "Je m'appuie contre le mur." "What is the difference between *livre* and *cahier*?" asks another. We take the two objects represented respectively by these two words and say: "Voici un livre et voici un cahier; voilà encore un livre; cela aussi est un livre; cet object-ci n'est pas un livre, c'est un cahier; voilä encore un cahier"; or we may say: "This is *un livre* and that is *un cahier*. Look at the two objects. Is this *un cahier* or *un livre*? Do you write your exercises in *un cahier* or in *un livre*?"

This is demonstration of the most direct nature possible, and the most effective in practice, ensuring as it does the most concrete and most permanent impressions.

This mode may be expressed in graphic form:

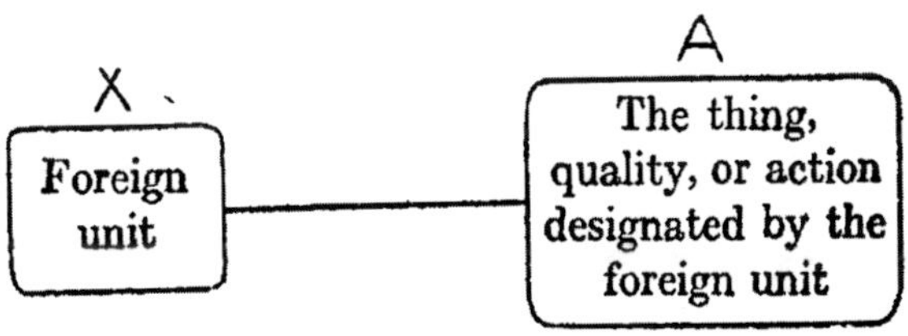

(*B*) Demonstration by Translation

This consists of associating the foreign word or sentence with the word or sentence of the mother tongue to which it most nearly corresponds.

Je ne comprends pas means the same thing as *I don't understand.* If ever you want to tell a Frenchman that you don't understand what he says, you may say to him: "Je ne comprends pas."

Venez ici means the same thing as *Come here.*

Lundi is the French name of the day we call in English

Monday. It may also mean the same as the English adverbial polylog *on Monday*.

Je ne m'en suis pas rendu compte means the same as *I didn't realize it*, or *I haven't realized it*.

Vous n'auriez pas dû le faire is equivalent to the English *You ought not to have done it*.

"What does *chapeau* mean?" asks a pupil. We answer: "It means *hat*."

"Does *brillant* mean *brilliant*?" . . . "No, not quite; it is just about equivalent to the English word *shiny*."

"What is the meaning of *vouloir*?" . . . "The word has many meanings, some of which cannot be expressed very easily in English. Give me the sentence in which the word occurs." . . . "Je l'ai fait sans le vouloir." . . . "That is equivalent to *I did it without meaning to*, or *I did not mean to do it*."

"Does *brique* mean the same thing as the English word *brick*?" . . . "Yes, generally."

"What does *Pierre* mean?" . . . "It may mean the same thing as the English words *stone* or *rock*, or it may be a proper noun etymologically identical with the English name *Peter*."

"Does *actuellement* mean *actually*?" . . . "No, it does not; *actuellement* may be taken to mean the same thing as *at present*."

These are a few specimens of a rational procedure of semantic demonstration by means of translation into the mother tongue.

For the sake of contrast, we append a few specimens of thoroughly bad semantic demonstration as practised by the old-fashioned classical school:

"*Prendre* is the French for *to take*."

"*Quinze jours* is *fifteen days*."

"*De* means *of* or *from*."

"*Encore* means *again*, *yet*, or *still*."

"*Prairie* is the French for *meadow*."

"*Se demander* means *to ask oneself*."

"*Beaucoup* stands for *much* or *many*."

"*Je me lève* is the French for *I raise me*, which is their way of expressing *I rise*."

"*Temps* is the French for *time*."

And yet, in face of the obvious benefits to be derived from

a rational use of translation as a means of explaining the meanings of new units, a generation of reformers has been and is fighting against any form of translation. A generation of teachers has been trained to consider any form of translation as an evil. A generation of school-children has been warned never to open a dictionary.

This mode of demonstration may be expressed in the following graphic form:

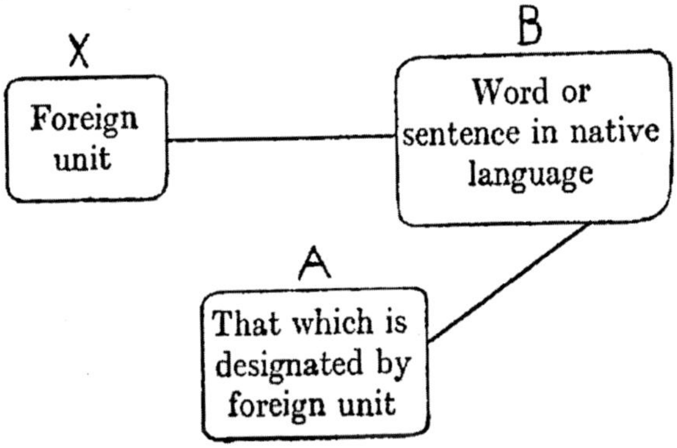

(*C*) DEMONSTRATION BY DEFINITION

Another mode consists of demonstrating the meaning of a foreign unit by means of its foreign definition, synonym, or paraphrase.

"*Pleuvoir* exprime la chute de l'eau contenue dans les nuages."

"*Vert* est la couleur qui résulte du mélange du bleu et du jaune."

"*Scie* = outil consistant essentiellement en une lame avec un bord tranchant disposé en zigzag qui sert à couper des substances résistantes."

"*Lever* = hausser."

"*Tuer* = ôter la vie à."

"*Se souvenir de* = ne pas oublier."

"*Savoir* = ne pas ignorer."

"What is the meaning of the French word *pont*?"—"*Un pont* c'est une construction en bois, en pierre, ou en acier disposée de manière à permettre aux personnes, aux bêtes ou aux voitures de traverser facilement un cours d'eau, une route, un chemin de fer, etc."

This mode may be represented graphically thus:

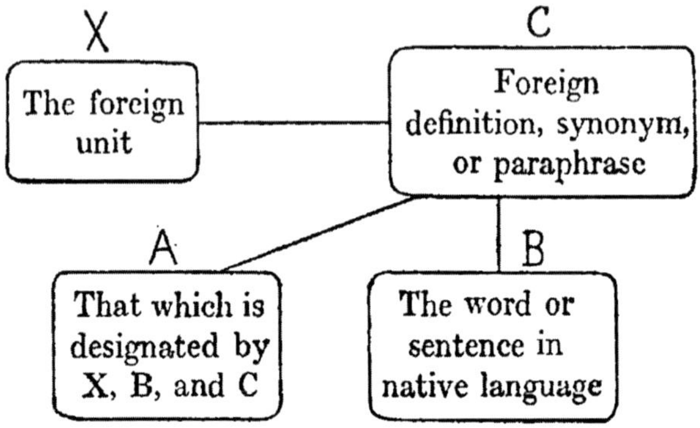

(*D*) Demonstration by Context

The fourth and last mode consists of using the foreign unit in a series of sentences in such a way that its meaning may be inferred by implication (as distinct from direct definition or description).

Alternative terms may be *demonstrating by illustration* or *by use.*

The meaning of the unknown word *parapluie* may be taught by the following examples of its use, none of which are equivalent to a definition:

"Voyant qu'il pleuvait j'ai ouvert mon parapluie. Il est prudent de ne pas sortir sans parapluie quand on croit qu'il va pleuvoir. N'oubliez pas votre parapluie, car je pense que nous aurons de la pluie."

(To teach the word *parapluie* by definition we should say: "Un parapluie est un objet qui nous protège de la pluie. Quand il pleut nous l'ouvrons, quand il cesse de pleuvoir nous le fermons.")

We may cause the meaning of the verb *recevoir* to be understood by saying: "Si je vous donne quelque chose, vous le recevez. Si je vous envoie une lettre ce soir vous la recevrez demain matin."

The meaning of *encre* may be demonstrated by the use of such sentences as, "Quand j'écris une lettre il me faut non seulement du papier, une enveloppe, un timbre, et une plume, mais il me faut encore de l'encre." This is not a true definition; the nature of ink is not described; we merely imply its nature by associating it with the other indispensable adjuncts connected with letter-writing.

It frequently happens that a series of sentences containing a given word constitutes the equivalent to its definition. For instance, if we said, "Quand on sort, on met presque toujours un chapeau sur la tête. Le chapeau protège la tête des intempéries. Un chapeau est fait généralement en feutre ou en paille," this would be tantamount to the definition, "Un chapeau est un vêtement, fait généralement en feutre ou en paille, qui se place sur la tête quand on sort, pour la protéger contre les intempéries."

This mode may be represented graphically thus:

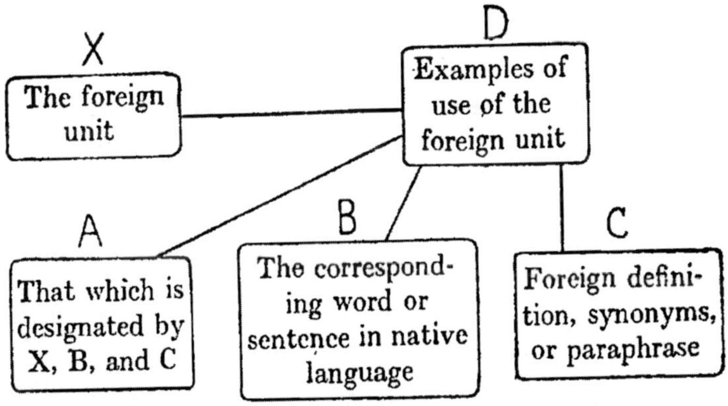

The non-differentiation of modes A, C, and D constitutes the 'Fallacy of the Direct Method.'

Many adherents of what has come to be called the Direct Method would have us believe that of the four modes of semantic demonstration, mode *B* (translation) is indirect and therefore to be avoided, and that the three other modes are direct and therefore to be encouraged.

This statement is not always set forth in categoric terms; it is generally implied rather than asserted. It is precisely this tacit assumption of unproved premises that constitutes what we shall venture to term *the Fallacy of the Direct Method.*

The origin of this fallacy is very simple and very obvious. Mode *B* (translation) is generally inferior to mode *A* (material association) in point of directness; hence *A* is termed *direct* and *B* is termed *indirect.* A minor premise is then assumed: What is not *B* is *A*, and is inevitably followed by the conclusion, What is not *B* is direct.

But the minor premise is false. What is not *B* may be *A*, *C*, or *D*; hence the conclusion "What is not *B* is direct" is false also.

Now an examination of the four modes will show us that as *A* is superior to *B* in point of directness, so is *B* to *C* or *D*.

We may then say that the 'Direct Method' is founded to a large extent on the confusion between the modes *A*, *C*, and *D*.

The following passage written by an advocate of the Direct Method is interesting:

"The teacher will endeavour to connect the words of the foreign language directly with the ideas they express, or with other words of the same language, not with those of the mother tongue. Translation will therefore be replaced, as far as possible, by object-lessons, picture-lessons, and explanations in the foreign language."

At first sight this principle would seem convincing, but on analysis it is seen to contain the invalid syllogism:

> Words should be connected directly with the ideas they express;
> Translation is indirect; therefore
> Words should be taught by . . . explanations in the foreign language.

Reduced to symbols it stands:

> *X* should be explained by *A*;
> *B* is not *A*; therefore
> *X* should be expressed by *A*, *C*, or *D*.

A severe critic might even object to the minor premise "Translation is indirect" on the ground that translation is not indirect in an absolute sense, but only in relation to the more direct *A*.

Not only must we avoid using *demonstration by translation*, and *direct demonstration* as correlative terms, but it will be found expedient even to avoid the use of the ambiguous terms *direct* and *indirect*.

Material Association

The great value of material association consists in its compliance with a law of mnemonic psychology known as Spatialization. This law may be expressed as follows: If two or more new terms are learnt in the same place, they will tend to become associated and confused; if they are learnt in two different places they will tend to become dissociated and distinct.

If we make the acquaintance of Mr A and Mr B at the same place, at the same time, and under the same circumstances, we shall tend to confuse these two persons with each other; if Mr A is introduced to us in London on Monday by our mutual friend X, and if we are introduced to Mr B at Manchester on Tuesday by our mutual friend Z, there will be no confusion whatever between their identities. The difference of time and of mutual friend is responsible to a certain extent for the differentiation, but the most important factor is the difference of place.

In order to appreciate the mnemonic aid rendered by *place-association*, let us make an experiment. Write on a sheet of paper six unfamiliar foreign words and their native translation. Learn them by continual reference to the paper, and note the time and effort required to associate each with its native equivalent and to dissociate each from the five others.

Then write six other equally unfamiliar words and their native equivalents on six separate slips of paper. Attach one to the door of the room in which you happen to be, another to the window-curtain, another over the mantelpiece, and the three others in three other parts of the room.

Learn the six words by reference to the slips and note how much less time and effort is required than in the former case. You will discover that the fact of their being dispersed in space or 'spatialized' will effectively prevent one being confused with the other, and consequently will remove that element of confusion which is after all the main obstacle in all memory work.

Many other interesting experiments may be made to demonstrate the immense value of this process of dissociation, but as these hardly come within the scope of our present inquiry we must refer the reader to treatises of rational mnemonics and the psychology of memory. It is sufficient at present to state that the operation of material association fulfils to a large extent the law of spatialization. The teacher points to the door and says "La porte." The eyes of the pupil follow him and associate *la porte* with the door to which he is pointing. He goes to the window and says "La fenêtre." It is as if the term *la fenêtre* is impressed on a new surface of the brain, and *la fenêtre* will not be confused with *la porte*, which might conceivably be the case were the two objects not so spatialized.

One of the reasons for the popularity of many 'direct methods' is explained by the fact that the first lesson is often devoted to the learning of the names of the parts of the room and of the objects dispersed around it. The great ease with which these names are learnt and associated by spatialization leads to the reasonable conclusion that all subsequent progress will be as rapid and as easily achieved.

The advantage of material association over translation may easily be exaggerated or over-estimated owing to the fact that the former mode is more often than not accompanied by spatialization ; the eyes of the student are directed successively to different objects *in different places*.

Experiments will prove that when spatialization is applied to the translation method, its results are eminently satisfactory, and in many cases comparable with those obtained by material association.

When it is convenient to use material association there is no reason whatever why this mode should not be given the preference, but when neither the objects nor pictures representing them are available, translation is by no means to be despised, and will very often be found more 'direct' than the two other modes which we are now about to examine and analyse.

The value of spatialization lies in the fact that it serves to separate, and consequently to identify, concepts liable to become confused with each other. *Buying* and *selling, pushing* and *pulling, going* and *coming, hot* and *cold, pleased* and *sorry*, although respectively contrary, complementary, or correlative terms, are so associated in our minds that there is a real danger of our confusing the pairs of foreign words which are used to express them. The writer confesses to having confused for quite a long time *kaufen* and *verkaufen*; *schieben* and *ziehen*. A pupil of his once confused the English words *bought* and *sold* to such an extent that he was only able to distinguish the two by spelling out in French the last three letters of *bought*: "*g, h, t,* = *j'ai acheté*"!

When the two terms liable to confusion are of a more abstract nature and represent subjective phenomena not clearly distinguished even in the terms of one's own language, some dissociative process is still more necessary. The writer has frequently had occasion to teach successively the three polylogs *hope to, expect to,* and *mean to.* When told that they correspond respectively to *espérer, compter,* and *avoir l'intention de* the French pupil has often maintained that he was unable to distinguish the three terms one from another. The terms in question being of an abstract and subjective nature, the demonstration of their meaning by material association is out of the question. There remain modes *B, C,* and *D.* As we have seen, mode *B* (translation) is inadequate, for the pupil cannot immediately distinguish his native terms. Recourse must then be had to definition or to context, either in English in order to fix the meanings of the English terms, or in French in order to demonstrate more concretely the meaning of the French terms.

In cases, however, where the two concepts are perfectly distinct or where a concept has a particularly striking character there is very little difference between *A* and *B* in point of directness. In practical teaching the equation *London*=*Londres* (mode *B*) may be more direct than *London*=[*the place to which I am pointing on this map*] (modification of mode *A*), and (if the pupil has any elementary notions of geography) is distinctly more direct than *London is the capital of England* (mode *C*). For the same reason, mode *B* is more direct than *The immense agglomeration called London, the seat of the British government, situated near the mouth of the Thames . . .* (mode *D*).

Translation is a more direct mode of conveying the meaning of a unit than Definition, and, a fortiori, more direct than context.

We may state once for all that translation is generally (but not always) inferior in point of directness to material association; hence in discussing the merits and demerits of translation as a mode of semantic demonstration, it would be well to confine ourselves to cases where material association must be excluded. As we have already observed, the use of this mode is confined to material things such as concrete objects, objective qualities and actions. When, therefore, the foreign units do not stand for such concrete concepts our choice must fall on modes *B*, *C*, or *D*.

In weighing the respective advantages of translation and definition our judgment must depend to a large extent on the following consideration. We must not unduly presume that the words of our native language must necessarily be fully or perfectly understood; were that the case there would never be any need to consult our native dictionary except in order to ascertain the spelling or pronunciation of a given word. If every word in our own language were perfectly associated with its meaning or meanings we should already have attained the ideal state imagined by logicians and should not require that ideal instrument of thought imagined by Pascal, Descartes, and others and termed by them the Philosophical Language. We must recognize that most of the words we use possess but the loosest of connotations, and that these are in a state of perpetual flux and evolution. How many quarrels, law-suits, polemics, controversies, and even wars are directly or indirectly caused by imperfect semanticizing! Misunderstandings due to different interpretations of the same term are responsible for most of our earthly troubles.

Study itself, in all its various branches and ramifications, is little more than the learning of the meanings of words. The whole educative process is one long learning of definitions.

There are words in our own language which have cost us many months or even years to semanticize adequately. We did not acquire the meanings of such words as *subjective*, *parabola*, *integrate*, *hypothecate*, *debenture*, *carbonate*, *mesozoic*, *syllogism*, etc., etc., without much reading and technical study. Thousands of our monologs and tens of thousands of our polylogs stand for most complex concepts and conceptual relations. Even apart from scientific and technical terms, we shall find numberless examples of everyday words and expressions the proper use of which has only become possible after long stages of perception and association. That we learnt so many thousands of these at a very early age and that most of them have been acquired by the subconscious rather than the conscious process does not affect the fact that in each case the association of term and concept had to be gradually developed over a long period of study (using the term study in its widest sense). Let the reader examine the last three sentences and seriously ask himself how he has come to understand the various abstract terms of which they are composed. Let him then consider more general and more popular terms such as *realize*, *afford*, *fancy*, *assume*, *agree*, *suggest*; let him imagine a case of complete aphasia or loss of memory and then let him realize the period of time and the amount of reading and study that would be required in order to re-form his associations.

Is it an exaggeration to suggest that each word of our vocabulary required on an average an hour's semanticizing spread over a long period before we were able so to associate it with its meaning that we could use it?

Now is it seriously maintained even by extreme exponents of

the Direct Method that we should go through all this work for each foreign language we study? We have learnt, let us say, mathematics, chemistry, or geology in our own language; we wish to read up or refer to works on these subjects written in some foreign non-cognate language. Are we, then, to study these sciences anew *ab ovo* in order to avoid the pernicious act of consulting the bilingual dictionary?

Poser la question, c'est la résoudre. Let there be no illusion on this point; the most fervent partisan of the Direct Method translates, whatever his impressions to the contrary may be. He learns German by reading German books without a dictionary. He is reading a technical book dealing with chemistry; the word *Wasserstoff* occurs repeatedly. Our reader does not refer to a bilingual dictionary, it is true, but in the end he says to himself: "Ach so, das Wort *Wasserstoff* bedeutet sicher *hydrogen*!" That he has guessed the translation rather than sought it does not affect the fact that he has more or less associated *Wasserstoff* with *hydrogen*, and by so doing has attached to the former the semantic value of the latter.

Now the perfectly bilingual person, he who has learnt two languages under natural and ideal conditions, does not hesitate to use a bilingual dictionary in all cases where his erudition is not equally distributed over the two languages. He has had occasion to associate with a certain concept the English word *beaver*; he has not had occasion to associate it with the French word *castor*; he consults his bilingual dictionary, which tells him that he may attach to the word *castor* the group of semantic associations hitherto confined to the word *beaver* (in its zoological sense). He does the same thing in the converse case; if he has had occasion to form an association between a concept and a French word and not an English one, he will remedy this omission by reference to a bilingual and not a unilingual dictionary.

As an *argumentum ad absurdum* let us take the frequent case of an Englishman who by some accident of circumstances has come to associate the word *hêtre* with the thing designated by it. He finds one day that he is ignorant of the equivalent word in English. What is he to do? Go to a forest with an English companion better versed than he in wood-lore and search for the tree associated with the term *hêtre* and then ask his companion to name it in English? Once again, *poser la question c'est la résoudre*; he will reach down his French-English dictionary and ascertain that *hêtre = beech*.

Now if the most direct manner of learning the meaning of a native word is to associate it with its foreign equivalent, the same argument may surely apply to the semanticizing of a foreign word of the same nature.

We say advisedly "of the same nature," for there is another side to the question. The known word may possess no exact equivalent in the other language, its connotation may be wider or narrower than that of the word or polylog which most nearly resembles it in meaning, the native word may be ambiguous and the nearest foreign equivalent may be precise. In such cases translation is inferior to mode *C*, or even mode *D*.

Upon this point depends our judgment when weighing the respective advantages and disadvantages of translation and definition. We venture to suggest the following principle: *When the foreign word to be demonstrated is known to be for all practical purposes the equivalent of a native word, translation is a better mode than definition; when the word to be demonstrated is known to be a doubtful equivalent or when the value of the equivalence is unknown, it is more prudent to confirm the translation by definition or by context; when the word to be demonstrated is known to have no equivalent whatever in the native language, then we must have recourse to definition or to context.*

In speaking of demonstration by definition we have so far assumed that such definition must necessarily be in the foreign language. We can conceive a mode intermediate between mode *B* (translation) and mode *C* (foreign definition, synonym, or paraphrase). This may be designated by the symbol *E*, and would consist of demonstrating the foreign unit by a native definition, synonym, or paraphrase of the native equivalent word.

Instead of *chaise = chair* (mode *B*) or *chaise = meuble consistant en un siège, quatre pieds, et un dossier, sur lequel on s'assied* (mode *C*), we may use *chaise = piece of furniture consisting of a seat, four legs, and a back, used for sitting purposes* (mode *E*):

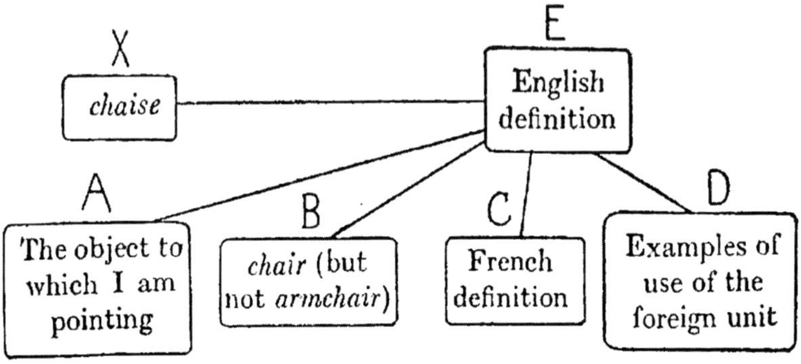

We are told by Direct Method extremists that *B* is less 'direct' than *A* or *C*; hence *C* is superior to *B*. But if the foreign definition is direct, then the native definition must necessarily be far more so; therefore *E* is more direct than *B*! This is indeed an argument *ad absurdum*, and in using it we are but pushing to its logical conclusion the *Fallacy of the Direct Method*, which assumes that *C* is more direct than *B* because *A* is (generally) more direct than *B*!

But it may be claimed that mode *C* constitutes an interesting and valuable exercise in the faculty of intuitive comprehension, that it inculcates the very necessary habit of successful guessing. This is perfectly true, but let us remember that systematic exercises for the development of the faculties of subconscious comprehension is one operation, and the documentation of a student in the course of his conscious work is another.

There is a time for everything and a function for each operation. It might be argued that geography, history, mathematics, etc., might be taught to English children through the medium of the French language, and with salutary and economical results. To a certain extent this is true *during the later stages of study*, but on the other hand there is a limit to the number of birds that one may conveniently kill with one stone. To impair one operation in order to make it serve two very different purposes is ingenious; so also is the using of a hairbrush to hammer in a nail; but neither of these acts is either economical or efficacious.

The course of study should and must include systematic and progressive exercises in immediate comprehension, as it must also include systematic pronunciation exercises and systematic substitution exercises and systematic ergonic exercises, but the worst time to choose for any of these is precisely the moment when we are teaching the meanings of the units contained in the elementary vocabulary of the student. Semantic demonstration is a means to an end and not an end in itself.

The exclusion of translation as a regular means of conveying the meaning of units is an uneconomical and unnatural principle.

The principle that translation should be excluded as a mode of demonstrating may conceivably be justified on two counts—the dictates of necessity, and pedagogic grounds. On pedagogic grounds also such exclusion is to be condemned.

Let us first examine the two arguments in favour of its exclusion.

It frequently happens that the teacher is ignorant of the native language of his pupil, or that the pupil's knowledge of the teacher's language is superior to the teacher's knowledge of the pupil's language. In such cases it may be urged that as it is materially impossible for the teacher to convey the meanings of words by the mode of translation this mode must of necessity be excluded.

It may be argued that one of the essential qualifications of the teacher should be an adequate familiarity with the language of his pupil. This particular argument will, however, scarcely hold good. It is true that the teacher whose business it is to give lessons in elementary English to French or German students ought to possess a working knowledge of French or German, but it cannot be seriously urged that he should also have learnt Spanish, Italian, Russian, Arabic, Urdu, Japanese, Chinese, etc., etc., before accepting an appointment or setting up in business as a language-teacher. Now in class teaching it frequently happens that while the majority of the members of the class are, let us say, French, one or two members may hail from parts of the world very far removed from France. An Icelander can hardly have grounds for complaint if he fails to find in an English provincial town an English teacher with a sound knowledge of Icelandic. If the Icelander insists as a *sine qua non* that his teacher of English should be perfectly acquainted with the Icelandic language, he must have recourse, not to a teacher of English nationality, but to an Icelandic teacher of English.

Is a teacher, then, to refuse to give lessons to any person with whose language he is unacquainted or imperfectly acquainted? That, of course, is primarily a matter for the student to decide. If I apply to a Russian for lessons, knowing full well that he has no knowledge of English, I do so at my own risk, and withhold from myself the advantages of translation in all its aspects.

Which, then, is better: to learn Russian from a Russian who is ignorant of English, or to learn it from an Englishman who has previously studied Russian? The answer to this question depends, of course, on the extent of the Englishman's knowledge of Russian; if he speaks broken Russian with an English pronunciation he must be rejected as a teacher.

But much of this is not to the point. We are discussing as if dictionaries had never been invented or printing were an undiscovered art. It is not necessarily the function of a teacher to semanticize all our words; this can be accomplished by any dictionary or manual composed expressly for that purpose.

You, a teacher of English, are giving lessons to a Norwegian. Your pupil asks you the meaning or the meanings of the English verb *to realize*. Do not waste twenty precious minutes in forging definitions which will be imperfectly understood; refer your pupil to a good English-Norwegian dictionary, of which there is no lack.

The only case in which we must exclude translation for reasons of *force majeure* is when the pupil's language is one for which no bilingual dictionary has either been composed or is accessible.

But the exclusion of translation as a mode of semantic demonstration (also as the vehicle for explanations) is often demanded on pedagogic grounds. It is frequently maintained by exponents of the Direct Method that translation in all its forms and functions is a vicious and harmful proceeding. We will not contest this point anew, but simply refer the reader to what we have already said on this particular subject.

We would, however, add that many teachers justify on pedagogic grounds a procedure dictated by necessity. We do not maintain that they do so knowingly or with any insincerity. An English teacher accepts an appointment at Moscow. He has hitherto taught English to French students, and, knowing French perfectly, has never hesitated to utilize translation as a mode of teaching. He arrives at Moscow; he knows no Russian; he can no longer use the mode of demonstrating to which he is accustomed, nor can he any longer use the native language for conveying explanatory matter. What happens? Is it by coincidence or is it as a natural consequence of his position that he suddenly discovers the pedagogic merits of the Direct Method? And when in after years he acquires a sound knowledge of Russian will he still remain faithful to its leading principle?

What is, now, the great disadvantage of excluding translation as a means of semantic demonstration? We all recognize the bad habits that may be engendered by associating the foreign with the native word; we fully realize that the exclusion of translation often tends toward a sounder knowledge of the foreign language. On what grounds, therefore, do we maintain with such insistence throughout these pages that mode *B* should not be rejected?

In the foregoing pages we have examined an argument in favour of translation, or, expressed conversely, an argument against its exclusion.

But there is another reason, entirely unconnected with the first, which compels us to reflect very seriously before relinquishing this valuable mode of demonstration.

As we have already mentioned, the term *direct* is an ambiguous and dangerous one. It may be applied to two quite different things—viz. to *Semanticizing* or to *Programme*. *Direct semanticizing* means *the demonstration and teaching of meanings without the use of translation.*

By *Direct Programme* we mean the course of study which conducts the student by the shortest and easiest route to a practical mastery of the most useful matter of the language.

A Direct Programme can only be drawn up by an observance of the principles of frequency and ergonic combination. The former tells us to assimilate the more useful before the less useful units of the language. The latter tells us that we should give priority to those units which are readily combinable with their fellows in order to form sentences.

In another place we shall show that these two principles are in themselves somewhat contradictory; that one can only be fully observed at the expense of the other; that the ideal programme is nothing other than a judicious series of compromises between their rival claims.

Now if, when drawing up our programme, we had not only to adjudicate between the exigencies of frequency and ergonic combination, but also to make both of these subservient to the non-translation principle, our task would become an impossible one; we simply cannot conform simultaneously to the three principles.

Let us express this point in more concrete terms. When the teacher (or method-writer) is about to draw up a programme for a beginners' course, he has the following alternative choice of material:

(*a*) Units possessing the two qualities *utility* and *combinability* (such as *faut-il*, *hier*, *comprendre*, *savoir*, *pouvoir*, *prêt*, *temps*, *gare*, etc.).

(*b*) Units of which the meaning may be demonstrated and taught by *Material Association* (such as *tableau*, *livre*, *œil*, *prendre*, *toucher*, *rouge*, *coin*, *plafond*, etc.).

If he chooses his units from class (*a*) the *Programme* will be Direct, and the *Semanticizing* Indirect [1]; in the contrary case the *Programme* will be Indirect, and the *Semanticizing* Direct, for only a relatively small number of units are common to both classes. Which are we more justified in sacrificing: Direct *Programme* or Direct *Semanticizing* ?

[1] For the purposes of our argument we will concede to partisans of the Direct Method the equation *translation = indirect semanticizing*.

When we have submitted to a critical analysis the principles of frequency and ergonic combination, we shall certainly conclude that these must at all costs be observed, and that the claims of the Direct Programme must be given priority over any claims whatever.

An additional argument in favour of mode *B* is one which would appear to have escaped the attention of many writers on this subject. The tendency of the average student, more especially in the early stages, is to associate the foreign word with its native equivalent. We may, if we so choose, assure him that this is a vicious tendency; we may go to great trouble to replace it by the three other modes; we may refuse to give the native equivalent and forbid the use of the bilingual dictionary. But we do not and cannot prevent the student from forming bilingual associations if he wishes to do so. We may say, "Voilà la fenêtre, regardez la fenêtre, j'ouvre la fenêtre," etc. The pupil will think to himself, "*Fenêtre* means *window*." One day when wishing to express in French *shop window*, he will say *fenêtre du magasin*, and in so doing prove our 'direct' tactics to have been ineffective.

We say, "Je prends le livre; je le prends; prenez le livre; je prends un livre quand je veux lire; je prends le train quand je veux voyager," etc., etc. The pupil will think to himself, "*Prendre* means *take*," and will one day say, "Prenez cette lettre à la poste," or "Mon père m'a pris à Londres." Again our efforts to prevent such misuse of *prendre* have been in vain.

Let us make an experiment in order to see whether our supposition is true. We will teach our pupil a number of French words without translation; among them may be the word *user*. At a given moment we will spring upon him the question, "How would you say *user* in English?" He will probably answer immediately, "*To use*," thus proving that in spite of our efforts he has associated *user* with its cognate *use*, instead of its semantic equivalent *wear*.

As a matter of fact, the instant that our pupil heard the word *user* he thought to himself, "That must mean *use*," and from that moment he paid no great attention to the examples that we adduced in order to demonstrate the meaning of the word.

Cases occur in which the absence of an authentic and officially given translation gives rise to the most absurd misconceptions.

Many years ago, when my notions of French were more rudimentary than exact, a Belgian office-boy would come to me in order to obtain permission to go to dinner. "Est-ce que je peux retourner, monsieur ?" he asked. I considered this a somewhat curious question, and answered : "Non seulement vous pouvez retourner, mais vous devez retourner." The boy looked puzzled, but went off. The next day the same question : "Puis-je retourner, monsieur ?" It began to occur to me that the Belgian office-boy was a different sort of creature from his English *confrère*. "Mais oui, certainement vous pouvez retourner ; il faut toujours retourner après le dîner." With a look of despair the boy went off to the chief and asked permission to *retourner*. "Oui, oui, retournez maintenant ; il est déjà passé l'heure !"

It then began to dawn on me that the equation *retourner* = *return* was a false one, and that it should stand, *retourner* = go *home*, or *go back*.

Another experiment, this time with a French pupil. We wish to teach the English polylog *go to sleep* (= *s'endormir*), in accordance with the precepts of the Direct Method. We withhold its translation in order that the pupil may semanticize it correctly and effectively without confusing cross-associations. We say to him : "When we are sleepy we go to sleep. In order to go to sleep we shut our eyes. Some people find it difficult to go to sleep, others can go to sleep at any time. Don't go to sleep now ; you must not go to sleep during the lesson."

Now these examples should surely suffice to show that *go to sleep* equals *s'endormir*. Our pupil, however, at the first example jumps immediately to the conclusion that *go to sleep* equals *aller dormir*. His analytic faculties tell him that if *go* = *aller* and *to sleep* = *dormir* (both of which equations are justified) then *go* + *to sleep* = *aller dormir*. With his preconception he pays little attention to the precise bearing of our examples.

We ask him : "Comment diriez-vous *go to sleep* en français ?" He answers : "*Aller dormir*" ; *s'endormir* has not even occurred to him.

Demonstrate by the Direct Method the English word *ascertain*, and the result will probably be the false equation *ascertain* = *s'assurer* (instead of *ascertain* = *s'informer*). Teach a German the sentence "I let him come" without translation, and the result will probably be "Ich lasse ihn kommen" (= "I make him come").

These are not exceptional examples; hundreds of others may be quoted to illustrate the point. Books exist the sole object of which is to correct misunderstandings of this kind.

It is an incontrovertible fact that in cases of this sort translation is the *direct* mode of demonstration and modes *C* and *D* (in some cases even *A* !) are indirect.

Let us recognize frankly that the withholding of an 'official' or authentic translation does not prevent the student from forming faulty associations, but that, on the contrary, such withholding may often engender them.

By a rational application of the principle of translation we not only furnish the true equivalent, but we also warn the student against false equivalents. When we tell the pupil that *fenêtre* means *window*, we are careful to add that this only applies to an ordinary window, and not to a shop window or an attic window.

When telling him that *prendre* is generally the equivalent of *take*, we must warn him that this does not include *take* in the sense of *carry*, *convey*, or *conduct*.

We warn the pupil that in spite of appearances *user* is never or hardly ever the equivalent of *use*, that *retourner* is not *return*, that *go to sleep* is not *aller dormir*, that in spite of appearances *ascertain* has nothing to do with *make certain* and that *lassen* is not always *let*.

Unless we put him on his guard a German will consider *to mean* as the equivalent of *meinen*. A Frenchman unhelped by an authentic translation will consider the English perfect tense as the semantic equivalent of his *passé indéfini* and will say: "I have seen him last year."

When we tell the pupil what is the equivalent word in his native language we are using this operation in its *positive* sense; when we warn him against error by telling him what it does *not* mean, we are demonstrating negatively. It will be found for purposes of negative demonstration that translation is a surer and more 'direct' mode than any of the others.

For these reasons, therefore, we may maintain in the face of all that is urged to the contrary that the exclusion of translation as a mode of semantic demonstration is unsound both pedagogically and for reasons of expediency.

No hard and fast rule can be adopted as to the mode of giving the meanings of units; each in its turn may be superior to the others.

How then shall we teach meanings? What principles are we to adopt as a general guide? Which is the right system?

The answer is obvious: adopt none exclusively, reject none absolutely. Each variety has its uses, each has its place in the general scheme, and each in its turn may be the most rational one.

The choice of the mode depends almost entirely on that group of factors which is the subject of the third chapter of our inquiry. The most important of these is that concerning the degree of knowledge already possessed by the student.

We may be giving lessons to an absolute beginner, to one whose knowledge of the language is represented by zero.

In his case modes *C* and *D* are of little utility (during the first lesson of no utility at all); we are confined to modes *A* and *B*. If the words figuring in the first lessons represent concrete concepts we may well semanticize them by material association.

If we are asked the meaning of the French word *chaise* and there happens to be a chair in the room, we will point to it and say: "Voilà une chaise" (or, "That's a chair"). If no chair is at hand we will say: "*Chaise* to all intents and purposes is equivalent to the word *chair*, exclusive of armchairs, deck-chairs, and other non-normal varieties."

If we do not speak the language of our inquirer or if we are unable to think of the equivalent word in his language we may draw a picture of a chair, or, better still, refer him to his dictionary. If, on the other hand, the pupil can already understand and speak the language we may teach him the word *chaise* by definition. But, needless to say, if the student has already reached such an advanced stage that he understands our definition he will certainly long since have learnt the word *chaise*.

The general principle, then, may stand: During the early stages use modes *A* and *B*, and avoid *C* and *D*; during the later stages use whichever of the four modes happens to be most convenient.

It must be perfectly understood, of course, that in order that the translation may be efficacious we must associate the foreign word with the true native equivalent word or definition, and not with an imaginary or merely traditional one. *Way* for *chemin* or *will* for *vouloir* will never do. If, as is generally the case, the native word has other meanings than that corresponding to the foreign word we must qualify our information accordingly. If we are asked the meaning of the French verb *savoir* it is not sufficient to say that it corresponds in meaning with the English verb *to know*; we must add: "in the sense of *to have knowledge* or *to be aware of*, and not in the sense of *to be acquainted with*."

The more integral such translations the more successful will be the result. The string of words to which we wish to attach the meaning must be compared, not with the native equivalents of each of the units taken separately, but with the native equivalent of the whole. "Je suis ici depuis quinze jours" must not be demonstrated by connecting each word with its assumed English equivalent. We must not say: "*Je* = *I*, *suis* = *am*, *ici* = *here*, *depuis* = *since*, *quinze* = *fifteen*, *jours* = *days*." This is an analytical operation which has nothing in common with semanticizing. We must say: "Je suis ici depuis quinze jours = 'I have been here a fortnight.'"

We have already alluded to the fact that vast numbers of our native words the pronunciation and spelling of which we are perfectly familiar with are either unsemanticized or only partially semanticized; they either convey but a vague meaning or convey no meaning at all to us. We may hear, read, or even use such words as *beech*, *bowline*, *flail*, without having any precise notion of what these things look like or what are their particular attributes. Many words are vaguely suggestive of meanings rather than expressive of them.

In such cases it is a moot point whether our duty is to give the native equivalent or to employ one of the other modes. By adopting the latter course the foreign word becomes better known than the native equivalent. Let us suppose that we are teaching the French word *pignon*. We tell our pupil that it means *gable*, and discover that he has no precise notion of what a gable is. The word *gable*, therefore, is inadequate to demonstrate the meaning of the word *pignon*. We teach *pignon* then by definition or by illustration. While we are doing so we are fulfilling the function not merely of a language-teacher but also that of a teacher of architecture. When we teach the meaning of *mongoose* to a Frenchman who has never learnt the French word *mangouste*, we are giving a lesson in zoology. It is an open question to what extent the language-teacher should overstep the limits which separate the dictionary from the encyclopædia.

In conclusion let us take a concrete example in order to show and to compare the four modes of demonstration. We will presume our pupil to be an English student of French.

Regarder

MODE *A* (Material Association)

Je regarde la fenêtre. Je regarde mon livre. Regardez le plafond. Regardez le plancher. Je vous regarde. Regardez-moi.

MODE *B* (Translation)

Regarder means *look* or *look at* as in the sentences "Look at me," "Look at your book," "Look out of the window," "What are you looking at?" It does not mean *look* in the sense of *seem, appear*, or *look like*; it does not mean *look* in the sense in which the word is used in "Look for your book" or "It looks good."

MODE *C* (Definition)

Regarder veut dire se servir consciemment des yeux.

MODE *D* (Context)

Si je regarde par la fenêtre je vois des maisons. Si je veux savoir l'heure je regarde à ma montre. Quand on veut savoir la couleur ou la grandeur d'un objet on doit le regarder.

In this case mode *A* is probably the best of the four.

Section 18.—Learning by Heart, or 'Catenizing.' Learning by heart is the basis of all linguistic study, for every sentence ever uttered or written by anybody has either been learnt by heart in its entirety or else has been composed (consciously or subconsciously) from smaller units, each of which must at one time have been learnt by heart. We may term primary matter all units learnt by heart integrally, and secondary matter all units built up or derived by the pupil from primary matter.

In considering the functions and advantages of memorizing (or 'catenizing') as opposed to reasoning, the important fact is often overlooked that *all* study directed toward the acquisition of the power of *using* the language is necessarily based on the faculty of memorizing.

As we have already noted, the progress of the student can only be measured by his capacity for understanding and producing fluent sentences. The amateur linguist, it is true, may maintain that his progress should be measured by his capacity for understanding and of producing *words*. He is inclined to say: "Let us memorize *words* and let us reason out *sentences*."

It is quite certain, however, that in both cases the study of language is ultimately based on memorizing, for the difference between memorizing 'words' (whatever the term *word* may mean) and memorizing sentences is one not of *kind*, but of *degree*.

Modern psychologists incline toward the 'integral' theory, and can produce data showing that a given 'chain' is more quickly memorized in its entirety than when we memorize its 'links' one by one.

One of the more important duties of the method-writer or of the language-teacher is to determine of what the pupil's *primary matter* shall or shall not consist.

The 121 identities contained in the first 11 multiplication tables (commencing at $2 \times 2 = 4$ and concluding by $12 \times 12 = 144$) constitute our arithmetical primary matter as far as the operation of multiplication is concerned; all other multiplicative identities must necessarily be treated as secondary matter.

In the classical method of teaching shorthand, the primary matter consists of the consonant and vowel signs plus the arbitrary grammalogues; all the other outlines are treated as secondary matter.

The actor's lines must all be treated as primary matter; were 'gagging' legitimate this would constitute secondary matter.

The essential difference between the (more or less) phonetic system of writing most languages and the ideographic system of writing Chinese lies in the fact that in the former case a very small quantity of primary matter results in the almost unlimited production of secondary matter, whereas in the latter case every individual unit has to be learnt by heart as it stands; that is to say, every Chinese character is a unit of primary matter.

The solving of all problems set by the teacher must be performed by the faculty of reasoning; the solutions to such problems therefore constitute secondary matter. Should the pupil treat the solutions as primary matter by memorizing them he will be cheating, and as a measure of precaution the teacher rightly withholds the key.

Conversely, if instructed to learn a given unit by heart, the pupil will be cheating if he replaces the process by calculating. When the teacher instructs the schoolboy to memorize the five times table he has a sound reason for doing so; the schoolboy avoids the memorizing operation and when examined produces the table in question by a series of eleven operations in mental addition. However praiseworthy his faculty of rapid mental addition, and however correct the result, the schoolboy is cheating.

The use of either process, then, constitutes an illegitimate act when the pupil has received precise instructions to work by the other.

We cannot state as a general principle that either process is superior to the other; each of them has its particular functions, advantages, and disadvantages. What these are cannot be determined with precision on *a priori* grounds.

We now have to examine the respective functions of the two processes as applied to the study of a foreign language, and to come to some conclusion as to what units are to be treated respectively as primary or as secondary matter.

Let us repeat the fundamental and obvious fact that the total number of units that we are able to use in a given language have either been acquired as primary matter or derived from this as secondary matter; no third term can possibly exist.

At first sight one is tempted to assume that, applied to language-study, *primary matter* means *words* and that *secondary matter* means *sentences*, for it is generally assumed that *words* are learnt purely by the faculty of memory and that by the faculties of reasoning we build up sentences from these.

It is assumed, for instance, that we learn by heart words such as *il*, *est*, and *ici*, then from these we derive by synthesis the sentence *il est ici*.

We now have to ascertain whether this assumption is borne out by facts or whether it is still another of those popular illusions which render the whole question of language-learning so obscure and the subject of so much contradictory discussion.

If we discover this assumption to be true it will enormously simplify the issue. It will constitute a principle upon which the whole science of language-learning must be based. It will also prove that the natural method by which the child learns its mother tongue is the wrong method and that our mastery of our own language has been obtained in defiance of this fundamental law.

If we discover this assumption to be false we must expose its falseness and make up our minds not to allow reasoning to be influenced by it.

If we discover it to be partially true and partially false we must decide what are the respective functions of memory and reasoning, and must determine what matter it is expedient to treat respectively as primary and secondary.

How did you learn the French words *lune*, *avec*, *savoir*, *jaune*, *vour*, *souvent*, and *mais*? By piecing together smaller units already acquired? By decomposing them out of compound units already acquired? By adapting them from other units already acquired? Most probably not. It is almost certain that you did not derive them from other units; you learnt them as they stand by the process of memorizing; they form a part of your primary matter.

How did you learn longer polylogical or sentence units such as *venez avec moi, je ne le lui ai pas encore expliqué, c'est impossible, savez-vous pourquoi*, or *parlez plus lentement, s'il vous plaît*?

It is probable (but not absolutely certain) that you have never learnt these as integral units, but that, having acquired the power of piecing together smaller ready-learnt units with the help of English, you built up such polylogs as you required them. If this is so, these sentences form part of your secondary matter.

How did you learn *aujourd'hui*? As secondary matter by piecing together the five words *à le jour de hui*? Most probably not; it is possible that you have never even thought of *hui* as being a distinct word.

The unit *aujourd'hui* is almost invariably learnt integrally long before learning the component unit *hui*.

Did you learn *maintenant* as an integral unit or by piecing together its component elements *main* (= *hand*) and *tenant* (= *holding*)? There is a strong presumption that you learnt it by the former process. Did you learn to form your native word *understand* by building it up from the component units *under* and *stand*, or did you acquire it integrally? We may, I think, presume the latter process.

Examine the following list of units and consider in each case by which of the two processes you are enabled to use them (either actively or passively): *pardessus, rez-de-chaussée, à moins que, parapluie, seulement, avant-hier, à propos, lentement, je ne sais pas, s'il vous plaît, s'il vous voit, malheureux, comprenez-vous?, tant mieux, il n'y a pas de quoi, il n'y a pas d'argent, qu'est-ce que c'est que ça?, comme il faut, ça m'est égal, peut-être, blanchir, ici, machine à écrire, quatre-vingts, soixante-quinze, prononcerai, voudrais, un peu, il y a, sera-t-il, en haut, bicyclette, bonheur, douzaine, pomme de terre, venir, celui, l'eau, Lemaire, le maire, plume, Lemaître, le maître, Lacroix, la croix, gendarme, char-à-banc, boîte aux lettres, porte-manteau, mépris, déménager, revenir, refaire, remarquer, mais, repartir, rentrer, abonnement, encaisser, s'agir, se lever, se demander, s'amuser, affaire, avenir, comment allez-vous ?, à bon port, tout le monde, le mien, mon, beaucoup, chapeau, chou-fleur, lundi, quand même, pas du tout, parce que je le lui ai donné, vous auriez dû venir, tout de suite, tout à l'heure, toujours, je viens de, au-dessus, quelque chose, quelqu'un, quelque part, autre part, quart d'heure, à cette époque-ci, ce matin, au contraire, la semaine prochaine, au fur et à mesure, nom de plume, de trop, au large, coup de main, coup d'œil, mal de mer, vaurien, suis allé, quinze jours, à moins que, quoi que, quoique, bien que, aussitôt que, aussi tôt que, avant que, dès que, jusqu'à ce que, sauter aux yeux, chef-d'œuvre, maître chanteur, en face, d'habitude, en outre, pieds nus, peu à peu, tant soit peu, de peur que, avoir peur, en premier lieu, à coup sûr, s'en voulair, vouloir bien, vouloir dire, lorsque, lors de, journaux, hiboux, familière, fondamentaux, comprenne, ça se fait, depuis.*

The examination of this list opens up a wide field of facts and conjecture. It will be found that many of the monologs have been learnt integrally and that many of the polylogs have not so been learnt. So far this would bear out the popular assumption.

But in contradiction to this you will have discovered that some of the monologs have been built up synthetically, and so constitute secondary matter ; a still more striking fact is that a larger number, probably the majority of the polylogs, have been learnt integrally, and so constitute primary matter.

Is it better to have learnt *il y a* integrally, or would it have been better to have learnt the three component parts *il*, *y*, and *a*, and to put them together as *il y a* when required ? The answer is obvious ; had you never learnt *il y a* as an integral unit, no process of reasoning would ever have enabled you to construct this unit synthetically.

It appears that you have learnt two words *bien que* as an integral conjunction polylog in the sense of *although*. Was this latter procedure necessary ? Would it not have been sufficient to learn the adverb *bien* (= *well*) and the conjunction *que* (= that) as primary matter, and to have derived from these as a synthetic product the compound conjunction *bien que*? Obviously this would not have been the right course; your knowledge of the individual words would not have enabled you to guess that the two words combined correspond to an entirely new concept equivalent to *although*.

Did you learn *vous auriez dû venir* as primary or as secondary matter? Probably as primary matter. Had you wished to produce the French equivalent of *you ought to have come* by the synthetic method the result would probably have been not *vous auriez dû venir*, but *vous devriez être venu*.

It is difficult to see how you could have treated *coup de main* or *coup d'œil* otherwise than by memorizing them integrally.

Are you ever tempted to say *le semaine prochain*? If so it proves that you have learnt to produce the French equivalent of *next week* by synthesis, for had you learnt it as an integral unit it would be impossible for you to make the mistake in question.

If you ever hear an English student say *à la contraire* or *sur le contraire* you may safely conclude that he has just formed the polylog by synthetic construction. If you ever hear any one say *tant le mieux* you may conclude that this person has considered it expedient not to treat the French equivalent of *so much the better* as primary matter.

Il n'y a pas d'argent might be formed synthetically from *il y a*, *ne pas de*, and *argent*, but it is difficult to see how *il n'y a pas de quoi* can become part of our linguistic baggage except by treating it as primary matter and so learning it integrally.

Most French children seem to be unconscious that *quatre-vingts* is composed of the two units *quatre* and *vingt*; they have learnt it as an integral polylog. Probably the average French child is no more conscious of the parts of *tout le monde* than is the English child of *everybody*. It is with a certain shock of surprise that the French child discovers that *s'il vous plaît* is nothing other than *si la chose vous plaît*.

When we use the adverb *next door* we are not thinking of the door which is nearest to our own house; the polylog has been assimilated as primary matter. So also the Frenchman has no cognizance of the ultimate units *beau* and *coup* in *beaucoup*.

Neither the Frenchman nor the Englishman connects the Franco-English word *char-à-banc* with its individual parts when using it.

Ask the Frenchman the meaning of the French words *fur* and *rez*; for a moment he will be as puzzled as the Englishman when asked the meaning of the English word *fro*. The average Englishman may use the polylog *to and fro* all his life without cognizing the existence of the element *fro*.

The Frenchman is no more conscious of the decomposition of *parce que* than is the Englishman of *because*.

The young child learning his mother tongue certainly does not confine the memorizing process to monologs. As a matter of fact, the young child does not distinguish monologs from polylogs. He learnt *la croix* by the same process as that by which he learns the proper noun *Lacroix*; he learns *pomme de terre* not as a word group signifying *pomme qui vient de la terre*, but as an integral word in itself like *haricot* or *orange*. Indeed, when the child first begins to write, it is exceedingly difficult for him to know which are the conventional orthographic units that we call monologs.

If we pass from French and English to languages of which the graphic unit is the syllable we shall find new data to convince or bewilder us. And what of unwritten languages in which obviously no graphic units exist at all?

The monolog of one language corresponds in meaning and function to the polylog or the miolog of another. The French *tartine* is equivalent to the English *piece of bread and butter*; French *difficilement* is equal to English *with difficulty*; English *while* generally expresses the same thing as *pendant que*. Furthermore, the polylog of one century becomes the monolog of the next, and the miolog of the future. The monolog *cupboard* used to be the polylog *cup board*. At the present day a Frenchman treats this unit, not as a synthetic product of *cup* and *board*, but as an integral primary unit.

Turning to the converse side of the question, we may discover vast numbers of monologs which we produce synthetically by composition or by derivation.

A foreigner having learnt *harmless* integrally will not hesitate to recognize or to produce *harmlessly*; knowing the monolog *bright* and the miolog *ness*, he will produce by synthesis *brightness*; knowing *polir*, we may forge *repolir*, or knowing *repolir* we may hazard *polir* with a fair chance of success. The cumbrous but none the less convenient German compound monologs are cognized and learnt in exactly the same manner as their polylogical English equivalents.

All these considerations tend to show among the other things that the accident of graphic continuity has little to do with the point we are examining, that primary matter is not restricted to monologs and that secondary matter may include them. Were every German monolog to be treated as primary matter our study would be as infinite as the number of German monologs. Were every French polylog to be treated as secondary matter our French compositions would be as lucid to a Frenchman as pidgin English is to a Cockney, and all French reading matter would be as hard to decipher as Assyrian cuneiform.

To what conclusions must we come and what principles may we enunciate as a result of examining the foregoing examples?

Let it be stated as axiomatic that, *ceteris paribus*, the integral assimilation of the matter of a given language is just as difficult or just as easy as the integral assimilation of the matter of any other language.

Some languages are said to be more difficult or more easy than others. As a concrete instance, Russian is said to be extremely difficult and Danish relatively easy for an English student. This statement is rightly based on the fact that Russian is a highly inflected language, whereas Danish is not.

And yet a Russian child and a Danish child will learn their respective native languages in their colloquial form with the same or approximately the same ease.

The deriving of a regular plural noun from the singular is a remarkably simple operation in English and a remarkably difficult one in German, and yet the German child learns his native plural nouns with approximately the same ease as the English child learns those of English.

The order of words in a French sentence is irregular in a very high degree; in English the word-order is far simpler, and yet the French child learns to form his sentences with approximately the same ease as the English child.

Stated in general terms, the fact is that the native user of a language subject to complex laws will, all other things being equal, make almost as few mistakes as the native speaker of a language subject to very simple laws. It may indeed, be regarded as an axiom that all languages in their colloquial form are equally or almost equally easy when considered from the point of view of their respective native users.

This most significant phenomenon can only admit of one explanation, and can point to but one conclusion. Let us ask ourselves under what conditions the respective solutions of a complex and of a simple problem are equally easy. The answer is clear—viz. *when we learn the respective solutions by heart*!

The obvious conclusion is that when we learn our native language, whatever it may be, in learning how to solve its problems we learn by heart the solutions of the problems. Reducing this statement to more precise terms, we may state as an incontrovertible fact that we treat the fundamental matter of our native language not as secondary, but as primary matter.

The essential difference between a difficult language and an easy one lies in the respective difficulty with which secondary matter is derived from the integrally assimilated units.

If German is a difficult language, it is because, having learnt singular nouns, we are unable without much calculation to derive from them their plural form; because having learnt as primary matter *der*, *die*, *das*, *Buch*, *Tinte*, and *Bleistift*, we are forced to calculate in order to derive as secondary matter *der Bleistift*, *die Tinte*, and *das Buch*.

The comparative ease and difficulty of languages, apart from phonetic and orthographic considerations, can only be estimated by reference to the formation of secondary or unseen matter. However complicated the mechanism of a given language, the natives themselves learn it with precision at an early age because they use the two processes in their natural and right proportions. Students of foreign languages generally produce results which are far inferior because they depend too little on primary matter and too much on secondary matter.

There would then appear to be three distinct advantages in assimilating integral units rather than in deriving secondary matter by inference:

1. Exclusion of any possibility of error.
2. Relief from the burden of abstract calculation.
3. Immediate utility of matter so learnt.

Let us illustrate the three points by concrete examples.

1. Exclusion of Error

No one who has treated integrally the polylogs *la dent* and *le tonnerre* can possibly say or write *le dent* or *la tonnerre.* No Frenchman who has learnt as primary matter *I always go to England* will ever produce *I go always in England.* No Englishman who has learnt *Ich bin mit meinem Freund gekommen* will ever be tempted to say *Ich habe gekommen mit mein Freund.* Were the Frenchman to learn *ought to, hardly ever, I want him to go,* integrally he would never say *I ought go, I go nearly never,* and *I will that he go.*

2. Relief from Calculation

In the second place, the integral process relieves us from an intolerable burden of abstract calculation.

The following sentence formed by an English student by synthetic construction will necessitate twenty-five separate efforts of the mind:

Ich habe mit grösstem Vergnügen seinen freundlichen Vorschlag angenommen.

1 to 9. Choice and recollection of the nine words in their employed uninflected form (presuming *Vergnügen, freundlich, Vorschlag,* and *annehmen* to have been previously acquired as primary matter).

10 to 18. Respective position of each.

19. Derivation of superlative from *gross*.

20. Recollection of the neuter dative singular case-inflection of an adjective when not preceded by article, etc.

21. Determination of gender of *Vergnügen*.

22. Recollection of the masculine accusative singular case-inflexion of the possessive adjective *sein*.

23. Ditto for the adjective *freundlich*.

24. Determination of the gender of *Vorschlag*.

25. Derivation of the past participle *angenommen* from the infinitive *annehmen*.

By learning the whole sentence as an integral unit, these twenty-five efforts would be reduced to one—viz. the production of the complete sentence in response to some stimulus.

3. Immediate Utility

An Englishman ignorant of French finds it necessary to pay a short visit to a remote French village where no interpreter is likely to be found. A few days before his departure he asks our advice on the linguistic question. We shall not advise him to study the French conjugation, nor the rules for the formation of the plural of nouns and adjectives; the short time at his disposal will preclude all possibility of doing any synthetic work. We may perhaps advise him to purchase some sort of tourist's pocket phrase-book and to make use of it by showing any appropriate sentence to the natives.

But this is not language-learning at all; it is merely a convenient substitute. The only advice we can give him from the point of view of language-study is to learn by heart such integral units as *oui, non, je ne comprends pas, je suis Anglais, y a-t-il quelqu'un ici qui parle anglais, donnez-moi ça, où?, combien?, comme ça, j'ai faim*, etc., etc.

This is primary matter. He need not know whether he is using monologs or polylogs. He will be unable to vary or to adapt any of these units; he must use them just as they are, and do the rest by gesture and by reference to his book.

Twelve categories of units may profitably be treated as primary matter.

We may now perhaps venture to draw conclusions from the various facts which we have examined and to lay down a few general rules concerning the respective functions of the two processes of study in order to determine what units should be treated respectively as primary or secondary matter.

There would appear to be twelve cases in which integral assimilation has an advantage over the complementary process.

1. When a monolog constitutes an entity undecomposable into significative parts and underivable from its etymological members it must necessarily be treated as primary matter. No possibility exists of deriving by synthesis such fundamental units as *bon, ici, où, comme, le, faire, commencer, souvenir, campagne, suis, viens, verrez, vu, pris, meilleur, lui*; *go, come, be, book, good, with, went, came, children, men, women, better, worse, am, is, ought.*

2. When a monolog can be decomposed into its ultimate units only by the aid of historical etymology, it would be well to treat it as primary matter. *Maintenant, toujours, bonheur, gendarme, aujourd'hui, affaire, avenir, beaucoup, lundi, remarquer, depuis, abonnement, rendez-vous, celui* should be learnt integrally, as should such English words as *perhaps, Wednesday, thirteen, because, afternoon, somewhere, forget, funny, alone, understand, hardly, yesterday, fortnight, never, neither.*

3. When a frequently used monolog, although decomposable without any special knowledge of etymology, is not generally regarded by the natives themselves as a compound, more especially when the meaning of the word does not represent the sum of the meanings of its component parts, it will be well to treat it as primary matter. The following are examples: *chou-fleur, quelque chose, quelqu'un, lorsque, pardessus, parapluie, paravent, blanchâtre, encaisser, déménager, bicyclette, malheureux, seulement*; *cupboard, waistcoat, forehead, something, upstairs, downstairs, seventeen, presently.*

4. When a monolog is a derived or compound word of which the elements can only be ascertained by reference to the

ancestral or some other foreign language it should be treated as an integral unit. Examples: *imprimer, exprimer, entrer, bibliothèque, téléphone, itinéraire, vicinal, traduire, candidat, fauteuil, réclamer, impossible, satisfaire, géographie,* and all words artificially composed in imitation of Latin, including nouns ending in *tion, sion, ence, ance, age, ure,* etc., adjectives ending in *able, ible, eux,* etc.

5. When a polylog constitutes a unit of which the semantic value is not the sum of its component monological parts or of which the component parts are not present to the minds of the native, it must be treated as a primary unit. *Bien que* no more represents the sum of *bien* and *que* than *understand* represents the sum of *under* and *stand.* Examples: *quand même, tout de suite, tout à l'heure, venir de, tenir à, il y a, tout le monde, quinze jours, s'agir, s'en aller, un peu, pomme de terre, comme il faut, qu'est-ce que c'est, qui est-ce que, peut-être, à moins que; next door, of course, all right, how much, last night, good-bye, had better, would rather, used to, on account of, in spite of.*

6. When a polylog constitutes a unit of which the individual parts are likely to be misplaced or confused with others, it should be taught as an integral unit. To ensure that such polylogs may be treated as primary and not secondary matter, it often becomes necessary to write these as one word; this is a very convenient device when using the phonetic script. Examples: *la fenêtre, la porte, le mur, la dent, le tonnerre, du pain, de l'argent, de la crême, commencer à, finir de, à la fin, au milieu, la semaine prochaine, assez de, près de, me le, le lui, suis venu; ought to, had better, would rather, at the end, in the middle, tell him to, on Sunday, half a dozen, hardly ever, more than, as much as.*

In this category we may place a vast number of polylogs composed of what Sweet calls *adjunct-words* and *head-words,* such as *article* and *noun, preposition* and *noun,* etc.

7. When a polylog is composed of elements rarely used in any other context it is advisable to treat it as primary matter. Examples: *je suis, suis-je, sera-t-il, il faut, rez-de-chaussée, induire en erreur, au fur et à mesure, to and fro.*

8. When the polylog is the natural equivalent of a native monolog it will be found expedient to treat it as a primary unit.

Examples: *en haut, en bas, laisser tomber, le mien, jusqu'à ce que, ce que, vouloir dire, coup d'œil; go in, go out, come back, get up, sit down, shall go, how much, ought to, on Monday.*

9. When a sentence is of idiomatic or irregular construction—that is to say, not to be composed by any laws of reasoning nor analogy—it should be learnt as if it were a simple monolog as primary matter: Examples: *Je n'y puis rien*; *S'il y a lieu*; *Il n'y a pas de quoi*; *S'il vous plaît*; *Je veux bien*; *Qu'est-ce que c'est que ça?*; *C'est pour rire*; *Ça m'est égal*; *Ça ne me fait rien*; *Il ne vaut pas la peine*; *I can't help it*; *It doesn't matter*; *It isn't worth while*; *How do you do?*; *I wish you a happy New Year*; *Turn to the left*; *It looks like rain*; *What's the matter?*

Into this category we place such stereotyped expressions as proverbs and well-known quotations.

10. A certain number of regular sentences serving as characteristic illustrations of important lexicological laws should be learnt by integral assimilation. In order to ensure their treatment as primary and not as secondary matter, these sentences should be thoroughly inculcated and assimilated at a very early stage. Examples: *Je ne le lui ai pas donné*; *Personne n'est venu*; *Je le lui ai dit hier soir*; *Que lui avez-vous dit?*; *Je ne peux pas venir ici demain matin*; *Je l'ai vu la semaine dernière*; *Il faut que je le fasse*; *Où voulez-vous qu'il aille?*

11. A certain number of regular sentences may be thoroughly assimilated at a fairly early stage in order to enable the student to make immediate use of his knowledge. This is more especially necessary in the case of adults who are contemplating a visit to the foreign country or are expecting foreign visitors. Examples: *Je ne vous comprends pas*; *Je suis anglais*; *Parlez plus lentement, s'il vous plaît*; *Qu'est-ce que cela veut dire?*; *Donnez-moi cela*; *Je désire une chambre*; *Eveillez-moi à huit heures*; *J'ai un peu faim*; *Je suis fatigué*; *Que puis-je avoir à manger?*

12. A certain number of regular sentences should be thoroughly assimilated in the early stages as primary matter in order to serve as model sentences to be developed by the student in the form of substitution tables.

The integral memorizing of a number of models is the best means of obviating the pernicious habits to be described in a later section under the heading "The Six Vicious Tendencies."

There is evidently no reason why categories 10, 11, and 12 should not coincide. The sentence *Je ne vous comprends pas* serves as an illustration of the general rule for the formation of negative sentences. It may serve as a model for the deriving of secondary matter by substitution, and it is probably the most useful sentence which anybody can learn when about to pay a first visit to France.

We may sum up these twelve lists or categories by stating that primary matter should consist of

(*a*) All simple and underived monologs and a vast number of compound and derived monologs.

(*b*) A vast number of polylogs (practically all those which are semantically equivalent to monologs).

(*c*) An indefinite number of sentences, both regular and irregular.

What then remains to be treated as secondary matter? When shall the student begin to use his reasoning faculties?

The answer is clear, and may be put in as concise a form as the question: the student is to use his reasoning faculties in order to learn the residue.

Of what does this residue consist?

It consists in the first place of all monologs derived or composed by the normal and regular laws of derivation and composition; it consists also of all the polylogs which do not come under headings 5 to 8; and, lastly, it consists of all the countless millions of sentences not included under headings 9 to 12.

In view of the great advantages offered by the assimilation of primary matter over the production of secondary matter, why shall we confine the process to the twelve categories enumerated above?

The obvious answer is that the number of units which can be assimilated integrally during a whole lifetime represents but a tiny fraction of the infinite number of combinations possible in any given language.

Sooner or later our integrally assimilated units must be supplemented by a vastly greater number to be produced by the student himself by the inferential process.

Is this, however, not in contradiction to what has been stated earlier? Have we not concluded that we learnt our native language as primary matter? Not so. We have never ventured to make such a sweeping and absurd assertion. We have concluded that we treat as primary matter not the *whole* but the *fundamental* matter of our native language.

Even in this case we must not assume that the matter of a language can be dichotomized into fundamental and non-fundamental units. The two terms are purely relative, for no unit can be considered as fundamental in itself.

Nor do we wish to suggest that the child assimilates fundamental units up to a certain moment and from that moment onward abandons the process in favour of inferential production. The two processes are used concurrently during the whole of our lives. What we do maintain is that in the very early stages the assimilation of primary matter is used in a larger degree, and that its use decreases in proportion to our general linguistic progress. Conversely the comparatively small amount of productive work of the early stages increases little by little in direct ratio to this progress.

We may now inquire whether existing methods, both ancient and modern, treat as a fundamental factor the distinction between the two classes of matter, and consider with any measure of consistency the two processes of study.

The critical analysis of a large number of methods over a period of many years conveys the impression that this factor, in common with other vital factors, has been completely overlooked.

Indeed, in many modern methods the only sentences apparently considered fit matter for integral memorizing take the form of archaic proverbs and infantile nursery rhymes!

We noted earlier in the present section the extreme importance of a thorough understanding of these two processes; we hinted that the conclusions which result from their perfect differentiation and a knowledge of their functions would have a most vital bearing on the whole question of language-study.

We will now venture to assert that in all but the most exceptional cases no method can possibly be sound which does not treat as primary matter most or all of the twelve categories of units that we have enumerated and described. All methods which assume monologs alone to constitute essentially the primary matter to be assimilated integrally, and which leave categories 5 to 12 to be treated as secondary matter to be derived by the student himself, must be rejected as unsound and unpractical.

We may repeat the reason upon which our judgment is founded: *Unless a vastly greater number of units are treated by the pure faculty of memory than is generally the case, the student will acquire, not the capacity of forming correct sentences, but the capacity of making unlimited mistakes, and by so doing will form habits which it will require perhaps years to eradicate!*

Section 19.—Gradation. In order that the pupil may proceed by the line of least resistance, he should pass from the known to the unknown by easy stages, each of which will serve as a preparation for the one immediately following.

It is considered by many that gradation implies passing from the incorrect to the correct, from broken speech to that used by natives, from hesitation to fluency. It has often been stated that perfection can only come from the gradual elimination of the factor of error. We would urge that the factor of error should never be allowed to obtain any footing at all. All errors other than those made by native speakers are abnormalities, and the results of a faulty method. We cannot and must not tolerate any system of teaching which will lead a student to pass off infinitives as past tenses, to use singulars instead of plurals, or to consider the nominative to be the universal case.

It is chiefly in this respect that a *general standard programme* differs from a *special corrective course.* The latter is designed expressly to eliminate the factor of error from the speech of the victims of faulty methods; the former is a system of teaching designed to result in correct speech and nothing but correct speech; hence the inclusion in our basic principle of the clauses "as spoken by natives" and "as written by natives."

What is *error*? Of what does it consist? Surely error is nothing other than the using of forms which are unknown to the native speaker or writer. An English student of French says [iːt nəː fou pɑː]; the Frenchman says [infopɑ]; consequently the former constitutes an error or a series of errors. An English student may say or write *la tonnerre*; no Frenchman says or writes *la tonnerre*, consequently this is an error. No Frenchman would ever say "J'ai été ici pour deux jours" in the sense of "I've been here for two days"; consequently the sentence is erroneous.

Error, however, is not confined to the using of non-native sounds, non-native combinations, and non-native meanings. The unit of language as used normally *by natives* is the fluent sentence; consequently the normal use of non-fluent sentences constitutes error. *The progress of students can only be measured by their capacity for understanding and for producing fluent sentences.*

The following passages extracted from *How to Learn a Language*[1] emphasize the value of this dictum as considered from the point of view of the student of missionary linguistics:

"Unless speaking, like piano-playing, is automatically correct, the result is not enjoyable. The only way to ensure this automatic accuracy in pronunciation, vocabulary, and construction is to learn all sorts of sentences, by frequent repetition, until an inaccurate sentence becomes an impossibility. When one has thus memorized his sentences they become matrices for thoughts. They are well-formed moulds into which all statements of that character readily fall. No pains spent on absolutely fixing these in the memory can be too great."

"Every art and science has its fundamentals. He who would be a master of any art must gain an automatic command of its basic principles. And just as the master of computation must have the sum, difference, and product of the nine digits at his tongue's end, so must the master of every language have

[1] A clear and concise *exposé* of a remarkably sound system of language-study, published in New York in 1916 by Thomas F. Cummings.

as ready a command of its pronunciation, construction, and vocabulary. To get one's phrases correctly at the second or third trial is about as satisfactory as a like readiness would be in making change for railroad tickets. If, however, one knows his language expressions as well as he knows his multiplication tables, he may rest satisfied. Anything else is annoyance and vexation."

"Our standard of attainment is *five syllables per second.* He who can deliver his language material at this rate of speed may rank as a skilled workman. Less than this is not efficiency."

"The only way to learn accuracy is by being fluent, for fluency is an integral part of accuracy. He who does not sing to time is inaccurate. He who does not speak to speed is also inaccurate."

"Recognition of failure is the first step toward success, but some foreign residents are so far from such recognition as to say: 'These people do not understand their own language.' True enough! Not as spoken by a raw foreigner."

If the work of a serious student is characterized by a certain proportion of error, it is a fairly trustworthy sign that he is doing work which is too difficult for him: there has been faulty gradation. All work performed by pupils in accordance with a properly graduated method under ideal conditions should be marked by extreme facility and extreme accuracy.

Gradation does not imply the learning of the easier aspects of language as a preparation for the more difficult. To consider the written form as a stepping-stone to the spoken form is one of the most popular fallacies of the amateur student of language, and the one which leads him the most surely to broken or pidgin speech.

What we can do, however, to ensure gradation on sound and salutary lines is to regulate the quantity of units in accordance with the capacities of the average student, to work from the easier toward the more difficult forms of exercise, to select the more used in preference to the less used ergons, and to avoid abrupt transitions.

In order to draw up an ideal programme in accordance with

the principle of gradation and all that this term implies, we may conveniently divide the whole of the scholastic period into three stages, to be termed respectively *Elementary*, *Intermediate*, and *Advanced*.

When the student is able to understand about three-quarters of what he hears and reads, and is able to express correctly about half of whatever he wishes to say or write, the remainder of his study may (if this is considered expedient on other grounds) proceed almost entirely on the basis of the subconscious process. The moment considered favourable for the entry of the pupil into this new phase may be termed the *Point of Transition*.

Section 20.—The Microcosm. In order that the pupil may reach the 'point of transition' with the least delay, the vocabulary must be selected with the greatest care and perspicacity ; it should include none but the commonest and most characteristic units, representing the most important ergonic classes. A vocabulary of this nature may be termed the Quintessence or the Microcosm of the language. This Microcosm should be formed and organized systematically in accordance with and as a compromise between the principles of Frequency, Ergonic Combination, Concreteness, Proportion, and General Expediency.

In view of the fact that a large number of units will have to be the object of conscious study, and in every way thoroughly assimilated, and also that most of these are destined to be combined with each other in order to produce an almost unlimited stock of secondary matter, the utmost care must be exercised in the selection of these units by the method-maker.

The best method of selecting the matter is first to draw up on fairly broad lines a rough microcosm of the language, and then to make a definite choice of units more or less in accordance with the five somewhat conflicting principles of *Frequency*, *Ergonic Combination*, *Concreteness*, *Proportion*, and *General Expediency*. The result will be a nucleus of the language, a quintessence of its most useful and most characteristic parts—in short, a practical if not perfect microcosm of the language.

We will examine each of these principles in detail.

Frequency

The lexicological units of all degrees of graphic continuity and of ergonic completeness may be classified according to their degree of frequency or rareness—*i.e.* according to their degree of utility. It is evident that it is more useful for a foreigner to be able to use words like *go*, *is*, *here*, and *I* than words like *fidelity*, *quarry*, or *transit*. It may also be asserted that the more frequently used words will be the more easily learnt, from the mere fact that they are frequent, for since the frequent words are to be found in every text either spoken or written, the foreigner will be more likely to assimilate them than those only figuring at rare intervals.

Since the memorizing or catenizing of words is at best a tedious process, it is obviously the duty of an instructor, when choosing the matter to be memorized by the student, to select the more frequent and to reject the rarer units of vocabulary. If the memorizing of five hundred of such units is deemed to be a necessary stage in the study of a particular language there are at least two reasons why each of these should be chosen from among the frequently used and not the rare ones, the first reposing on utilitarian and the second on pedagogic considerations.

We will imagine that we have before us two books, each written with the intention of teaching us some foreign language. In the first few pages of the first we find a vocabulary roughly equivalent to the following :

> *Cherry, diligent, idle, roof, mouse, plough, jump, swim, nightingale, formerly, Dutchman, buckwheat, beautiful, Mary, Charles, lest, uncle, acorn, grasshopper, door-nail, huntsman, rejoice, unsubstantial, wearisome, praise, enemy, feign, honeysuckle, turbot, beseech, weep, daily-growing, shudder, prating, misbecome, peevish, wild boar.*

The other book, in its first pages, contains a vocabulary roughly equivalent to the following :

> *I, you, he, somebody, something, nobody, nothing, am, is, are, have, has, come, go, know, understand, do, see, hear,*

take, it, this, that, not, never, good, bad, ready, tired, very, too, quite, here, there, mine, yours, what, who, where, when, can, must, will.

Is it not evident that our choice would fall on the second book without a second's hesitation ? What is there about this vocabulary which attracts us, and what is it that repels us in the first ? Is it not merely the respective degrees of frequency and rareness ?

We feel that even if we only succeed in mastering the first few pages of the second book we shall know something worth knowing, and that in the first case if we even succeed in learning the heterogeneous group of words we shall certainly have forgotten them long before ever having the occasion to use them.

May we then consider it possible to divide all the words of a language into two categories, the useful and the useless ? At first sight it would appear possible to do so, but a moment of reflection will show us that between the two extremes there must be an imperceptible transition, that instead of two distinct categories respectively of frequent and rare words there is an infinite number of degrees of frequency. A few experiments in the practice of drawing up lists of the 100, 250, 500, and 1000 most used English etymons or ergons would be the best demonstration of the difficulties of such classifications and prove the necessity of working in accordance with precise principles, and, when the possibilities of reason are exhausted, even of invoking the arbitrary.

It should be noted that all frequency statistics in order to be valid must be based on considerations of relative speciality and generality. The more a word is special, the more difficult it is to assign to it its true frequency value. The word *French* is a most important word for a Frenchman, and of comparatively little importance to a Chinaman, for instance. The word *Folkestone* is a most frequent one in the speech of Folkestonians. *Hammer*, in the speech of a carpenter, is of far greater frequency than in that of a tailor.

If we wish to compose a list of the 500 most frequent English monologs, is the word *like* to figure once or twice ? If we are contenting ourselves with a list of mere morphons, it will appear once only; if our list is based on etymological considerations, it will also appear once only, for the verb *like* and the preposition *like* are both identical in origin. If our list is to be based on ergonic grounds it must appear at least four times, as infinitive, as present tense, as adjective, and as preposition. If we include semantic considerations the word must figure as many times as it has meanings. There is a vast difference between a list of morphons, etymons, ergons, and semanticons, and we must decide in advance according to which of these aspects we are working. Some would include as separate units the eight words *be, being, been, am, is, are, was, were*; others will include only the word *be* and refer to the seven others as mere ptosonic varieties. A list of words to be used for systematic pronunciation exercises will contain as a single unit the word *mine* and ignore the ergonic and semantic differences between the two varieties as in *This is mine* and *This is a mine.* But such a list will treat *foot* and *feet* as two units, as would the ergonic list; the semantic list would include *foot* at least twice, once with the meaning of *pedal extremity* and the other with that of *twelve inches.*

Ergonic Combination

Given the words *it, this, that, is, was, not, good, bad, large, small, new, ready, here, there, in, out, away, back,* it is possible to combine them into 288 perfectly rational and eminently useful sentences.

Given the words, *he, am, take, go, come, no, of, the, my, very, quite, now,* it is impossible to form (apart from a few laconisms) one single sentence, although these words represent an even higher degree of frequency than the first list.

The most carefully calculated frequency statistics based on etymons or morphons represent but lists of minor ergons, and as our pupil can never be encouraged or expected to learn isolated minor ergons on any considerable scale they will be of little or no practical value in a book of instruction.

If we decide that the first pages of such a book should contain the word *am,* we must also include the word *I,* without which *am* is a perfectly useless word. If we decide on presenting the present tense of the verb *be*, we must choose at the same time a group of adjectives or of adverbs of place, together with a few words to serve as subjects, in order that *be* may be studied in the form of sentences.

If, on the other hand, we decide on *take*, *see*, *know*, *understand*, *tell*, etc., as our first vocabulary, we must provide a few subjective and objective ergons with which the verbs may be combined.

In observing the principle of ergonic combination we must not neglect the principle of frequency, although the latter must be subordinated to a certain extent to the former. Were we to carry out the principle of frequency to its logical conclusion the pupil would hear nothing of nouns nor see a single example until fully 200 other words had been learnt, and yet without nouns certain words of the highest frequency degree, such as *a*, *the*, *my*, and *your*, remain but meaningless particles. We must be prepared to make mutual concessions of frequency and of ergonic combination so long as such concessions are not too one-sided. We cannot, for instance, exclude from our first lessons half a dozen nouns on the pretext that their presence will invalidate our frequency statistics, nor may we introduce a large number of rarer words in order to utilize fully the principle of ergonic combination.

This principle may be stated as follows: Certain groups or categories of ergons possess the power of almost unlimited combination; other groups of equal frequency have not this power of combination. The most interesting exercises are those which consist of combining words and ringing changes on a small number of words on the basis of previously memorized models.

In every programme there is generally a place where a word may be introduced to the best advantage. The right moment to introduce *very*, *rather*, *too*, and *quite* is when the pupil has just learnt his first group of adjectives; the right moment to introduce *here* is when the pupil has just learnt *come*. The best time to teach *some* is when the pupil is learning the polylogs *there is* and *there are*. Plural nouns and numerals combine well; *yesterday*, *last week*, etc., should be learnt with the first preterites; *not yet* combined with the anterior tenses form most useful and natural sentences.

The best way to gain a first-hand knowledge of the nature of this principle is to draw up a set of substitution tables; this interesting work will result in many curious surprises and shed much light on the powers of ergonic combination possessed by the most frequently used words.

Concreteness

Let us examine the following two lists of words and inquire into the essential difference between them.

1. *I, you, here, there, this, that, door, window, ceiling, wall, floor, arm, hand, pocket, take, put, go, come, move, shake, push, pull, open, shut, on, under, over, against, one, two, three, large, small.*
2. *People, language, man, something, everything, somebody, water, shop, train, bird, know, understand, do, think, expect, mean, like, wonder, ask, answer, for, with, without, of, to-day, yesterday, Monday, town, country, very, too, good, bad, ready, busy, beautiful, ugly.*

There does not seem to be any great difference in their relative degrees of utility. On the whole, the second group appears to be somewhat favoured in this respect. The first group seems to possess better possibilities of ergonic combination. Beyond these two facts there does not seem to be any marked difference between them.

But let us suppose that it falls to us to teach these words to a foreigner who so far knows no word of English and whose language is unknown to us. A very striking difference between the two groups then becomes manifest. If we are in a room (and lessons are not generally given in the street) a few elementary gestures and actions will make clear to our pupil the meaning of the words contained in the first group, whereas the most violent gesticulations would be necessary in order to give even the faintest notions of the meanings of those in the second group. A beatific expression of admiration may convey the idea that the object of our contemplation is beautiful, but even then our conception of beauty may not agree with that of our pupil. An expression of disgust and loathing may suggest that we are trying to convey the idea that something to our mind is ugly; or we may convey the expression that we have been poisoned or that we are awaiting a visit from a dentist. Our onomatopoetic rendering of the idea *train* will result in puffings and snortings which may suggest a grampus or a futurist orchestra. Even a professional gesture specialist might exhaust his powers of mimicry without conveying anything but the vaguest impressions of the second group of words.

It would appear to be a psychological fact that we learn with comparative ease the names of concrete things, qualities, and actions, and with comparative difficulty the names of things which are not present, qualities which are not visible, and actions which we do not see performed. It will therefore be necessary at certain moments, more especially in the earlier stages, to sacrifice both the frequency principle and that of ergonic combination in order to introduce words of which the only merit is their facility of immediate comprehension.

The teacher will find it convenient to introduce the names of all the objects in the schoolroom, to give undue importance to words such as *ink*, *chalk*, *blackboard*, *handle*, *ceiling*, and *desk*, not because of their intrinsic utility, not because of their value in substitution tables, but because of their *concreteness*. Better than all pictures, better than all definitions, and suggestions by context, are the things themselves. It is quite impossible to reconcile the principle of frequency with that of concreteness, for, generally speaking, the most frequently used words are precisely those which it is the most difficult to concretize, and *vice versa*. The only escape from the dilemma is to work on parallel lines, alternating concretizing exercises with others of which the object is to present material in accordance with the laws of frequency and of ergonic combination.

Proportion

A teacher who spends nine-tenths of his time and energy in the teaching of verbs, who has made a speciality of their manifold classifications, modifications, and aspects, doubtless does good work. But by crowding all the other categories of ergons as mere appanages to the verb, he is not an ideal teacher; his interest being centred upon his speciality, the verb, he offends against the principle of proportion. A language method should treat each ergonic division according to its importance, and not develop any particular one at the expense of others.

The various parts of speech and their subdivisions should be introduced proportionately, the development of each should proceed on parallel lines. A given lesson may introduce, let us say, a group of adjectives, a few adverbs of degree with which to modify them, a few nouns as objects of modification, and a sprinkling of the members of the verb *to be* to show the predicative relation. The next lesson should change the subject and deal, let us say, with a new group of verbs, or a new tense of verbs already studied. The next lesson should concern, let us say, prepositions and a new set of nouns, to be followed by another, relating, let us say, to conjunctions and subordinate sentences. A series of complements of time might well follow, succeeded by the study of a new group of pronouns. Having run round the ergonic circle, we may again revert to adjectives and increase the nucleus formed some half dozen lessons before.

In this way each part of speech receives due and proper attention, so that each may play its part in the development of the pupil's knowledge of the language.

The principle of proportion should be applied not only to the ergonic categories, but also to other aspects of language and its study. Phonetics is a very interesting study and one of the foundations of sure progress, but an overdose of phonetics may be detrimental instead of beneficial. A doctor is not satisfied with the impatient patient who swallows a whole pint of tonic instead of the prescribed three tablespoonfuls a day.

General Expediency

In addition to the more or less precise claims of Frequency, Ergonic Combination, Concreteness and Proportion, there are certain minor requirements which we may treat under the heading of General Expediency.

When drawing up a list of words or a substitution table it

often happens that the inclusion of a comparatively rare word will complete and round off a category. If by considerations of the frequency principle we omit it, not only will this cause a more or less perceptible gap in the category, but later on it will be difficult to find a place for it.

The word *hundred* is of far less importance than *one*, *two*, or *three*; the word *thousand* is less useful still, and *million* is a comparatively rare word. The ideal principle of frequency will not allow us to present at the same moment words of such widely separated degrees of utility, and yet to omit the words *thousand* and *million* in a lesson devoted to the teaching of numerals would constitute a lacuna hardly to be justified by any considerations of frequency.

For a second example let us suppose that we are devoting an early paragraph to the words *always*, *generally*, *usually*, *often*, *sometimes*, and *never*. Frequency statistics tell us that these words are, roughly speaking, of the same importance, but consign *ever*, *hardly ever*, *scarcely ever*, *rarely*, and *frequently* to an outer radius, and *seldom*, *ordinarily*, and *occasionally* to a still more remote radius. And yet all these fourteen words belong to the same ergonic family (adverbs of frequency generally in the pre-verbal position) and are mutually interchangeable in a substitution table. Whether the comparative rareness of the latter words induces us to relegate the whole group to a later lesson, or whether the comparative frequency of the former words leads us to introduce it in an early lesson, we transgress in either case the laws of frequency. But if such transgression results in our cutting up the group into three we may be offending against the laws of common-sense by spoiling an otherwise perfect substitution table in which there is exactly room for all the fourteen.

In such cases in order to round off our subject instead of leaving it with ragged edges, we may certainly subordinate frequency to expediency. As a matter of fact it is difficult enough to compose a substitution table in such a way that all the combinations will make rational sentences without further handicapping ourselves in our efforts toward an impossible perfection.

Other cases will readily occur to teachers, in each of which the inclusion in our microcosm of some unit is justified by reasons which do not fall directly under any of the principles we have named and examined.

Section 21.—Subconscious Comprehension. The pupil's powers of subconscious (or immediate) comprehension will be developed concurrently with his conscious study of the microcosm, and quite independently of the matter contained therein.

The student may become proficient in the use of the foreign language either consciously or subconsciously. In the former case he converts unknown into known matter by dint of conscious efforts directed more or less systematically by the teacher in a series of specific and appropriate exercises; in the latter case the language is assimilated spontaneously and automatically without any conscious efforts on the part of the pupil.

By intuition and not by intelligence the young child comes to understand his mother tongue; by intuition and not by intelligence he may come to understand a foreign tongue. The adult, relying not on intuition, but on intelligence, makes much slower progress and attains inferior results.

Of the vocabulary possessed by any person proficient in the use of a foreign language, a very small proportion has been acquired by conscious study, probably less than five per cent; the bulk of his vocabulary has been acquired by subconscious assimilation. A rational programme should therefore be designed with a view to enabling the student to utilize with the least delay and to the fullest extent his subconscious faculties.

During the whole period of study, one of the most profitable and interesting forms of work will be that which has for its main object the development of the pupils' capacities of understanding fluent speech. It will matter little whether the units of which it is composed have been the object of previous study or not. If the teacher realizes the exact functions of this form of work, recognizes the limitations of his audience, and pursues the system regularly and consistently, the pupils will in a remarkably short space of time come to follow intelligently and with ease the fluent speech of the teacher.

It must be clearly understood from the outset that the object of this type of work is not to provide material for conscious assimilation, not to furnish a vocabulary which the pupils will be expected to retain either as a whole or in its individual units, but to give the pupils an ideal series of opportunities for exercising and developing those powers of direct and subconscious understanding without mental analysis or calculation. It is designed to appeal to intuition and not to intelligence; the result produced may be considered as an end in itself, or may be considered as an auxiliary to the conscious and intelligent study which will be pursued concurrently.

The attitude of the pupils will be that of a passive receptivity; they will listen and watch, and by dint of listening and watching will gradually come to follow the trend of what is being said to them, and understand the gist of what they hear. In the first instance their comprehension will be vague and of the nebulous order, but as time goes on the diffuse nature of their comprehension will become more precise, and after some fifty short periods of this type of work they will be able to follow the thoughts of the speaker with ease.

Although the main object of this form of exercise is to foster habits of direct comprehension without the mediation of analysis or reasoning, we may also assume that a secondary group of results will be attained by these same means.

These talks, repeated day by day, will serve as a series of subconscious ear-training exercises; unfamiliar sounds and unfamiliar combinations of sounds will gradually come to be familiar; these continual immersions in the sea of sounds will in many cases result in the absorption of the sounds; they will linger in the ears, and the organs of speech will tend to conform themselves to the auditive impressions. Let us remember that it is almost exclusively by this process that each of us at an early age learnt to articulate and to produce the sounds of our mother tongue.

Although primarily designed as a purely semantic exercise, this will probably (if not certainly) entail the assimilation or the partial assimilation of many ergonic and etymological facts. The continual audition of [lafnɛːtr] or [mɔ̃liːvr] will tend to ensure future correctness in distinguishing masculine or feminine. It is intelligence and consciousness (not intuition and subconsciousness) that have ever produced *le fenêtre* or *ma livre.*

Similarly, at a later period, when the pupil is taught that objective personal pronouns do not follow the verb, but precede it, the previous ear-training provided by these talks will serve as a conclusive and effective corroboration. The teacher will say: "You have never heard me say *Je prends le,* have you? It would sound funny if I were to say *Je donne lui le,* wouldn't it?" and this appeal to the ear will be found more effective than all the ingenious rules of etymology or ergonics ever written.

The procedure of the teacher will be somewhat as follows:—He will first compose a rough-and-ready series of talks, either in outline or in the more developed form. In the earlier lessons these will be based on the conditions actually present: the schoolroom, its occupants, the furniture, and all or any of the concrete objects to be found therein. Each of these talks will suggest others, either extensions of the first or entirely new ones. The resourceful teacher will probably accumulate an extensive stock of these exercises to suit the particular needs of his various classes, and adapted to any special or local conditions.

In the earlier lessons much care must be exercised to fulfil the four essential conditions of subconscious (or intuitive) as opposed to conscious (or intelligent) work. These four conditions we will proceed to examine.

1. Gesture

Were the teacher at the first lesson to sit at his desk and reel off, with impassive features, without gesture, movement, or pause, a description of a country ramble or a railway journey, it is quite certain that no result whatever would be obtained. If, on the contrary, the teacher talks about the objects of the schoolroom, and illustrates his talk by an abundance of appropriate gestures and facial expressions, there is every chance that he will make himself perfectly understood from beginning to end.

This, then, is the first condition to be observed. When

speaking about the window the teacher will invariably point to or look toward the window; when alluding to a book he will point to, take up, or touch a book; he will point to himself at each occurrence of the words *je, me, moi, mon,* etc.; *ici, là, là-bas,* etc., will each have their appropriate gesture; negative sentences will be accompanied by a shake of the head, and questions by a raising of the eyebrows.

But there are, alas! teachers who plead an inability to use gesture or facial expression, or who confess to a rooted dislike of such histrionic artifices. We hear them say: "We are teachers, not cinema actors; we teach, we do not perform." We must answer that such people must be classed among those who have no aptitude either for using or for teaching colloquial French; they are to be numbered among those who have mistaken their vocation.

2. Interest

In order to maintain interest, all semblance of monotony must be avoided. Variety is one means of ensuring interest, and movement is another. A lifeless enumeration of the names of objects, of their qualities and attributes, will not result in a successful lesson. This does not mean that the teacher is to perform acrobatic feats and excite the pupils' sense of the ridiculous. He need not jump over chairs to illustrate the verb *sauter,* nor crawl along the floor to demonstrate the meaning of *ramper.* Between such exaggerations, however, and the tedious repetition of some hundreds of nouns there is a wide difference, and few teachers, if so minded, will experience any difficulty in steering a middle course.

3. Semantic Order

The words, sentences, and other units used by the teacher in the course of these talks should not be enunciated in any mechanical order. It is no part of this type of work to demonstrate facts of ergonics or etymology; our immediate purpose is to develop the pupils' powers of subconscious comprehension, not of the theory of speech, but of speech itself. At another moment and by other tactics we shall teach the pupil to calculate and to reason, but we cannot profitably combine in one and the same exercise appeals to the consciousness and to the subconsciousness.

At first sight it would appear an admirable idea to proceed by series of pairs, such as :

Voici le crayon, *voilà la plume.*
Voici le papier, *voilà la boîte.*
Voici un crayon, *voilà une plume.*
Voici un livre, *voilà une boîte.*

This, however, would be but a form of etymological or ergonic drill smuggled into and spoiling an exercise designed for other ends. Nor might it be successful even as drill, for the pupils might gain the impression that *le* must be used after *voici* and *la* after *voilà*.

Voici le crayon, *voici les crayons.*
Je prends la plume, *je prends les plumes*, etc.,

may be a good form of drill when exercised at the right moment, as may also be

Ceci est le crayon, *ceci n'est pas le crayon.*
Ceci est la plume, *ceci n'est pas la plume*, etc.

These and all similar forms of mechanical demonstrations are excellent in their place and considered as appropriate means to a predetermined end, but the fostering of the ability to understand rapid and fluent speech is quite independent of any forms of grammar drill.

4. Uninterrupted Passivity

Many teachers will feel an almost irresistible desire to include in this form of exercise an occasional question, to be answered by the class or by an individual pupil. Encouraged by the evident success of his efforts to be understood by the pupils, the teacher will be sorely tempted to test his success by giving his pupils a chance to respond by means of speech.

This would be a fatal error of tactics. It would immediately change the whole character of the exercise. It would interrupt the current of thought; it would convert subconscious into conscious effort. The pupils, anticipating future interrogations, would immediately abandon that passive attitude so favourable for the subconscious reception of impressions; they would henceforth make efforts to grasp and to memorize the individual words, and these efforts would tend to destroy the collective impression conveyed by the talk as a whole. *Ils ne verraient plus la forêt à cause des arbres.*

Instead of the nebulous recognition of the sentence "*Je ferme la porte,*" there will be a conscious retention of two isolated units [fεəm] and [pɔːt], with mental translation and mental mispronunciation. As an ultimate result of the pure subconscious comprehension of *la porte* the sight of the door will evoke the reaction [lapɔrt], whereas the conscious comprehension will probably produce as an immediate reaction either [pɔːt] or [ləː pɔːt].

In addition to these considerations, we must also bear in mind that any interruption whatever in the current of passive thought will militate against the success of the whole exercise. There must be fluency and continuity. We cannot stop to experiment nor afford breaks of twenty seconds in order to correct faulty answers. Unless there is a constant and uninterrupted flow of sentences the purpose of this type of work will be frustrated.

The subconscious and conscious processes of study have each their advantages and disadvantages; consequently the ideal programme must include both and reject neither. In order to ascertain to what extent and in what degree each of these is to be employed in a language course, we may draw up and frequently consult the following list:

SUBCONSCIOUS STUDY

Advantages	*Disadvantages*
Cumulative rapidity.	Comparative slowness during the first stages.
Little intelligence requisite on the part of the pupils.	Of little educational value as mental gymnastics.
Naturalness of resultant products.	Inaptitude for purposes of a corrective course.
Immediate comprehension of normal rapid speech.	

Conscious Study

Advantages	*Disadvantages*
Comparative rapidity during the early stages.	Comparative slowness during the later stages.
Concrete progress.	Beyond the capacity of dull pupils.
Of educational value as mental gymnastics.	Unnaturalness of resultant products.
Utility in reacting against vicious tendencies.	Inaptitude for fostering habits of immediate comprehension of normal rapid speech.
Value for purposes of a corrective course.	

PART V

AN IDEAL STANDARD PROGRAMME

HAVING reviewed the main principles of Linguistic Pedagogy, we will now endeavour to draw up a working programme embodying the conclusions suggested by our inquiry. We will consider as a standard programme that which will prove to be the most suitable for school-children. It will comprise the study of the foreign language (which we will assume to be French) in its oral and written aspects with a view to active and passive use. The whole period of study will be divided into three stages.

Section 22.—The first or elementary stage, of the duration of at least one term, will consist of:

(*a*) Easy exercises in subconscious comprehension.
(*b*) Imperative drill.
(*c*) Easy articulation exercises.
(*d*) Easy exercises in the use of phonetic symbols.
(*e*) Simple talks on the five lexicological theories.

The inexperienced but enthusiastic amateur worker, impatient of results and fired with the energy and ambition of all enthusiasts, is no sooner in possession of his apparatus than he flies to work in order to achieve concrete results the same day, the same morning, within the hour if possible.

The expert worker, less enthusiastic, but more practical, is desirous of achieving more rapid effective results, and so spends the first hour or the first day in cleaning the apparatus, overhauling the instruments, sharpening the tools, arranging the workroom, labelling the bottles, and providing himself with the hundred and one little things that will ensure economical and uninterrupted work.

At the end of the second day the expert is contemplating with pride the result of his finished labours; at the end of the second day the amateur finds it necessary to scrap his work and start afresh.

The inexperienced but enthusiastic language teacher, impatient of results, and fired with the energy and ambition of all enthusiasts, is no sooner in the presence of his pupil than he flies to work in order to get him to speak, read and write, and understand the language within three months, within one month, within the space of one lesson if possible.

The expert teacher, less enthusiastic, but more practical, is desirous of achieving more rapid *effective* results, and so spends the first lesson, the first month, or the first three months, in teaching the sounds of the language, in cultivating the pupil's faculties of auditive perception and imitation, in grounding him in the first principles of practical phonetics, semantics, and ergonics, in initiating him in the first principles of language and of language-study, in doing the hundred and one little things that will ensure economical and uninterrupted work.

At the end of the first year the expert teacher and his docile pupil are congratulating each other on the result of their joint and successful labours; at the end of the first year the amateur is wondering why his pupil can neither speak, read, write, nor understand the language, and the pupil, if intelligent, is probably looking out for another teacher.

The apparatus used in language-learning consists primarily of the pupil's organs of speech and hearing. An auxiliary set of apparatus consists of the pupil's faculties of discrimination and analogy. To these may be added the necessary complement of documentary matter enumerated and described in a later chapter of this book.

If the student wishes to do effective work and make effective progress, the initial stage of his study must be devoted to getting into working order the apparatus upon which his success depends. If his aims comprise the using of the spoken language, a sound preliminary knowledge of its sounds is indispensable; no progress is possible until each one has become perfectly familiar. The sounds stand to the spoken language in the same relation as the letters to the written language; in the same way that the capacity of tracing letters is an indispensable preliminary to the study of writing, so also is the capacity of articulating sounds an indispensable preliminary to the study of speaking. As our first efforts in the case of the native language were directed to the mastery of our native sounds, so also must the first efforts of the student be devoted to the sounds of the foreign language.

The first lessons will be devoted almost exclusively to *systematic pronunciation exercises*, first by learning to recognize and to reproduce the individual sounds, then by learning to combine them in monosyllabic words, and subsequently in polysyllabic words and short polylogs, and finally to acquire the art of correctly reproducing the longer polylogs and complete sentences.

No sharp line of demarcation can be drawn between pronunciation exercises proper as understood by the phonetician and *catenizing* exercises as understood by the language teacher. The faculty of catenizing, or learning sentences by heart, is merely a development of the faculty of remembering isolated sounds and short words; there is no difference of kind but of degree.

While learning the foreign sounds, the student must also learn to associate them with the graphic forms by which they are represented. This does not necessarily mean that he must at once commence the study of the conventional system of orthography. The student of the Chinese language may postpone for a while the study of the ideographs invented by the Chinese, as these are merely a graphic auxiliary to the language proper. Nor would we suggest that the student engaged in the study of the French spoken language should disperse his efforts at this early stage in devoting any attention to that cumbrous and curious system known as French orthography.

The graphic forms that we recommend are the symbols corresponding to the sounds themselves and known as *phonetic symbols*. The most suitable system will most probably be found to be that of the International Phonetic Association, not only on account of its intrinsic merits and adaptability, but also in view of its widespread diffusion in all countries.[1]

For the sake of economy it is desirable that the words and

[1] See Appendix for list of phonetic symbols.

sentences used during the pronunciation exercises should be selected from those forming part of the ergonic tables of the second stage; in all but exceptional cases there appears to be no objection to providing the integral translations of the units serving as phonetic examples, nor is there any grave objection to be urged against learning such bilingual equivalences as (what is termed commercially) a side line.

Some time must necessarily elapse before the student is perfectly familiar with all the sounds of the foreign language, but the more his attention is focused on the immediate object of his study the sooner will the desired result be obtained.

Since it would be dangerous to embark on a more ambitious type of exercise until the mastery of the sounds is complete, we may utilize the preliminary period to teach the broad fundamental principles of the lexicological sciences. We may introduce the theory of phonetics and show how sounds are classified; we may compare foreign sounds with their nearest native equivalents, laying particular stress on the differences between them. We may give him simple and interesting exercises dealing with the phonetics of his own language in order that he may better understand the phonetic system of the foreign language. We may document the student on the nature of semantics, and provide him with a simple series of exercises designed to show him the relations between words and thoughts, and the difference between meanings and functions. He will gradually become expert in the art of finding synonyms, and of paraphrasing in his own language. He must be made to understand, for instance, that the difference between *because* and *on account of* is an ergonic or functional difference, that the difference between *I would like him to go* and *I wish he'd go* is one of emotional degree; we may demonstrate that the true negative of *I must* is *I need not* (and not *I must not*), that the true negative of *it must be here* is *it can't be here*, etc., etc. By interesting exercises of this sort we shall anticipate and circumvent many misunderstandings and difficulties.

We may also introduce the leading principles of inflexions, derivations, and ergonics, taking our examples from, and basing our exercises on, the student's own language. In doing so we shall demonstrate that each language has its own characteristics, and that we must not expect any close analogy between languages which are not cognate.

In certain cases we shall find it profitable to instruct the pupil in the theory of language-learning. If our examples and exercises are judiciously chosen we may enlarge the horizon and quicken the ideas of our student; we may even cause him to share our enthusiasm and create an interest in the range of subjects treated in the present work. By so doing we shall give the soundest of all incentives to successful work; an intrinsic interest in language and language-learning in the abstract.

These indications, suggestions, and exercises may be given either systematically or at odd moments with the intention of breaking the monotony of the phonetic drill. The first stage is the right moment to choose for such talks, for it is now or never that we are to succeed in giving the right orientation and by means of preventive measures to react against the vicious tendencies to which allusion has already been made, and which will be more fully described in Part VII.

The opening move in the ideal standard programme which it is now our intention to outline may well consist of a first lesson in subconscious comprehension. We suggest that this should last from fifteen to thirty minutes.

If considered necessary, the teacher may tell the pupils to listen and to watch, that they are not to translate what they hear, and that under no circumstances whatever will any answer be given to such questions as "Please, what does that mean?" or "Please, what's that in English?"

It is understood that each of the sentences given in the following specimen lesson will be accompanied by the necessary gestures and movements.

Specimen of a First Lesson

"Regardez! Voilà la fenêtre. On appelle ça une fenêtre. Regardez tous! C'est la fenêtre.

"Regardez! Voilà la porte. C'est une porte. Ce n'est pas la fenêtre. C'est une porte. Je touche la porte. J'ouvre la porte. Je ferme la porte.

"Je vais à la fenêtre. Je regarde la fenêtre. Regardez la fenêtre. Je la touche. C'est une fenêtre.

"Regardez la porte! Regardez la fenêtre! Regardez le plafond! Ça c'est le plafond.

"Ceci n'est pas le plafond. C'est le plancher. Je regarde le plancher. Je regarde le plafond. Je regarde la fenêtre. Je regarde la porte.

"Est-ce la porte, ça? Oui, c'est la porte. Je vais à la porte. Je l'ouvre et je la ferme.

"Voici une chaise. Ce n'est pas une fenêtre. C'est une chaise. Regardez la chaise!

"Voici la table. La table. La chaise. Je vais à la table et je la touche. Je prends la chaise et je la mets près de la table.

"Le livre. Voici le livre. On appelle ça un livre. Je mets le livre sur la table.

"Voici ce qu'on appelle un crayon. Je prends le crayon et je le mets sur la chaise. Regardez le crayon qui est sur la chaise! Regardez le livre qui est sur la table!

"Je prends une feuille de papier. Regardez la feuille de papier! Je vais mettre le papier sur la table. Non—je ne le mettrai pas sur la table. Je le mettrai par terre, sur le plancher.

"La plume. Voilà la plume. Je prends la plume et le crayon. Regardez la plume et le crayon! Je les mets sur la chaise. Voilà!

"La porte. La fenêtre. La chaise. Le crayon. Le livre. La plume. La feuille de papier.

"Je prends maintenant un morceau de craie. Regardez la craie! Avec la craie j'écris au tableau noir. Voilà le tableau noir. Regardez tous le tableau noir!

"Je mets la craie sur la table. Je ramasse le papier et je le mets sur la table à côté de la craie.

"Voilà le mur. Je vais au mur et je le touche. Ce n'est pas le plafond. Voilà le plafond et voilà le plancher. Ceci, c'est le mur.

"Il y a quatre murs ici. Un, deux, trois, quatre. Je vais du mur à la fenêtre. Je suis maintenant à la fenêtre et je la touche.

"Je prends le livre. Je l'ouvre. Je le ferme. C'est mon

livre. Je mets le livre dans ma poche. Je mets aussi le crayon dans ma poche.

" Voici un tiroir. J'ouvre le tiroir. Je mets la feuille de papier dans le tiroir et je le ferme.

" Un cahier. On appelle ça un cahier. Ce n'est pas un livre. C'est un cahier. Je prends le cahier et je le mets sur la chaise.

" Une clef. Voici une clef. C'est ma clef. Regardez la clef ! Je vais mettre la clef sur la table.

" La fenêtre. La porte. Le plafond. Le plancher. Le mur. La chaise. La table. Le tiroir. Le crayon. La plume. Le papier. La craie. La clef. Le tableau noir.

" Voici une lettre. J'ai tiré cette lettre de ma poche. Regardez la lettre ! Voici l'enveloppe. Voici le timbre. Je mets la lettre sur la table.

" On appelle ceci un encrier. Un encrier. Voici l'encrier. Il est sur la table. Je mets la plume dans l'encrier.

" Regardez cette boîte-ci ! Je l'ouvre. C'est une boîte. Qu'est-ce qu'il y a dans la boîte ? Regardez ! Il y a de la craie. Il y a beaucoup de morceaux de craie dans la boîte. Je la mets sur la table.

" Voici encore une boîte. Je l'ai tiré de ma poche. C'est une petite boîte. Qu'est-ce qu'il y a dans cette boîte-ci ? De la craie ? Non. Des livres ? Non. Des plumes ? Non.

" Regardez ! J'ouvre la boîte et je regarde ce qu'il y a dedans. Ce sont des allumettes. Regardez les allumettes ! Je prends des allumettes dans la boîte et je les mets sur la table. J'en prends une, deux, trois, quatre, cinq, six. Six allumettes.

" Je vais compter. Une fenêtre. Deux fenêtres. Une boîte. Deux boîtes. Un mur, deux murs, trois murs, quatre murs. Un livre, deux livres, trois livres, quatre livres. Une feuille de papier, deux feuilles de papier, trois feuilles de papier, etc., etc.

" Regardez maintenant ce que je vais faire. Je vais arranger tous les objets qui sont sur la table.

" D'abord je prends le livre et je le mets ici. Le crayon ; je le mets ici. La plume ; je la mets à côté du crayon. La clef ; je la mets ici. La lettre ; ici. La boîte—avec la craie dedans ; ici. L'autre boîte, la boîte à allumettes ; je la mets ici, etc., etc.

" La feuille de papier. Où est-elle, la feuille de papier ? Où est la feuille de papier ? Ah, la voici ! La voici dans le tiroir. Voici la feuille de papier.

" Voilà ! Regardez sur la table ! Regardez tous les objets ! Le livre, la craie, la plume, la clef, etc., etc.

" Maintenant je prends la lettre et je la mets dans ma poche. Le livre ; je le mets dans le tiroir. L'encrier ; je le laisse là, sur la table. La clef ; je la mets dans ma poche, le crayon aussi. Le cahier ; dans le tiroir.

" La boîte ; je la mets dans l'armoire. Oui, l'armoire. On appelle ça une armoire. Ce n'est pas le tiroir. Voilà le tiroir. Voici l'armoire.

" Regardons maintenant tous les objets dont j'ai parlé : la fenêtre, la porte, le mur," etc., etc.

This exercise in subconscious comprehension will probably not occupy the whole of the period generally allotted to the French lesson ; indeed, it would be unwise to dwell more than from fifteen to twenty minutes on any one type of work. The remainder of the first lesson may be devoted to other exercises suggested in these pages. We would advise as a useful sequel to the above talk a first lesson in conscious ear-training. This may be given in the following way :

" While I was talking in French to you just now, you must have heard that I was using a number of sounds that we never use when we are speaking English. I am going to pronounce some of these sounds to you now, and I want you to notice them particularly. You are not to pronounce them after me at present, but just to listen carefully. This will sharpen your ears and make it easier for you to imitate me when we start learning French pronunciation :

" [iː], [iː], [eː], [eː], [ɛː], [ɛː], [aː], [aː], etc., etc.

" All the sounds I have just made are used when we speak French, and we can't speak French without making them.

" I expect you will have noticed that some of them are just

like some English sounds. Listen again, and you will tell me which ones you think sound like English ones :

"[iː iː]. Yes, that sounds very English, doesn't it? That is the English vowel-sound that we make when we say *see* or *be*.

"[eː eː]. No, that doesn't sound at all English—at any rate not like the English that we speak in this part of the country. If you went to Scotland you would probably hear people there using the sound [eː] when they speak English.

"[ɛː ɛː]. Yes, something like the vowel in the word *pen*, isn't it? It's really more like a sound you hear when I say *fair* or *Mary*. Listen again :

"[aː aː]. Have you ever heard that in English? As in the word *up*? Yes, very much like the vowel in *up* or *cut*, especially as we pronounce such words here in the south of England."

If the lesson is given in the north of England the French sounds will be compared with those of the local pronunciation. [ɛː] will be compared with the *a* of *take* (in some parts of Yorkshire), [a] with the vowel of *cat* (north of England), etc.

The Second Lesson

This, as before, may start by a period devoted to an exercise in subconscious comprehension. It may be the repetition of the one given the day before, or may be a modified form of it, with the addition of a few new words and forms.

The second part of the lesson may be the continuation of the exercise in ear-practice. We may now say :

"I am now going to read to you some lists of French words. In a few days' time you will have to repeat these words after me and pronounce them just as I do, so I want you to listen very carefully :

"Lit, qui, si, oui, pris, mis, fils, guide, livre, cerise, etc.

"Clef, chez, nez, blé, secouer, jouer, lier, etc.

"Belle, sec, sept, elle, laine, aide, même, prêt, mais, fouet, etc.

"Bal, mal, place, chaque, salle, drap, moi, voix, cage, etc.

"Classe, phrase, âge, tasse, pas, mois, etc.

"Bonne, donne, note, mode, noble, etc.
"Chaud, veau, faute, cause, rose, chose, autre," etc.

And so on for other French sounds.

The Third Lesson

This will continue the series of exercises in subconscious comprehension. We suggest the following outline:

"Regardez la craie. Elle est blanche. Le papier est blanc. Le plafond est blanc. Est-ce que la craie est blanche? Oui, elle est blanche. Est-ce que le plafond est blanc? Oui, il est blanc.

"Le tableau est noir. L'encre est noire. Voilà encore quelque chose qui est noir. Le tableau n'est pas blanc. Il est noir.

"Le livre est grand. C'est un grand livre. L'armoire est grande. Ce livre-ci n'est pas grand. Il est petit. Etc., etc.

"Est-ce que ce crayon-ci est long ou court? Il est long. La craie n'est pas longue. Ce morceau de craie est court. Voici deux crayons. L'un est court. L'autre est long. Je mets le crayon long sur la table et le crayon court sur la chaise. Etc.

"Le plafond est haut. La chaise n'est pas haute. Elle est basse. . . .

"Je prends le livre. Je le tiens. Je le regarde. Je l'ouvre. Je le ferme. Je le mets dans le tiroir.

"Je prends une feuille de papier. Je la regarde. Je la tiens. Je la touche. Je la déchire.

"Je prends mon canif. Je l'ouvre. Je prends une allumette et je la coupe avec mon canif. Avec mon canif je coupe l'allumette. Je coupe le papier. Je coupe la craie. . . .

"Je mets le papier sur la table. Je mets un livre sur le papier. Je mets une boîte sur le livre. Je mets le crayon sur la boîte.

"Je mets la chaise près de la fenêtre. Je mets l'autre chaise près de la porte.

"Je vais à la porte. Je vais à la fenêtre. Je vais au pupitre. Je vais au mur. Je reviens à ma place.

"Je m'assieds. Je me lève. Je marche. Je m'arrête. Je retourne à ma place. Je m'assieds.

"Je regarde la fenêtre. Je regarde le plafond. (Le plafond est blanc.) Je regarde le tableau. (Le tableau est noir.)

"Je prends le livre. (Le livre est grand.) Je le mets sur la chaise. (La chaise est basse.)

"Où est le livre ? Il est sur la table. Et le crayon ? Il est sur la chaise. Et le papier, où est-il ? Il est par terre.

"Où est la fenêtre ? Voilà la fenêtre. Où est la porte ? Voilà la porte. La porte est là. Où est le plafond ? Voilà le plafond.

"Où est le livre ? Voici le livre. Et le crayon ? Le voilà. Et la plume ? La voilà.

"Comment est la craie ? Elle est blanche. Comment est le plafond ? Il est blanc.

"Combien de livres y a-t-il ici ? Il y en a deux ; le livre bleu et le livre rouge.

"Combien y a-t-il de chaises ? Il y en a trois. Il y en a une près de la porte. Il y en a une autre près de la fenêtre, et l'autre est ici, près de moi." Etc., etc.

Ear-practice may be continued on the same lines as before, and we may now introduce easy articulation exercises.

Specimen First Lesson in Articulation

"All pronounce after me the sound [ɑː].

[The pupils do so.]

"Yes, very good; but I want to hear it pronounced more steadily and with more force. Try again, and make the sound last until I raise my hand.

[The pupils produce a long [ɑː], lasting from two to four seconds.]

"Now [addressing individual pupils] see whether you can produce a nice [ɑː].

[Various pupils do so.]

"Yes, that's very good. When I want you to pronounce that sound I shall write this letter on the blackboard: [ɑ]. If I put two dots beside it, [ɑː], that will mean that you must make it long."

[The symbol will remain on the blackboard.]

Sounds such as [iː], [uː], [æː], [ɔː], [v], [z], [ʒ], [ʃ], etc., will be treated in the same way.

The pupils must now come to realize that the English [aɪ], [ɛɪ], etc., are not pure vowels, and that [tʃ] and [dʒ] are not simple consonants.

"Now pronounce [aɪ].

[The pupils do so.]

"Make the sound last as long as I hold up my hand."

Result, three seconds of [a] and three seconds of [ɪ]. We call the attention of the pupils to that fact, and make repeated trials in order to demonstrate the point clearly.

A 'narrow' transcription of the English sounds is to be recommended. This may seem a strange procedure, but it is nevertheless a sound one, resulting in clearer and quicker comprehension.

English *oo* in *good* must be indicated by [ʊ]; the vowel in *bit* should be written [ɪ]; similarly the vowel in *pen* should be [ɛ] and the English *r* should be [ɹ].

If we adopted the conventional simplifications generally used in teaching English to foreigners ([u] for [ʊ], [i] for [ɪ], etc.), we should deprive ourselves of a valuable means of demonstrating some of the essential differences between English and French vowels.

All phoneticians will probably agree that a broad transcription is sufficient when examining the sounds of any one language, but that a narrow transcription becomes desirable when comparing the sounds of two or more languages.

At a subsequent moment, when a pupil pronounces the English vowel in *bit* instead of the French vowel in *si*, we may write the two vowels [ɪ] and [i] on the blackboard and point out that the former was pronounced instead of the latter. If, on the other hand, the pupil unduly lengthens the French vowel in *si*, we shall write the two forms [iː] and [i], and call the pupil's attention to the fact that the latter is required and not the former.

Without a narrow transcription there will always be a certain confusion between [ɪ], [i], and [iː]; between [ʊ], [u], and [uː]; between [ɹ], [r], and [ʀ], etc.

The Fourth Lesson

Exercises in Subconscious Comprehension

These will continue on the lines suggested in the preceding pages, the vocabulary gradually becoming more extensive. The teacher will perform such actions as dropping, picking up, breaking, raising, pushing, pulling, rubbing, scratching, writing, rubbing out, etc., etc. He will speak of the relative positions of various objects ("Le crayon est sur la boîte, sous la boîte, devant la boîte. La chaise est entre la porte et la fenêtre," etc.), and will introduce possessives and similar modifying units.

Ear-training Exercises

These may now include the passive audition of polysyllabic words grouped according to their phonetic structure:

Allez, prenez, lisez, écrivez, donnez.
Honneur, couleur, odeur, valeur, vapeur, moteur.
Final, royal, journal, moral, spécial.
Humain, africain, marin, musicien.
Heureux, joyeux, précieux, vicieux.
Actif, passif, tardif, négatif. Etc., etc.

Articulation Exercises

As before.

Imperative Drill

This new type of exercise may now be introduced. Although it is similar to the exercise in subconscious comprehension, the object in view is not the same, nor will the pupils maintain their attitude of purely passive receptivity. The teacher will issue commands in French to be carried out by the class as a whole, or by individual pupils. Needless to say, each one of the orders will be accompanied in the first instance by appropriate gestures.

"Regardez le plafond! Regardez la fenêtre! Regardez la porte! Regardez moi! etc.

"Prenez votre livre! Ouvrez votre livre! Lisez votre livre! Fermez votre livre! Levez votre livre! Mettez votre livre sur le pupitre! etc.

"Prenez votre crayon! Levez votre crayon! Regardez votre crayon! Laissez tomber votre crayon! Ramassez votre crayon! Mettez votre crayon dans votre poche! etc.

"Levez la main gauche! Levez la main droite! Baissez la main gauche! Baissez la main droite! Baissez les yeux! Levez les yeux! Fermez les yeux! Ouvrez les yeux! Ouvrez la bouche! Fermez la bouche! etc.

"Retournez-vous! Regardez-moi! etc.

"Touchez votre banc! Touchez votre pupitre. Touchez le plancher! Touchez votre livre! Touchez votre tête! etc.

"Frottez-vous les mains! Battez des mains! Prenez votre crayon! Tournez votre crayon! Frottez votre crayon! Poussez votre pupitre! Tirez votre pupitre! Penchez-vous du côté gauche! Penchez-vous du côté droit! etc.

"Levez-vous! Sortez de votre banc! Allez à la porte! Allez à la fenêtre! Allez à la table! Allez au mur! Allez à l'armoire! Retournez à votre place! Asseyez-vous!" etc.

Fifth and Sixth Lessons

These may be devoted to a general recapitulation of all the exercises previously described.

Seventh and Eighth Lessons

Exercises in Subconscious Comprehension

The teacher will continue these daily talks on the same lines as before. He may speak of the parts of the body, articles of clothing, and the substances of which various objects are composed.

Ear-training Exercises

Longer words may be introduced, such as:

Instructif, interrogatif, déterminatif.
Civilization, conversation, explication, proposition, traduction.
Comparaison, combinaison, conjugaison, déclinaison.
Imaginable, inévitable, déplorable, incapable, improbable.
Impossibilité, difficulté, sensibilité.

Articulation Exercises

As before.

When the pupils have learnt to isolate and to produce with ease the sounds they know, and can read and write the isolated symbols representing them, the foreign sounds are introduced one by one.

"Pronounce [iː].

[The pupils do so.]

"Are your lips rounded and bunched up, or are the corners wide apart?

[The pupils note that they are wide.]

"Pronounce [iː] with the lips rounded and bunched together, like this.

[The pupils do so more or less successfully.]

"We must try that again. Be sure that it is really [iː] that you are pronouncing, and be sure that your lips are rounded just as if you were going to whistle.

[A more successful [yː] is the result.]

"Now, does that appear to be an English sound? Do you use [y] when you are speaking English? No, of course you don't; it isn't an English sound; it's a sound that French boys and girls use when they speak their own language. Let us do it again. Now then, all together: [yː].

"When I want you to pronounce this sound, I shall write on the blackboard the letter [y]. We shall not call it y (pronounced [wai]), but the letter [y].

Now I am going to pronounce a strange sound to you. It doesn't exist in English, or at any rate in this part of England; it is a sound that you have probably never heard before. Listen: [eː]. Do you think that you can make that sound? [eː]. Look at the shape of my lips when I pronounce it: [eː]. See whether you can make a noise like that.

[The pupils are more or less unsuccessful.]

"No, no, that won't do at all; you are pronouncing quite a different sound. Listen again: [eː], [eː], [eː]. Don't you hear what a shrill, squeaking sort of sound it is? Try again; make it shriller and more squeaky.

[The result is better.]

"Yes, that is better, but it is not squeaky enough. Some of you are not screwing back the corners of your lips enough. Draw back your chins and squeeze the sound. [eː], [eː].

"Look at my hand [which is hanging limply]; it is in what we call a limp or lax position. Look at it again and notice the difference; all the muscles are taut and strained, and the skin is stretched tight over the back of it; my hand is in a strained or tense position. Now when I pronounce an English [ɛ] (as in *pen*), the muscles of my mouth, chin, and tongue are as limp as my hand is now. But when I pronounce the sound [eː] they are all strained and tense, just as my hand is now. Try again: tighten the muscles of your tongue and chin; feel as if you were just going to put out your tongue; now then: [eː]."

In this manner each of the foreign sounds will be inculcated. The representation of the vowels on the triangle will serve to give an identity to each of them.

Imperative Drill

As before, but with fewer gestures.

Phonetic Reading

The teacher will write a series of phonetic characters on the blackboard, and require the pupils (collectively or individually) to read them aloud. In the first instance these should represent native sounds.

Ninth to Twentieth Lessons

Subconscious Comprehension

The teacher will use the various simpler forms of exercise that he has prepared in advance. He must judge from the general attitude of the pupils whether the matter given is too difficult or the contrary.

Ear-training Exercises

As before.

Articulation Exercises

The next exercises will be to produce combinations of a given vowel with consonants: [iːp], [iːb], [iːt], [iːd], [iːk], [iːg], etc.; [piː], [biː], etc.; [piːp], [piːb], etc., and so on with each of the French vowels.

Dictation Exercises

The pupils should now be initiated into the art of writing phonetically to dictation. The first exercises will consist of monosyllabic words; these will be succeeded by others containing words (actual or artificial) of two and three syllables.

When a certain proficiency has been attained, these phonetic exercises will gradually merge into exercises calculated to quicken the pupils' faculties of auditive perception and reproduction. Whole sentences may be repeated several times by the teacher, and will be reproduced by the pupils in chorus and individually. The sentences chosen will be the models forming part of the microcosm.

Imperative Drill

As before, but with still fewer gestures.

Phonetic Reading and Dictation

The first exercises in phonetic reading can now be attempted; the pupils will articulate isolated sounds written by the teacher on the blackboard.

Comparisons should constantly be made between the English and the French sounds generally liable to be confused.

"Pronounce the sound I have just written on the blackboard: [e]. Now the one I have written beside it: [ɛ]. Now the English [ɛɪ], [e], [ɛ]; [e, ɛ, ɛɪ], [e, ɛɪ], [ɛɪ, e].

"Pronounce the *r* in *red* [ɹɹɹ]. Now the French *r* [rrrr]. Again. Again. Now [ɑːrrr], [iːrrr], [ɛːrrr]; [rrrɑː], [rrriː], [rrrɛː]. Now [ɹɹɹɑ]," etc., etc.

This exercise is varied by phonetic dictation. It will consist of pronouncing various sounds, each of which is to be written by the pupils in phonetic characters.

Obviously the teacher alone can decide at what rate the programme is to be developed. With bright and responsive pupils a new stage will soon be reached; in the contrary case it will be necessary more than once to recapitulate everything from the very start.

We will therefore content ourselves with indicating briefly in what directions the various exercises that we have suggested may be expanded, and what new ones may be introduced during what we have designated as the first or elementary period.

Exercises in Subconscious Comprehension

At about the twentieth lesson the transition from concrete to the abstract may begin. It may be initiated somewhat in the following way :

" Je touche la table. Je touche le plancher. Je touche le mur. Je touche le plafond—Non ! Je ne touche pas le plafond. Je ne peux pas toucher le plafond. C'est impossible. Il m'est impossible de toucher le plafond. Le plancher ; oui, je peux toucher le plancher ; ce n'est pas difficile. Vous pouvez toucher le plancher, n'est-ce pas ? Ce n'est pas difficile de toucher le plancher ou le mur. Mais vous ne pouvez pas toucher le plafond.

" Si je reste ici, à ma place, je ne peux pas toucher la porte ni la fenêtre. Il m'est impossible de toucher la porte si je reste ici. Vous ne pouvez pas toucher la porte si vous restez là où vous êtes.

" Je soulève la chaise. Je soulève l'armoire—Non ! je ne peux pas soulever l'armoire, la chose est impossible.

" Je regarde le plafond. Je regarde la fenêtre. Si je mets la main devant les yeux, ou si je ferme les yeux, je ne peux pas regarder le plafond ; je ne peux pas regarder la fenêtre.

" Donnez-moi votre crayon ! Donnez-moi votre plume ! [The teacher takes them away from the pupil.] Maintenant écrivez ! Vous ne pouvez pas écrire. Il vous est impossible d'écrire.

" Je n'ai pas de craie. Je ne peux pas écrire au tableau. Puis-je écrire avec le doigt ? Non, n'est-ce pas ? Puis-je écrire avec le livre ? Non, n'est-ce pas ?

" Je n'ai pas de livre ; je ne peux pas lire. Je ferme les oreilles ; je ne peux pas entendre. Je ferme les yeux ; je ne peux pas voir.

"Je ne peux pas toucher le plafond. Pourquoi? Parce qu'il est trop haut. Je ne peux pas toucher la porte. Pourquoi? Parce qu'elle est trop loin. Je ne peux pas soulever l'armoire. Pourquoi? Parce qu'elle est trop lourde. Je ne peux pas écrire au tableau. Pourquoi? Parce que je n'ai pas de craie.

"Pourquoi ne pouvez-vous pas écrire? Parce que vous n'avez pas de crayon. Pourquoi est-ce que je ne peux pas voir? Parce que j'ai les yeux fermés. Pourquoi est-ce que je ne peux pas entendre? Parce que j'ai les oreilles fermées.

"Si je n'ai pas de craie, je ne peux pas écrire au tableau. Si je n'ai pas de livre, je ne peux pas lire. Si je n'ai pas de clef, je ne peux pas fermer la porte. Si vous n'avez pas de crayon, vous ne pouvez pas écrire. Etc., etc.

"Sans livre il est impossible de lire. Sans crayon ou plume il est impossible d'écrire. Sans clef il est impossible d'ouvrir la porte. Etc., etc.

"Si je veux écrire, il faut que je prenne une plume. Si je veux lire, il faut que je prenne un livre ou un journal. Etc., etc.

"Je ne peux pas toucher la porte sans y aller. Je ne peux pas écrire sans prendre un crayon ou une plume." Etc., etc.

At about the same period the following talk will probably be fairly well understood:

"Nous sommes ici dans la classe, vous et moi. Nous sommes dans l'école. La classe est dans l'école. Nous sommes ici pour parler français. Je parle français. Je vous parle en français et vous écoutez ce que je vous dis. Nous sommes ici dans la classe; la classe est dans l'école. L'école est à Londres. Nous sommes à Londres. Londres est une ville. Manchester aussi est une ville; Birmingham est une ville; Liverpool est une ville. Nous ne sommes pas à Manchester; nous ne sommes pas à Birmingham; nous sommes à Londres. Est-ce que Londres est une ville? Oui, Londres est une ville. Est-ce que Londres est une école? Non, Londres n'est pas une école; Londres est une ville, une grande ville, une très grande ville. La classe est-elle grande? Oui, elle est grande, n'est-ce pas? La ville de Londres est-elle grande? Oui, n'est-ce pas?

"Londres est la capitale de l'Angleterre. Ce n'est pas la capitale de la France. Londres est une ville anglaise. La capitale de la France est Paris. Paris est une ville française. Paris aussi est une grande ville. Nous ne sommes pas à Paris; nous sommes à Londres. Londres est en Angleterre. Nous sommes en Angleterre. Vous êtes en Angleterre; moi, je suis en Angleterre; nous sommes tous en Angleterre.

"Vous êtes anglais; vous n'êtes pas français. Vous parlez anglais, c'est votre langue. Les Français ne parlent pas anglais; ils parlent français. Les Anglais ne parlent pas français; ils parlent anglais. Les Italiens parlent italien. Etes-vous italiens? Non, n'est-ce pas? Vous êtes anglais. Etes-vous français? Non, n'est-ce pas? Vous êtes anglais. Vous parlez anglais, vous ne parlez pas français.

"Londres est une ville; Paris est une ville. L'Angleterre est un pays. La France aussi est un pays. L'Italie encore, c'est un pays. La Belgique est un pays. Le Portugal est un pays. L'Angleterre est-elle un pays ou une ville? Un pays, n'est-ce pas? Londres est-il un pays ou une ville? Une ville, n'est-ce pas? Nous sommes ici à Londres; nous sommes en Angleterre; nous sommes dans la capitale de l'Angleterre." Etc., etc.

Imperative Drill

The direct imperative may now be replaced or alternated with various indirect forms such as:

"Voulez-vous venir ici? Je vous demande de venir ici. Il faut venir ici. Vous devez venir ici. Faites-moi le plaisir de venir ici. Je vous dis de venir ici. Ça ne vous ferait-il rien de venir ici?"

The commands may now embrace actions of a more precise nature and more difficult of illustration by gesture:

"Donnez votre livre à X!

"Apportez-moi cinq morceaux de papier!

"Allez à la fenêtre sans faire de bruit!

"Voulez-vous venir ici, prendre mon livre et mon crayon, et les donner à l'élève qui est derrière vous?

"Il faut venir ici, prendre la craie et puis écrire un mot anglais au tableau noir."

Articulation and Ear-training Exercises

These may now be combined with phonetic reading and dictation, the whole set to be considered as *General Phonetic Exercises.*

There will be a daily drill embracing one or more forms of these types of work, passing from isolated sounds to syllables, and from these to longer units.

Two forms of ear-training exercises may be recommended; both of these, devised by Mr Daniel Jones, Reader in Phonetics at University College, London, have been used in his classes with conspicuous success.

The first of these consists of writing on the blackboard a series of numbered phonetic symbols:

1	2	3	4	5	6	7	8	9	10	11	12	etc.
i	e	ɛ	a	ɑ	ɔ	o	u	y	ø	œ	ə	

The teacher enunciates these sounds in a mixed order, and as he does so the pupil or pupils respond by quoting the number of the symbol representing the sound which they hear, or imagine they hear. For instance:

Teacher. [ɛɛɛɛ].
Pupil. No. 3?
Teacher. Right. Now: [oooo].
Pupil. No. 7?
Teacher. Quite right. Now: [øøøø].
Pupil. No. 9?
Teacher. Listen again: [øøøø].
Pupil. No. 10!
Teacher. Yes, No. 10. Listen to the difference between No. 9 and No. 10: [y, ø, y, ø, y, ø]. Etc., etc.

The second exercise, named *Nonsense Dictation,* consists of dictating artificial and meaningless words composed in advance by the teacher, such as: [ytvɛljɛ̃, søvezɔ̃d, ikmɛ̃ʒruʃ].

These words must be written phonetically by the pupils. When they make mistakes, the teacher should repeat the word with the right and the wrong sound alternately so that the difference may be clearly audible.

Fluency Practice

This is the natural development of articulation exercises when carried into a later stage. When the pupils have become fairly proficient in the production of isolated sounds and syllables, they may go one step farther and practise groups of connected syllables. These may be nonsense sentences or real sentences; but as no particular end is to be gained by the former, we may prepare a number of real sentences and proceed to work on these.

Although nominally a type of phonetic exercise, a secondary purpose will be well served by this fluency drill: the daily repetition of a number of sentences will result in their being memorized. If the sentences are well chosen the pupils will acquire, during their phonetic lessons, a considerable stock of useful vocabulary in the form of complete ergons.

We need hardly point out the direct and indirect advantages of learning by heart a number of characteristic sentences. Not only will such sentences form the nucleus of their stock of primary matter, but each of them will serve at a later stage as the models from which they will derive an almost unlimited quantity of secondary matter.

Teacher. Listen to what I am going to say: [ʒənpøpɑvniː risidmɛ̃].

The pupils repeat, but with indifferent success. We may help them by isolating portions of the sentence: [niːrisi], [niːrisi], [niːrisid], [niːrisid], [isidmɛ̃], [isidmɛ̃], [ʒənpøpɑ], [ʒənpøpɑ].

Then with better success the pupils produce: [ʒənpøpɑvniː risidmɛ̃].

The unit is then dictated, written on the blackboard, and read, and the next sentence is taken.

Let us bear in mind that, with the exception of the articulation and fluency exercises, the first or elementary stage is not concerned with the active aspect of language-study. We are acting in accordance with the principle that no active work is profitable until the pupil has mastered the sounds of the language, and can produce them with fluency and accuracy.

Now even under the most favourable circumstances we cannot expect an average class of average pupils to acquire anything like accuracy or fluency in sound-production under at least a term. To allow or to force pupils to answer questions (or indeed to make any active oral use of French) before they are proficient in the production of the very basis of spoken language is to expose them to all the dangers which inevitably result from premature efforts. We cannot and must not allow our pupils to speak broken or 'pidgin' French; our ideal standard programme is based on the principle of *fluent accuracy or nothing.*

From the outset, then, we must be prepared to let at least three months pass before we can risk any other active oral work, on the part of our pupils, than articulation exercises. The object of these pages is to show what varied forms of useful exercises we may employ while awaiting the moment at which the pupils may be considered ripe for their entry on the second or intermediate stage.

For obvious reasons we have suggested no form of written work beyond the tracing of phonetic characters; however long we may have to wait ere we can risk active oral work, this active oral work must precede any written work.

The teacher will probably find that the various types of exercises that we have suggested will more than occupy the incubatory three months. Should this, however, not be the case, we would suggest a series of simple lessons (or periods of fifteen minutes) to be devoted to the teaching of the more important principles of language-theory. There is no reason why we should not take advantage of our three months' wait by giving simple lectures to our pupils on the theories of phonetics, ergonics, etymology, and semantics. These lectures, needless to say, will be given in and based on the pupils' native language and adapted to their standard of intelligence.

In the following pages we will see what sort of lectures it is possible to give to pupils of the age of eleven or twelve by giving a few typical specimens.

Phonetic Theory

Specimen Lesson

"Pronounce [mmm] and then tell me what happens to your lips. . . .

"Well, what happened? You closed them? Yes, you certainly closed them. Try and find out what other sounds are made by closing or by nearly closing your lips.

[The pupils discover [p], [b], and [w]].

"Very well, let us write these four sounds on the blackboard, and call them the *lip-lip sounds*; that means that one lip touches the other.

Lip-lip Sounds

p b

m

w

"Do your two lips come together when you pronounce [vvv]? No? What does happen then? . . . Yes, that's right, the bottom lip is pressed against the upper teeth. This we shall call a *lip-teeth sound.* Can you find any more lip-teeth sounds?"

[[f] is duly discovered.]

"Very well, let us put [f] and [v] together and call them the lip-teeth sounds.

Lip-lip Sounds	*Lip-teeth Sounds*
p b	
m	
w	f v

"Now try and find out what parts of the mouth have to touch in order to make other sounds.

[Various sounds are discovered and are duly displayed under their appropriate headings: *teeth-edge and tongue-tip sounds* [θ, ð], *ridge and tongue-tip sounds* [s, z, ʃ, ʒ, ɹ, l], etc., etc.]

"Do you make a sort of explosion when you pronounce [s s s]? No? Can you find out some sounds which do make an explosion? [b]? Yes, [b] is an explosive sound. Any more? *g* [dʒiː]? What do you mean by [dʒiː]? Do you mean [dʒ] or [g]? Ah, [g]; I thought you meant that. In future you must say [g], not [dʒiː], when you mean [g], or I shall not know whether you mean [g] or [dʒ]."

The plosives or explosion sounds are written in a row on the blackboard:

Plosives or explosion sounds	p b	t d	k g

The nasals, fricatives, and laterals are discovered and treated in the same manner. Subsequently, the vowels and diphthongs receive similar treatment.

A large diagram may be constructed progressively and hung up for reference.

A few minutes of phonetic reading and dictation will be very useful at this period. Of particular interest will be the names of the pupils written in phonetic script. Each pupil may subsequently be asked to write his address in phonetic characters.

Short talks on phonetics will be welcomed by the average pupil.

"Some people do not know the difference between a letter and a sound. And yet there is a great difference between the two things, isn't there? A sound is something we make with our mouth, a letter is something that we write.

"In English, French, and other languages the ordinary spelling of words with the letters of the alphabet doesn't agree at all with the pronunciation of the words. The word *one* is made up of the letters called [ou,] [ɛn], and [iː], but we do not pronounce it [ouɛniː], we pronounce it [wʌn]. How many sounds are there in *one*? Which is the first? The second? And the third?

"How many sounds are there in [fɔːt]? Yes, three sounds; let us write them in phonetic symbols on the blackboard. . . . Now each of you write the word in ordinary spelling with the letters of the alphabet. . . . Why, how is this? Some of you have written *fort* and others *fought*. What is the reason? . . .

Yes, just so, sometimes two different words are pronounced in exactly the same way, but are written in different ways. That never happens in phonetic writing. The phonetic symbols never shift about like letters; each one always represents a fixed sound, and always the same sound." And so on, *ad lib.*

It will be noted that this is not a French lesson at all, but an English lesson. It is intended that this should be so; we are engaged in sharpening our tools, labelling the bottles, tidying up the workshop, and all the other preliminary work which alone will make our future work rapid and effective.

Etymological Theory

Specimen Lesson

"*I give, you give, he give, we give, you give, they give.* Is there anything wrong in what I said? Did it sound right? What was wrong with it? . . . Oh, I should have said *he gives*, instead of *he give*. That evidently means that a word like *give* sometimes has to change its form. See if you can tell me any other ways to change the word *give*.

"*Gave?* Yes, *gave*. *Giving?* Yes, *giving*. *Given?* Yes, *given*. Any more? *Giveth?* Yes, there is *giveth*, and *givest* too, but as this is not the English we use every day we will take no notice of these old-fashioned forms. Let us write on the blackboard the five words in this order:

1. *give*
2. *gives*
3. *gave*
4. *giving*
5. *given*

"Let us see whether the word *stay* changes in the same manner. . . . There appear to be only four different forms this time; numbers 1, 2, 3, and 4. Where has number 5 got to? . . . Yes, that is right; number 5 is *stayed*, just like number 3.

[Other examples to be treated in the same way.]

"These five forms are called *inflexions*. Let us see whether we can find any inflexions for the word *under*. . . .

"No, we have not been able to find any. *Under* is a word which cannot be inflected. Let us try the word *mouse*. . . . *Mice?* Yes, *mice*. Any more? *Mouse's?* Yes, I think we can put down *mouse's*, although some people say that the apostrophe and the *s* are really a separate word and not part of the word *mouse*. We see, then, that the word *mouse* has three inflexions: *mouse*, *mice*, and *mouse's*.

"In French, Latin, Russian, and other languages there are far more inflexions to be found than in English. A little later on we shall make collections of French inflexions and arrange them just as we arrange collections of foreign stamps in our albums."

And so on.

Semantic Theory

Specimen Lesson

"When I say *I am going to get my hat*, what does the word *get* mean? . . . Yes, it means *fetch*. We see, then, that sometimes there are two ways of putting a thought into words. What word can we use instead of *nearly*? . . . Yes, we can use *almost*. What word can we use instead of *intend* in the sentence *I intend to go*? . . . No, we cannot use *expect*, because that changes the meaning of the sentence; *intend* and *expect* stand for two very different thoughts. . . . *Mean?* Yes, *mean* will do very well to replace *intend*; in fact, we far more often say *I mean to go* than *I intend to go*.

"Two words which mean the same thing, or very nearly the same thing, are called synonyms. Can you give me a synonym for *scarcely*? . . . For *sure*? . . . For *glad*?

"What can we put in the place of the word *far* in the sentence *Is it far from here?* Yes, that's right: *a long way*. So you see we can sometimes replace a single word by two or three words. *Far* is what we call a *monolog* or *single word*; *a long way* is what we call a *polylog* or *group-word*. Can you give me a *polylog* as a synonym of the monolog *enter*? Yes, *go in*. Yes, *come in*. Yes, *walk in*. You will find quite a lot of polylog synonyms of *enter*.

[Further examples to be given.]

"Now, we not only find monologs which are the synonyms of other monologs, and polylogs as synonyms of monologs, but we also find polylogs as synonyms of other polylogs. What can we say instead of *Will you go*? . . . Yes, we can say *Would you mind going?* What can we say instead of *all right*? . . . Yes, we can say *very well.*

[Further examples to be given.]

"Now, we saw that in *I am going to get my hat* the word *get* may be replaced by *fetch* without changing the meaning of the sentence. Can we always replace *get* by *fetch*? Can we say, *It is fetching dark* instead of *It is getting dark*? . . . No, of course we can't. Only one sort of *get* can be replaced by *fetch*. What does *get* mean in the sentence, *It is getting dark*? Yes, it means *growing* or *becoming*; this sort of *get* is a synonym of *grow* and of *become*.

"We see, then, that *get* number 1 and *get* number 2 are just as much different words as *fetch* and *become*.

"Have you ever thought how many *gets* there are? We have just examined two.

1. *Get* in the sense of *fetch*.
2. *Get* in the sense of *grow* or *become*.

"What others can we find? Yes, there is:

3. *Get* forming part of the polylog *get to* in the sense of *arrive at* or *reach*.
4. *Get* in the sense of *persuade* (*Get him to come*).
5. *Get* in the sense of *cause to be* (*Get it mended*).
6. *Get* in the sense of *make* (*Get it ready*).
7. *Get* in the sense of *receive* (*I got a letter this morning*).

"These seven words are called the semantic varieties of *get*.

[The semantic varieties of other words, such as *keep, care, mind, mean,* etc., etc., to be examined in the same way.]

"In French and in all other languages we find exactly the same thing; we find synonyms (two or more words having the same meaning) and semantic varieties of words. We shall have to pay great attention to these and be very careful not to mix them up.

"We have seen that some thoughts can be expressed in

English by two or more different words. We must not expect to find that exactly those same thoughts can be expressed in French by two different words. In English we can say *nearly* or *almost*, but in French there is only one word instead of two. Then we shall sometimes find two different French words to express one thought where in English we only have one word for it.

"We have seen that *get* and other English words have a number of semantic varieties, but we must not expect to find exactly the same words in French having exactly the same number and the same sort of semantic varieties.

"We shall sometimes translate from French into English, and from English into French, but we shall discover that one French word may be expressed in a number of different ways in English, according to its meaning. We shall also see that the meaning of one English word may be expressed in a number of different ways in French, and that we shall have to choose the one which has the same meaning as the English one. We shall sometimes have to turn English polylogs into French monologs, or do the contrary, and turn English monologs into French polylogs.

"Some children (and even grown-up people) think that for each English word there is a French word, with just the same meanings and just the same number of meanings. Those people, not knowing any better, sometimes ask very funny questions. They say, for instance, 'What's the French for *get*?' Of course we can't answer questions like these. We first have to ask which sort of *get* they mean; whether it is *get* number 1, or *get* number 2, or *get* number 3, and so on. Then we shall tell them how the French express that particular thought that is expressed in English by that particular sort of *get*."

Ergonic Theory

Specimen Lesson

"If somebody asked us the question 'When did you last write a letter to your uncle?' what different answers should we all give? Let us see what some of the answers would be. Each of you write down an answer to the question. Perhaps some of you haven't any uncles, and if you have, perhaps you never write to them, so those pupils need only write what they think some of the others are writing. . . .

"Yes, just as I thought; there are hardly any two pupils who have written the same thing. You have all started by saying, 'I wrote to him——' and then each one seems to have written something different. I will write on the blackboard some of the answers:

I wrote to him yesterday.
on Sunday.
this morning.
three weeks ago.
during the holidays.
last week.
in January.
at Christmas.
when it was his birthday.
last month.
on the 17th of July.
a long time ago.

"Now there is something the same about all the words that come after *him*. What is it that is the same? What do *you* say? . . . That they all tell us when somebody wrote to his uncle? Very well, and what do *you* say? . . . That they all answer the question *when*. Very well, and what do *you* say? That they are all different ways of saying *then*?

"Yes, they are all answers to the question *when*. Now, we must find a name to give to all the different ways of answering the question *when*. We will call them *complements of time*. If each of them were like the word *yesterday*, and contained one word only, we could call them *adverbs of time*, but an adverb is always a monolog or single word, and these are nearly all polylogs.

"Now, if a *complement of time* answers the question *when*, what question do you imagine we can answer with *complements of place*? . . . Yes, quite right; the question *where*. Now, each of you write an answer to the question: 'Where did you see it?'"

[In the same way treat complements of duration, frequency, manner, etc.]

Similar exercises can be given on other forms of complements, as well as on subjectives, predicates, and modifiers. In this manner clear notions will be inculcated concerning the chief ergonic categories and their names.

Section 23.—The second or intermediate stage, of the duration of from one to three years (according to the radius of the microcosm), will consist of:

(*a*) More advanced exercises in subconscious comprehension.

(*b*) Articulation and fluency exercises.

(*c*) The assimilation of primary matter by means of various catenizing devices.

(*d*) The production of secondary matter by means of a large number of varied exercises based on etymology, semantics, and ergonics.

During this stage the traditional spelling will be introduced and taught by means of various types of orthoepic exercises.

The second or intermediate stage is the beginning of what most people would term the study proper of the language.

It will commence when the student is able to reproduce with ease the sounds of the language, not only as isolated elements, but in groups of varying lengths, and is able to transform with tolerable accuracy the symbols into sounds and the sounds into symbols.

Although this stage may be of indefinite duration, we would suggest that it should not be unduly prolonged nor brought to a premature conclusion. As in the case of the first stage, its duration is not to be measured by days, nor even by the number of lessons devoted to it; it should begin when the pupil is ripe to begin it, and should terminate only when the pupil is ripe for the next stage.

At what moment will the pupil be considered ripe for the third stage? Bearing in mind the end we have in view and the broad principles of the differentiated programme, we may answer that the third stage may begin and the second stage terminate when the efforts of the student have enabled him to understand the greater part of what he hears and reads, and to use in a simple manner and with a relative freedom from error by the oral and written mediums, about 75 per cent. of the matter contained in the ordinary everyday speech of the average person.

The essential difference between the second and third stages lies in the fact that in the former the greater part of the study will be pursued on a basis of consciousness, and in the latter on the basis of subconsciousness.

During the second stage a relatively small number of carefully selected units will be presented one by one, each of which is there and then to be completely and thoroughly assimilated by means of those processes of study which we shall examine and analyse later on. During the third stage a relatively large number of unselected units will be brought within the range of the student's perceptive faculties in a haphazard order; their assimilation will be neither immediate nor thorough; they will gradually become inculcated by the slow cumulative process of natural absorption.

One of the chief aims of the intermediate stage is to ensure perfect fluency, both of expression and understanding.

In Section 19 we have spoken of the necessity for fluent *expression*; more important still is the necessity for fluent *comprehension*. It is possible to express ourselves in broken and halting sentences. By a desultory firing off of insecables, we may possibly make ourselves understood; the only sufferers will be the persons who have to listen to us.

But unless we have acquired the art of fluent comprehension, it is manifestly impossible to understand what is said to us by fluent native speakers—and many native speakers are incapable of any but ultra-fluent speech. Nor is it pleasant to be obliged to interrupt with continual exhortations to speak slower, to speak more distinctly, not to run the words together, to repeat, etc., etc. Lack of fluent comprehension is to be attributed to a faulty method rather than to slowness of perception. Students whose training in fluent comprehension has been sound should understand the foreign language better when spoken rapidly than when uttered word by word.

The second or intermediate stage will commence under the

most auspicious conditions. The pupils will have mastered the foreign sounds and will be able to use the phonetic symbols both actively and passively. Their hearing faculties will have been sharpened and their powers of auditive observation developed. They will be able to reproduce sentences, both seen and unseen, with accuracy and fluency.

Their elementary lessons on the various branches of lexicology will have sharpened their wits and they will be to a large extent immune from those vicious tendencies and errors which are invariably the result of misconception and misunderstanding of the nature of language.

The study proper of the French language in its active aspects will now commence. The pupils will be from one to three Terms behind those who have not been through the preliminary stage, but they will now be ideally prepared and perfectly ripe to enter the new stage of their study. No time will be lost on long parenthetical explanations nor in those vexatious interruptions which break the thread of an organized and systematic course of language-study.

Other things being equal, they will rapidly overhaul their less fortunate fellow-students, they will run while the others are crawling, and their progress will be proportionate to their speed.

This stage will be characterized by a number of varied but gradually converging lines of study. Most of them will be based on the microcosm, that nucleus of scientifically chosen units representing the quintessence of the language.

The lessons will generally consist of two or three parts, thus ensuring variety and interest. Catenizing work will be interspersed with exercises of a more lively character; appeal will be made to the auditive and visual faculties, to the powers of perception, imitation and reasoning.

In the same way that the instructor of scientific gymnastics devises special exercises, each of which is destined to act on a certain set of muscles, so also will the language teacher devise special exercises, each of which will play its part in the proportional development of the pupil's linguistic knowledge.

The microcosm, formed in advance, will be characterized by the various features and qualities described in Section 20.

An adequate number of graduated substitution tables in phonetic and orthographic script and with translations and notes will be in the hands of each pupil. These will be accompanied by a number of appropriate exercises, both for oral and written work.

There will be object-lessons, questions and answers both systematic and non-systematic. Abundant material for practice in material association can be found in any class-room.

Appropriate progressive exercises for homework will be provided in book or card form; the right exercise at the right moment will strengthen the associations of the pupil and lighten the work of the teacher. Each new fact perceived will be driven home by cumulative examples and concretized instances. Nothing taught from the microcosm is meant to evaporate when once cognized and inculcated. Absolute assimilation is to be the order of the day; the pupil is to digest, in the shortest possible time, with the least effort, and with a freedom from error, the greatest quantity of the most essential matter of the language.

It will be useful to note at this point that in order to utilize with rapidity and success many of the proposed exercises, a set of special books should be in the hands of each pupil. This being an *ideal* programme—that is to say, a programme of work to be carried out under ideal conditions—we must assume the existence of such books, and trust that ere long many of them will be available for school work. While awaiting this moment, the teacher may make good some of these deficiencies by writing out various tables and groups on the blackboard, to be copied by the pupils into special exercise-books provided for that purpose.

The second stage will be characterized, as we have said, by a number of varied but gradually converging lines of study. We will now describe and illustrate the more important of them.

Subconscious Comprehension

By the time that the pupil has arrived at the second stage, the type of exercise for which we have suggested the above title will have developed considerably. Having exhausted the subjects connected with the schoolroom and its contents, recourse will be had to pictures, of which, fortunately, there is no lack. The teacher will exhibit one of these and proceed to talk about the various objects, persons, and scenes portrayed thereon; he will describe country and town scenes, journeys, and various occupations.

Many lessons may be given quite independently of pictures. The habit of direct comprehension having been fostered and developed daily over a long period, it will be possible for the teacher to make himself understood even without recourse to material association. The following is an example of the sort of talk that will probably be fairly well understood during the intermediate stage.

"Le cheval est un animal utile. Dans les rues on voit beaucoup de chevaux. Ces animaux traînent les charrettes et les voitures. Les vaches sont aussi des animaux. Les vaches, comme les chevaux, mangent de l'herbe. La vache a deux cornes; le cheval n'en a pas. La vache nous donne du lait. Le lait est blanc. Nous buvons du lait. C'est la vache qui nous donne le lait que nous buvons. Le mouton aussi est un animal; il est plus petit que le cheval et plus petit que la vache. Le mouton nous donne de la laine. La laine est blanche. Avec la laine nous faisons du drap et de l'étoffe. Mon veston est fait en laine. Le mouton est un animal utile. Le chien est aussi un animal utile; il ne nous donne pas de lait ni de laine, mais le chien garde la maison. Il y a aussi des chiens qui gardent les moutons. Il y a des chiens qui sont très grands, il y en a d'autres qui sonts petits. Le chat est un animal; il n'est pas si utile que le chien. Les chats aiment beaucoup le feu; ils boivent du lait; ils attrapent les souris. La souris n'est pas un animal utile; au contraire, c'est un animal nuisible; on n'aime pas les souris." Etc., etc.

Systematic Questionnaire

A second line of study may be carried out concurrently conceived on the following lines:

Teacher. Est-ce la fenêtre?
Pupils. Oui, c'est la fenêtre.

T. Est-ce la porte ?
P. Non, ce n'est pas la porte.
T. Qu'est-ce que c'est ?
P. C'est la fenêtre.

T. Le plafond est-il blanc ?
P. Oui, il est blanc.
T. Le plafond est-il noir ?
P. Non, il n'est pas noir.
T. Quelle est la couleur du plafond ?
P. Il est blanc.
T. Qu'est-ce qui est blanc ?
P. C'est le plafond.

T. Le livre est-il sur la chaise ?
P. Oui, il est sur la chaise.
T. Le livre est-il par terre ?
P. Non, il n'est pas par terre.
T. Où est-il ?
P. Il est sur la chaise.
T. Qu'est-ce qui est sur la chaise ?
P. C'est le livre.

T. Est-ce que le professeur prend le livre ?
P. Oui, il prend le livre.
T. Est-ce qu'il prend la craie ?
P. Non, il ne prend pas la craie.
T. Qu'est-ce qu'il prend ?
P. Il prend le livre.
T. Qui est-ce qui prend le livre ?
P. C'est le professeur.

T. Ouvrez le livre ! Ouvrez-vous le livre ?
P. Oui, j'ouvre le livre.
T. Ouvrez-vous la porte ?
P. Non, je n'ouvre pas la porte.
T. Qu'est-ce que vous ouvrez ?
P. J'ouvre le livre.
T. Qui est-ce qui ouvre le livre ?
P. C'est moi.

T. Êtes-vous venu ici hier ?
P. Oui, je suis venu ici hier.
T. Êtes-vous venu ici samedi ?
P. Non, je ne suis pas venu ici samedi.
T. Quand êtes-vous venu ici ?
P. Je suis venu ici hier.
T. Qui est-ce qui est venu ici hier ?
P. C'est moi.

T. Avez-vous mis le livre sur le pupitre ?
P. Oui, j'ai mis le livre sur le pupitre.
T. Avez-vous mis le crayon sur le pupitre ?
P. Non, je n'ai pas mis le crayon sur le pupitre.
T. Qu'avez-vous mis sur le pupitre ?
P. J'y ai mis un livre.
T. L'avez-vous mis sur le pupitre ?
P. Oui, je l'ai mis sur le pupitre.
T. L'avez-vous mis sur la chaise ?
P. Non, je ne l'ai pas mis sur la chaise.
T. Où l'avez-vous mis ?
P. Je l'ai mis sur le pupitre.
T. Qui est-ce qui l'a mis sur le pupitre ?
P. C'est moi.

There is no limit to the number of model sentences which can be developed into systematic questions and answers. Any of those from the conjugation exercises will serve this purpose, as will also any incidental sentences whatever. In this type of exercise catenizing and semanticizing are performed simultaneously.

The questions may be classified and asked in the cross order:

Teacher	*Pupil*
Qu'est-ce que c'est ?	C'est la fenêtre.
Qu'est-ce que c'est ?	C'est la porte.
Qu'est-ce que c'est ?	C'est le plafond.
Etc.	Etc.

Teacher	*Pupil*
Où est le livre ?	Il est sur la table.
Où est la craie ?	Elle est sur le pupitre.
Où est la plume ?	Elle est sur la chaise.
Etc.	Etc.
Quelle est la couleur du plafond ?	Il est blanc.
Quelle est la couleur du mur ?	Il est jaune.
Quelle est la couleur du papier ?	Il est blanc.
Quelle est la couleur de la craie ?	Elle est blanche.
Quelle est la couleur du livre ?	Il est bleu.
Quelle est la couleur de la plume ?	Elle est rouge.
Quelle est la couleur de l'encre ?	Elle est noire.
Etc.	Etc.
Qu'est-ce que je fais ?	Vous vous levez.
Qu'est-ce que je fais ?	Vous marchez.
Qu'est-ce que je fais ?	Vous allez à la porte.
Qu'est-ce que je fais ?	Vous regardez le plafond.
Qu'est-ce que je fais ?	Vous prenez le livre.
Etc.	Etc.

Another form of systematic *questionnaire* will be based on a series of question-and-answer groups, of which the following are typical specimens:

Qu'est-ce que le cheval ?	C'est un animal.
Qu'est-ce que le chien ?	C'est un animal.
Qu'est-ce que le chat ?	C'est un animal.
Qu'est-ce que le mouton ?	C'est un animal.
Qu'est-ce que la vache ?	C'est un animal.
Etc.	Etc.
Qu'est-ce que la table ?	C'est un meuble.
Qu'est-ce que la chaise ?	C'est un meuble.
Qu'est-ce que le lit ?	C'est un meuble.
Etc.	Etc.

Teacher	*Pupil*
Qu'est-ce que le fer ?	C'est un métal.
Qu'est-ce que l'or ?	C'est un métal.
Qu'est-ce que l'argent ?	C'est un métal.
Etc.	Etc.
Qu'est-ce que le mur ?	C'est une partie de la chambre.
Qu'est-ce que le plafond ?	C'est une partie de la chambre.
Qu'est-ce que le plancher ? Etc.	C'est une partie de la chambre. Etc.
Qu'est-ce que le chapeau ?	C'est un vêtement.
Qu'est-ce que le veston ?	C'est un vêtement.
Qu'est-ce que le gilet ?	C'est un vêtement.
Etc.	Etc.
Quelle est la couleur du plafond ?	Il est blanc.
Quelle est la couleur du col ?	Il est blanc.
Quelle est la couleur du ciel ?	Il est bleu.
Etc.	Etc.
Quelle est la couleur de la neige ?	Elle est blanche.
Quelle est la couleur de la craie ?	Elle est blanche.
Quelle est la couleur de l'herbe ?	Elle est verte.
Etc.	Etc.
Où est Londres ?	Londres est en Angleterre.
Où est Douvres ?	Douvres est en Angleterre.
Etc.	Etc.
Où est Paris ?	Paris est en France.
Où est Lyon ?	Lyon est en France.
Où est Bruxelles ?	Bruxelles est en Belgique.
Où est Genève ?	Genève est en Suisse.
Où est Rome ?	Rome est en Italie.
Etc.	Etc.

Teacher	*Pupil*
Où est-ce qu'on parle français ?	On parle français en France.
Où est-ce qu'on parle anglais ? Etc.	On parle anglais en Angleterre. Etc.
Quelle est la capitale de la France ?	C'est Paris.
Quelle est la capitale de l'Angleterre ? Etc.	C'est Londres. Etc.
Qu'est-ce qu'on prend quand on lit ?	On prend un livre.
Qu'est-ce qu'on prend quand on écrit ? Etc.	On prend un crayon ou une plume. Etc.
Que fait-on avec un crayon ?	Avec un crayon on écrit.
Que fait-on avec une clef ? Etc.	Avec une clef on ferme la porte. Etc.
Quel est le premier jour de la semaine ?	C'est lundi.
Quel est le deuxième jour de la semaine ? Etc.	C'est mardi. Etc.
Quel est le premier mois de l'année ?	C'est janvier.
Quel est le deuxième mois de l'année ? Etc.	C'est février. Etc.
Combien de secondes y a-t-il dans une minute ?	Il y en a soixante.
Combien de minutes y a-t-il dans une heure ? Etc.	Il y en a soixante. Etc.
Que puis-je faire si j'ai un livre ?	Si vous avez un livre, vous pouvez lire.

Teacher	*Pupil*
Que puis-je faire si j'ai une brosse ?	Si vous avez une brosse, vous pouvez brosser.
Etc.	Etc.
Que dites-vous si vous voulez un crayon ?	Si je veux un crayon, je dis "Donnez-moi un crayon."
Etc.	Etc.

Under ideal conditions each pupil will possess a book containing a hundred or so of these groups properly graduated and accompanied by appropriate exercises. Each group (containing about ten members) will appear in phonetic script, with English translation either on the same page or at the end of the book. The manner of using these groups will be somewhat as follows :

Teacher. Turn to page one. I am going to read out to you the sentences that you will find in group one.

Qu'est-ce que le cheval? C'est un animal, etc.

Now you see from your book what these sentences mean. *Qu'est-ce que le cheval?* means *What is a horse?* The answer *C'est un animal* means *It's an animal.* I am now going to ask these questions, and to each of them you will answer *C'est un animal.*

Qu'est-ce que le cheval ?

Pupils. C'est un animal.

Teacher. Qu'est-ce que le chien ?

Pupils. C'est un animal. Etc., etc.

Teacher. We will now take the second group. I shall ask the question *Qu'est-ce que la table?* and you will answer *C'est un meuble.*

Qu'est-ce que la table ?

Pupils. C'est un meuble.

Teacher. Qu'est-ce que la chaise ?

Pupils. C'est un meuble. Etc., etc.

Teacher. Now I think that this is rather too easy for you. I'm going to mix the questions, so be careful to give the right answer, *C'est un animal* or *C'est un meuble,* as the case may be.

Qu'est-ce que le chien ?

Pupils. C'est un animal.
Teacher. Qu'est-ce que la table ?
Pupils. C'est un meuble.
Teacher. Qu'est-ce que le lit ?
Pupils. C'est un meuble.

New groups will be repeated and mixed together as before. In a very short time the result will be :

Teacher. Qu'est-ce que le chapeau ?
Pupils. C'est un vêtement.
Teacher. Quelle est la couleur du plafond ?
Pupils. Il est blanc.
Teacher. Où est Londres ?
Pupils. Londres est en Angleterre.
Teacher. Qu'est-ce qu'on prend quand on lit ?
Pupils. On prend un livre.
Teacher. Qu'est-ce que la vache ?
Pupils. C'est un animal. Etc., etc.

After some twenty or thirty periods of this type of work the pupils (either collectively or individually) should have no great difficulty in giving prompt and fluent answers to any of the thousand or so questions of which the collection may be made up.

Non-systematic Questionnaire

After a certain amount of systematic questioning has been given the teacher may venture on questions chosen at random. If a large number of mistakes occur this work should be dropped immediately and be postponed to a more propitious moment.

Qu'est-ce que c'est ?	C'est le plafond.
Est-il haut ou bas ?	Il est haut.
Quelle est la couleur du plafond ?	Il est blanc.
Pouvez-vous le toucher ?	Non, je ne peux pas le toucher.
Pourquoi pas ?	Parce qu'il est trop haut.
Qu'est-ce que c'est ?	C'est la porte.
Est-elle ouverte ou fermée ?	Elle est fermée.
Pouvez-vous l'ouvrir ?	Oui, je peux l'ouvrir.

Pouvez-vous toucher la porte si vous restez là ?	Non, monsieur, je ne peux pas toucher la porte si je reste ici.
Pourquoi pas ?	Parce que la porte est trop loin.
Qu'est-ce que c'est ?	C'est un livre.
A qui est-ce ?	C'est à moi.
Est-il ouvert ou fermé ?	Il est ouvert.
Où est-il ?	Il est sur le pupitre.
Qu'est-ce que je regarde ?	Vous regardez le livre.
Est-ce un livre français ou anglais ?	C'est un livre anglais.
Voyez-vous la fenêtre ?	Oui, je la vois.
Où est-elle ?	Elle est là.
Est-elle ouverte ou fermée ?	Elle est ouverte.
Le cheval, est-ce un animal ou une plante ?	C'est un animal.
Un animal utile ou inutile ?	Un animal utile.
Avez-vous un chien ?	Oui, monseiur, j'ai un chien.
Est-il ici ?	Non, il n'est pas ici.
Où est-il ?	Il est chez moi.
Etc.	Etc.

Substitution Tables

Another concurrent line of study will be the development and use of substitution tables. The principal object of this type of work is to contribute on a large scale to the enriching of the pupils' vocabulary in the form of fluent sentences. Some of the most suitable models during the early stages will be those taken from the conjugation exercises. The pupils will repeat, read, translate, and, in some cases, act, tables of the 'simple' type, such as :

Je suis prêt à	commencer.
	lire.
	écrire
	me lever.
	prendre le livre
	sortir
	partir.

J'ai	mon livre	devant moi.
	mon crayon	
	mon papier	
	mon cahier	
	ma plume	

Je mets le livre sur	le pupitre
	la chaise.
	le plancher.
	la table.
	les genoux.
	le cahier.

Je vais	à la porte.
	à la fenêtre.
	au pupitre.
	au coin.
	à la table.
	à Londres.
	en France.
	à la gare.

Je mets la craie	dans	la boîte.
	sur	
	devant	
	derrière	
	à côté de	
	près de	
	loin de	
	sous	

Je	dois	apprendre ces phrases tout de suite.
	veux	
	peux	
	ne dois pas	
	ne veux pas	
	ne peux pas	
	devrais	
	voudrais	
	pourrais	

Je dois apprendre ces phrases	tout de suite.
	maintenant.
	ce soir.
	demain.
	samedi.
	pour lundi.
	la semaine prochaine.

Je	la donne	au professeur.
	la passe	
	la prête	
	l'envoie	

J'écris	quelque chose	au tableau.
	mon nom	
	un mot	
	une phrase	
	des mots	
	des noms	

Needless to say, every table will first be presented and studied in the phonetic transcript with as few graphic separations as possible.

These and other tables will be developed progressively into their compound form :

Je ne peux pas	venir ici	demain
Je ne dois pas	aller là	lundi
Je ne veux pas	rester ici	la semaine prochaine
Vous ne pouvez pas	le faire	le mois prochain
Voulez-vous	l'avoir	l'année prochaine
Faut-il	le voir	mardi
Il ne faut pas	parler	maintenant
Il faut	le dire	aujourd'hui
Il vaudrait mieux	sortir	à deux heures
Il est difficile de	partir	samedi prochain

Je mets Je vois Je laisse	mon son votre notre leur le un	livre crayon cahier papier timbre	sur devant derrière	le pupitre la table la chaise la boîte l'armoire

Je dis que [1] Il dit que Dites-moi si [1] Savez-vous si Je ne sais pas si Il pense que Voilà pourquoi Vous voyez que Il ne savent pas que Personne ne sait que	je suis tu es il est nous sommes vous êtes ils sont	ici là chez moi à Londres en Angleterre en France fatigué(s) prêt(s) occupé(s) content(s)

Exercises of various kinds based on these tables will be given as homework, specimens of which are included in the list of exercises figuring in the next section.

Exercises in Material Association

Concurrently with the various lessons and exercises which we have briefly sketched out, the names of all available objects may be taught by material association. These will include the parts of the room; the various pieces of furniture, etc.; parts of the body; articles of clothing; small objects, including those to be found in the average pocket.

Qu'est-ce que c'est ?	C'est la main.
,, ,,	,, la tête.
,, ,,	,, le bras.

[1] At an appropriate moment the pupils will learn, once for all, the various rules of elision (*qu'* for *que*, *s'* for *si*, etc.).

Qu'est-ce que c'est ?	C'est la bouche.
,, ,,	,, la poitrine.
,, ,,	Ce sont les mains.
,, ,,	,, les bras.
,, ,,	,, les doigts.
,, ,,	,, les jambes.
Etc.	Etc.

A large number of verbs, indicating concrete actions, may be taught in the same way.

Qu'est-ce que je fais ?	Vous touchez la chaise.
,, ,,	,, levez ,,
,, ,,	,, portez ,,
,, ,,	,, renversez ,,
,, ,,	,, ramassez ,,
,, ,,	,, regardez ,,
,, ,,	,, tenez ,,

Certain more or less material adjectives may be treated:

Quelle est la couleur de ce livre-ci ?	Il est blanc.
,, ,, ,, ,,	,, ,, noir.
,, ,, ,, ,,	,, ,, rouge.
,, ,, ,, ,,	,, ,, vert.
,, ,, ,, ,,	,, ,, jaune. Etc.
Le plafond est-il haut ou bas ?	Il est haut.
La classe est-elle grande ou petite ?	Elle est grande.
Le livre est-il grand ou petit ?	Il est petit.
La fenêtre est-elle chaude ou froide ?	Elle est froide.

Many of these groups fall more or less into the classes of exercises already treated—subconscious comprehension, substitution tables, questionnaire, etc. The distinguishing feature, however, should be the fact that each word is consciously and materially associated with some object, action, or quality.

Systematic Conjugation Exercises

On one of the first pages of a book of which the above would be a suitable title will be found a series of sentences similar to the following:

1. Je suis prêt à commencer.
2. J'écoute le professeur.
3. Je comprends ce que j'entends.
4. J'ai mon livre devant moi.
5. Je sais ce que je dois faire.
6. Je prends le livre (*or* Je le prends).
7. Je commence à le lire.
8. Je finis de le lire.
9. Je le mets sur le pupitre.
10. Je me lève.
11. Je marche.
12. Je m'arrête.
13. Je vais à la porte.
14. J'ouvre la porte (La porte s'ouvre).
15. Je ferme la porte (La porte se ferme).
16. Je sors de la classe.
17. J'entre dans la classe.
18. Je viens au pupitre du professeur.
19. Je monte sur l'estrade.
20. Je reçois la craie.
21. Je la tiens dans la main droite.
22. J'écris quelque chose au tableau.
23. Je lis ce que j'ai écrit.
24. Je l'efface.
25. Je descends de l'estrade.
26. Je laisse tomber la craie.
27. Je la remasse.
28. Je la donne au professeur.
29. Je retourne à ma place.
30. Je m'assieds.
31. Je dois apprendre ces phrases tout de suite.

They will, however, appear in phonetic script and without any separation between the words. The transcription will be that of the most rapid speech.

1. ʒsɥiprɛakɔmɑ̃'se.
2. ʒekutləprɔfɛ'sœːr.
3. ʒkɔ̃prɑ̃skəʒɑ̃'tɑ̃. Etc.

All of these sentences may already have been catenized during the preliminary stage in the form of fluency practice.

The integral English translation will appear on the opposite page; the orthographic script will be given in another part of the book.

The page immediately preceding will contain the same series of sentences but in the interrogative form :

1. ɛːtvuprɛakɔmɑ̃'se ?
2. ɛkutevulprɔfɛ'sœːr ?
3. kɔ̃prənevuskəvuzɑ̃tɑ̃'de ? Etc.

The first lesson will be carried out somewhat on the following lines :

" Pronounce after me [ʒsɥiprɛakɔmɑ̃'se].

[The pupils do so.]

" That means *I am ready to begin.* Are you ready to begin ?

[One or more pupils will answer affirmatively.]

" Very well, then, tell me in French that you are ready to begin. . . .

[Addressing a particular pupil] : " What does that mean ? . . . Yes, it means *I am ready to begin.* Now I am going to ask you in French whether you are ready to begin. When I do so, each of you must answer in French. [ɛːtvuprɛakɔmɑ̃'se] ?

[The pupils answer " [ʒsɥiprɛakɔmɑ̃'se]."

" Yes, that's very good. You probably know the French word equivalent to the word *yes* . . . *oui*, that's right. Well, put that word in front of the sentence. Now then, again : [ɛːtvuprɛakɔmɑ̃'se] ? "

The pupils answer : " [wi, ʒsɥiprɛakɔmɑ̃'se]."

And so on for the first five sentences. At the sixth sentence, " I shall now ask you whether you are taking your books. You will answer [wi, ʒprɑ̃mɔ̃'liːvr], and in order that your answer may be true you will take the book which is lying before each of you. [ɛskəvuprənevɔt'liːvr] ? "

The pupils take their books and answer : " [wi, ʒprɑ̃mɔ̃'liːvr]."

The questions and answers may be gone over several times, sometimes with the class collectively and sometimes with individual pupils.

"I want you to pay particular attention to the way I ask the questions, because to-morrow I shall want some of you to take my place and ask *me* the questions instead. You will find all the questions on page . . . Your work for to-night will be to learn the first nine questions and their meanings."

The whole of the thirty-one sentences will be treated in this manner. After one or two lessons the interrogative will be replaced by some form of command, preference being given to some infinitive form :

1. Il faut maintenant être prêt à commencer.
2. Il faut écouter le professeur. Etc.

Some of the brightest pupils will be invited to take the teacher's place and ask the questions (or give the commands).

The book containing these conjugation exercises will give on successive pages all or most of the conjugational variations of each one of the sentences, one series per page.

At a subsequent lesson, some weeks later, the procedure will have reached the following stage :

"You, A, will give the orders to B, C, and D. You, B, will refuse to execute the order; you, C, will be obedient and do what you are told to do and will tell me what you are doing. You, D, will also do what you are told, and will tell me what C and you are doing. E, you will tell me what C is doing. F, you will tell me what C and D are doing. G, you will tell me that you haven't to do the action. H, you will tell me that you are not doing the action, but that you will do it to-morrow. I, you will ask J whether you are to perform the action, and you, J, will tell him that he mustn't. You, K, will tell me that you would do it if you had to." Etc., etc.

"Now, are you ready ? Start at sentence ten."

A. "Levez-vous !"
B. "Je ne veux pas me lever !"
C. "Je me lève."
D. "Nous nous levons."
E. "Il se lève" (*or* "C se lève.").
F. "Ils se lèvent" (*or* "C et D se lèvent").

G. " Je ne dois pas me lever."
H. " Je me lèverai demain."
I. " Faut-il me lever ? "
J. " Oui, il faut vous lever."
K. " Je me lèverais si je devais le faire."

At a later stage the terminology will be inculcated somewhat in the following manner :

" We will go through some of the actions again. Let me see, who's taking the part of the present tense, first person singular?"

" I am, sir."

" Very well, stand up. All the present tenses stand up. . . . You're a present tense, aren't you ? Stand up, then. Which person are you ? Third person singular. All right."

" Please, am I to stand up ? I'm the present tense negative."

" No, I shan't want you for a moment. Now you six, we will take the verb *marcher*. Conjugate ! "

Pupil No. 1. " Je marche."
" " 2. " Tu marches."
" " 3. " Il marche."
" " 4. " Nous marchons."
" " 5. " Vous marchez."
" " 6. " Ils marchent."

" Now the verb *aller*."

Pupil No. 1. " Je vais à la porte."
" " 2. " Tu vas à la porte."
" " 3. " Il va à la porte."
" " 4. " Nous allons à la porte."
" " 5. " Vous allez à la porte."
" " 6. " Ils vont à la porte."

And so on with several verbs.

" Now then, infinitives, get ready. Stand up. Why aren't you standing up, M ? "

" Please, sir, I'm not an infinitive ; I'm the past participle."

" All right, past participle, you'll come on presently. You, infinitive, over there, you were talking. What's your concomitant ? "

" Il ne faut pas."

"Well, you will bring me to-morrow three copies of the present tense of *Je ne dois pas parler pendant la leçon.* Now then, infinitives, let me hear your lines; we will take as an example the verb *se lever.*"

Pupil No. 16. "Je ne veux pas me lever."
" " 17. "Voulez-vous vous lever?"
" " 18. "Il ne faut pas vous lever."
" " 19. "Je voudrais me lever."
" " 20. "Faut-il me lever?"
" " 21. "Vous pouvez vous lever."
" " 22. "Il est difficile de se lever."
" " 23. "Il vaudrait mieux se lever."

And so on with several verbs.

"Past participles, stand up. Are you a complete tense?"

"No, sir."

"What do you want to make a complete tense?"

"A past participle concomitant."

"What are the past participle concomitants in French?"

"The two auxiliaries, *avoir* and *être.*"

"Do you know when to use one or the other?"

"I think I do, sir."

"Give me some examples of the use of *être*, then."

"*Je suis venu, Je suis allé, Je me suis levé, Je suis retourné, Je me suis assis.*"

"What is the name of that tense?"

"The *passé indéfini.*"

"You said just now *Je me suis assis.* What does that mean?"

"It means *I sat down.*"

"Do all French people say *Je me suis assis*?"

"No, sir; ladies say *Je me suis assise.*"

"What do we call the change from *assis* to *assise*?"

"Agreement, sir."

[To the whole class:] "Levez-vous! . . . Qu'avez-vous fait?"

"Nous nous sommes levés."

"Asseyez-vous! Qu'avez-vous fait?"

"Nous nous sommes assis."

"And if you were girls instead of boys, what would you answer?"

" Nous nous sommes assises."

" And if this were a mixed class of girls and boys ? "

" Nous nous sommes assis."

" Infinitive M, the imperative affirmative, the past participle, the present tense second person singular, stand up. Repeat the word you represent for the verb *donner*."

The infinitive: " [dɔne]."

The imperative affirmative: " [dɔne]."

The past participle: " [dɔne]."

The present tense, second person plural: " [dɔne]."

" But that's the same word ! Do you mean to tell me that each of you have to say [dɔne] ? "

A pupil: " It happens to be the same in this case, sir."

" Let's try another verb. We'll take the French equivalent for *to open*."

The infinitive: " [uvriːr]."

The imperative affirmative: " [uvre]."

The past participle: " [uvɛːr]."

The present tense, second person plural: " [uvre]."

And so on, eliciting one after another the various terms considered necessary for the understanding of French grammar.

The Ergonic Chart [1]

Shortly after the beginning of the secondary stage the Ergonic Chart will be introduced and gradually developed. A primitive chart may consist of a blackboard reserved specially for this purpose, a number of small squares of card, and a supply of drawing-pins. A more ambitious apparatus may be devised of stout straw-boards neatly covered with black paper and provided with grooved ledges, pegs, and holes.

The various lexicological units will be written in fairly large letters on small cards or slips of paper.

At the first lesson in which this branch of the programme is treated a few simple sentences will be chosen from among those already forming part of the pupil's stock.

The pupils will be invited to write words on slips and to come

[1] See Appendix I.

and attach them to the blackboard. The nature of the various ergonic classes will be introduced, explained, combined, and analysed.

As time goes on this rough synoptic table or scheme of 'visible grammar' will be developed slowly but surely. Each new abstract fact will become spatialized, concretized, and readily assimilated even by those who have hitherto seemed incapable of grasping the most elementary knowledge of the mechanism of speech.

Just as we designed various exercises to develop the auditive faculties, so will our ergonic chart strengthen and encourage the capacities of visualization.

The various lessons given in front of the ergonic chart will treat of the function of each of the parts of speech, the mechanism of the French system of inversion, the mechanism of the verb, and the verbal inflexions. The various phenomena connected with the interrogative and negative forms, modification by adjectives and adverbs of degree will all be shown so clearly that the learning of 'rules and exceptions' will be dispensed with and superseded by direct and spatialized understanding.

Living Ergonics

In a type of work which we may designate by the above title the pupils themselves take the place of the slips or cards, and the schoolroom floor serves as a background for the ergonic chart.

The following arrangement and general method of working will be found suitable for a class of about twenty pupils:

Pupil No.	*Rôle*	*Type-unit*
1.	Subject	*je*
2.	Negative	*ne*
3.	Imperative (second person)	*prenez*
4.	Present	*prends*
5.	Imperfect	*prenais*
6.	Future	*prendrai*
7.	Conditional	*prendrais*

Pupil No.	*Rôle*	*Type-unit*
8.	Past participle concomitant	*ai* (or *suis*)
9.	Infinitive concomitant	*peux*
10.	Adverbs	*pas, toujours*
11.	Past participle	*pris*
12.	Infinitive	*prendre*
13.	Direct object	*le livre* (or *le*)
14.	Indirect object	*au professeur* (or *lui*)
15.	Subjective complement	*blanc*
16.	Place	*ici*
17.	Duration	*pendant deux heures*
18.	Manner	*lentement*
19.	Time	*maintenant*

Later on it will be well to appoint one of the pupils as representative of such units as *Est-ce que*, *Je pense que*, *Il faut que*, etc. If the number of pupils is in excess of the number we have mentioned, minor *rôles* (such as adverbs of degree) can be created, or certain parts may be doubled by understudies.

The pupils should be taught to 'fall in' in the manner illustrated on opposite page.[1]

Each pupil should learn his ergonic name and be instructed in his part. During the first two lessons the parts should be confined as far as possible to the type units. Nos. 3, 4, 5, 6, 7, 12, and 13, however, must be prepared to produce their respective tenses (first person singular) of *prendre* (for use with the direct object), *venir* (for use with the place complement), *donner* (for use with the indirect object), *attendre* (for use with the duration complement), and *être* (for use with the subjective complement).

The Subject will be told that he occupies the first place in the sentence except in cases of inversion. He must also be told to 'fall out' whenever the Imperative is present.

The Imperative will be told that he can only be preceded by *ne*.

The Present, Imperfect, Future, and Conditional will be told that they are the Simple Tenses and must stand to the left of

[1] The pupils are presumed to be facing the left of the diagram.

the Subject except in cases of inversion, when they will change places with the Subject.

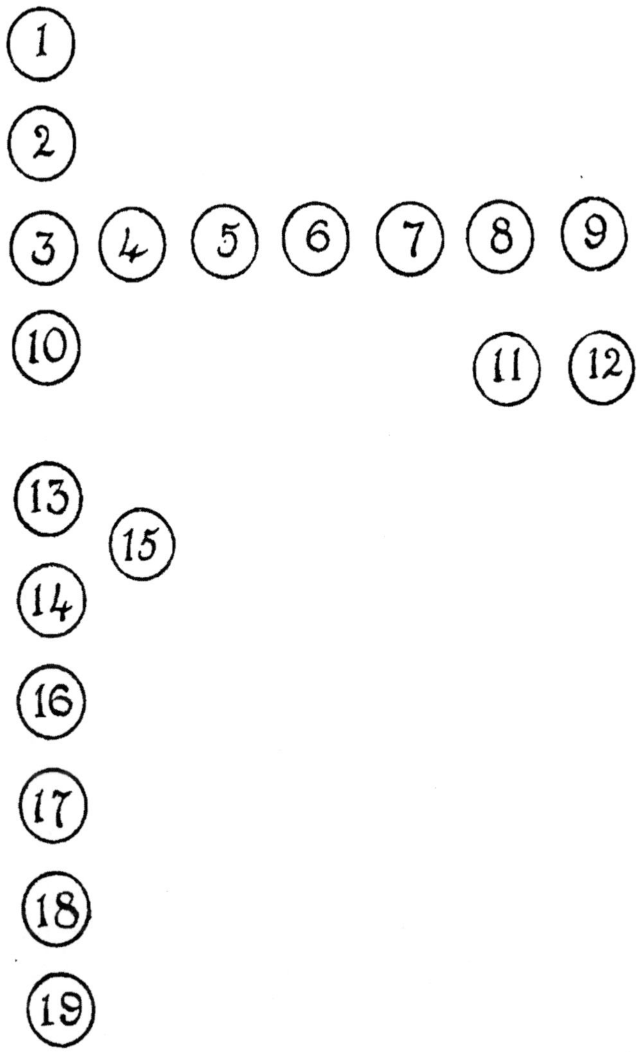

The Past Participle Concomitant will be told that he can never appear without the Past Participle, who will generally stand next to him on the left, but who may be separated from him by *pas* and other adverbs (10). He will also be told when to take the form of *ai* or of *suis*.

The Past Participle will be shown his place.

The last two pupils will be told that they form together the *Past Indefinite* Tense.

Similar instructions will be given to the Infinitive Concomitant and the Infinitive.

Ne will be told that his place is on the right of the Imperative, Present, Imperfect, Future, and Conditional Tenses, and of the two Concomitants.

Pas will be instructed to take up his position on the left of the above tenses.

The Direct Object must be instructed that his place is normally to the left of the verb, from which he can only be separated by *pas* and other adverbs. If he should represent a personal pronoun, however, he must stand to the right of the Simple Tenses and of the Past Participle Concomitant, but between the Infinitive Concomitant and the Infinitive. He will also be told to change places with the Indirect Object when the latter is represented by *me*, *te*, *se*, or *vous*.

The Indirect Object will be given similar instructions.

The other pupils will learn their respective positions and duties.

Obviously the whole of the class must pay attention to all these instructions, and each individual will be expected after a few lessons not only to be expert in his own part, but to be fairly well acquainted with the parts played by the other members.

A special exercise-book in which all the instructions will be noted should be compiled by each pupil. One page (at least) will be reserved for each ergonic part. The following is a characteristic specimen of one of the pages:

JOHN SMITH. *Infinitive Concomitant*

Type-unit: *peux*.

Conjugation of same: *peux*, *peux*, *peut*, *pouvons*, *pouvez*, *peuvent*.

Place: On the left of Subject. May be separated from Subject by *ne*, by Direct Object (when a personal pronoun), and by Indirect Object (when a personal pronoun).

Changes places with Subject in case of inversion.

On the right of Infinitive. May be separated from Infinitive by *pas*, Direct Object (when a personal pronoun), and Indirect Object (when a personal pronoun).

Most frequent units: *dois, dois, doit, devons, devez, doivent.*
veux, veux, veut, voulons, voulez, veulent.
faut.
espère, espères, espère, espérons, espérez, espèrent.

Specimen Lesson

" Subject, Present, Direct Complement, Time Complement, take your places ! "

[They do so.]

" Each pupil will recite his unit."

" *Je—prends—le livre—maintenant.*"

" The whole class will repeat *Je prends le livre maintenant.*"

[They do so.]

" What does that mean ? "

" *I take the book now,* or *I am taking the book now.*"

" Very well. Negatives, take your places."

" Each pupil will recite his unit."

" *Je—ne—prends—pas—le livre—maintenant.*"

" Negatives, dismiss ! "

[Addressing the Direct Complement :] " What part are you taking ? "

" Direct Complement, sir."

" Very well. Do you know by what other name you are known ? "

" Yes, sir ; Direct Object."

" That's right. Are you a noun or a pronoun at present ? "

" A noun, sir."

"Well, I now want you to represent the pronoun *le*."

[Direct Complement passes behind Present Tense and takes his place on the other side.]

"Each pupil will recite his unit!"

"*Je—le—prends—maintenant.*"

"Negatives, take your places!"

"Each pupil will recite his unit."

"*Je—ne—le—prends—pas—maintenant.*"

"Negatives, dismiss! Present Tense, dismiss! Fall in, Future!"

"Each pupil will recite his unit."

"*Je—le—prendrai—maintenant.*"

"Dismiss!"

"Form the following sentence: *Je peux venir ici demain.*"

"Each pupil will recite his unit."

"The whole class repeat *Je peux venir ici demain.*"

"Negatives, take your places."

"Each pupil will recite his unit."

"The whole class repeat *Je ne peux pas venir ici demain.*"

"Dismiss!"

"Form the French equivalent of the sentence *I did not give it to him yesterday.*

"That's right, Subject, extreme right as usual. What are you doing here, Imperfect? This sentence does not concern you; go back to your place. Now, then, Past Participle, we are waiting for you. Direct and Indirect Complements, what are you running round each other for? Direct to the right and Indirect to the left. *Ne*, a little more to the right, Direct and Indirect Complements have to stand between you and the Past Participle Concomitant. In order now? Each pupil will recite his unit."

"The whole class will recite the sentence *Je ne le lui ai pas donné.*"

"That wasn't very smart; we must go over that again. Dismiss! Once again; the French equivalent of *I did not give it to him.*"

Etc., etc.

The Script

The introduction of the orthographic script should be postponed as long as possible. Were the phonetic script merely an instrument to ensure a normal pronunciation it might be dispensed with as soon as habits of normal pronunciation had been acquired. But seeing that the phonetic aspect of language has an importance apart from questions of pronunciation, that many problems connected with the mechanism of the language can only be adequately understood by studying the true base of all linguistic phenomena, the *sound*, the introduction of the conventional spelling system should be delayed as long as possible—the longer the better. We would suggest that a minimum of two years should be accorded to the exclusive use of the phonetic transcription.

The traditional spelling requires no particular period of transition; we have data proving conclusively that the pupil who has been trained by the use of phonetic symbols, all other things being equal, is a better speller than the one who has not enjoyed the advantages of such a training. It will be found that when the more important lexicological units of a given language have been assimilated, the orthographic form of such units is acquired by the spontaneous or automatic process.

The pupils themselves will soon discover the essential facts of orthoepy; they will soon perceive that [y] is almost invariably written in French by means of the letter *u*, etc., etc.

The introduction of the traditional spelling may be the signal for a general recapitulation of all past work. It may take the form of exercises in which the phonetic is to be converted into the orthographic text, and *vice versa.*

Much can be done by a series of guessing competitions. We write on the blackboard various words and sentences, and ask the pupils to guess for what words they stand, or we devise homework to the same effect.

"Take care of the phonetics and the spelling will take care of itself" is a true saying and worthy of all respect.

Section 24.—The third or advanced stage, of the duration of from one to three years, will complete the scholastic training of the pupil. It will consist of:

- (*a*) **Subconscious work (rapid reading, mental and oral; listening to talks, stories, and lectures).**
- (*b*) **Free composition (descriptions of objects, pictures, and events).**
- (*c*) **Free translation (French into English and English into French).**
- (*d*) **Conversation.**
- (*e*) **Systematic study of texts.**

Under ideal conditions, the third or advanced stage will commence at the moment that the previous efforts of the student have enabled him to understand the greater part of what he hears and reads, and to express in a simple manner and with a relative freedom from error by the oral and written mediums about 75 per cent. of the matter contained in the ordinary everyday speech of the average person.

This 75 per cent. of matter consists of the relatively small number of units contained in the microcosm; the 25 per cent. which remains consists of the residue of the language, the mass of the vocabulary, the infinite number of ergonic combinations of all degrees.

The study of a language is never-ending; no one can claim to have a perfect knowledge even of his own language after a life-time of intensive study. All that one can hope to do is to acquire the faculty of converting thoughts into lexicological units, and *vice versa*, to such a degree that the attendant problems and difficulties are reduced to a practical minimum.

The ideal programme starts at a fixed point: that at which our knowledge of the foreign language stands at zero. The ideal programme has no concluding point; it continues throughout the lifetime of the student; every conversation in which he participates, every lecture of which he is an auditor, every book of which he is a reader, and every composition of which he is the author advances him on his way.

To determine the point at which the scholastic or tutorial study should be replaced by those types of study which consist of the using of the language in social intercourse, and the applying of language to intellectual ends would be but an arbitrary proceeding, and we shall not attempt it.

Nor do we propose to give in any detail any precise indications as to the manner in which the last section of the scholastic programme is to be carried out by teacher and by student. If the conclusions that we have so far reached are sound, and if the two stages so far described have been traversed in accordance with the principles already indicated, and in the manner which will be fully described in the later sections of this book, there will be little or no need to dwell at any length on the problems of the advanced stage.

Nor need we postulate any special process of transition. When the student has reached the point which is the signal for his entry into the third stage, he will be able to plunge straight into this without any further preliminary work.

If the first and second stages have been conscientiously treated by an expert method-maker, a competent teacher, and an average student, the third stage will take care of itself.

Starting this stage under the same happy auspices that marked the entry into the second, but increased in a tenfold degree, the student will henceforth progress with the same ease and rapidity as if the language were his mother tongue. The pupil's working power will have been fostered and cultivated. Everything that he has learnt has been designed not only to increase his linguistic knowledge, but also to increase his power of acquiring further knowledge. The daily investments made during the earlier periods have long since been yielding, and will continue to yield, compound interest, the rate of progress will continue on the same scale, and little by little the artificial element of study will give way to the natural and spontaneous course of study with all its stimulus and incentive.

The first two stages are necessarily and essentially of an artificial character. Except for the daily exercises in subconscious comprehension, the student does not work on the lines of a young child in the earliest period of his study of his native language. Arrived, however, at the end of the second stage, the student is more or less in the same position as the child at a later stage, and commences to enjoy all the advantages and facilities of the process of spontaneous and natural assimilation.

In order better to realize the differences and resemblances between the natural programme pursued when learning our own native language and the semi-artificial programme which it is the main object of this book to describe, we may aptly form an analogy between this subject and that concerning the growth of plants.

In the state of nature there is neither garden nor gardener; there is no hot-house, no watering-can, neither spade nor rake, nor any of those artificial appliances considered indispensable by the horticulturist.

The flower blooms and engenders seed; the seed may germinate, form a root, send up a stem, and finally develop into a hardy and worthy representative of its family. This is the natural method in all its simplicity.

The gardener wishes the phenomena of growth to be manifested at a given time and in a given place. Were he to take the seed, to treat it with chemicals in a laboratory, to tend it with a thermometer, with X-, N-, and Z-rays, and with doses of electrical energy, he would not be submitting the plant to the natural method of growth. The results might be satisfactory; perhaps one day some artificial method may supersede the other, but up to the time of writing these methods are not current among gardeners.

Does he then adopt the other extreme and leave the raising of plants to unaided nature? Is he a passive spectator of the chance fall of the seed, of its chance germination aided by chance showers? Does he not rather tend the soil with nitrates and garden tools? Does he not place the seed into the ground at a given and predetermined depth at a predetermined period of the year? Does he not ensure the future development by means of scarecrows, soot, lime, and weed-killers? Does he not subsequently prick out the embryonic plant, bind its fragile stem to a support, water it during the drought, and encourage it with a glass bell?

All these proceedings are of an artificial nature in that they differ in kind and degree from those of Mother Nature. And yet, in so far that each one of these proceedings is an intense application of the methods of nature, such proceedings may be termed *natural* in a somewhat qualified acceptation of the term.

But when the preliminary stage of soil preparation has been accomplished, and when the plant has attained the proportions of a hardy microcosm of its future self, the gardener may leave the plant to nature during the residuary stage and nature will do the rest.

The gardener has exercised all his arts in order to ensure a successful passage through the critical stage; he has curbed the vicious tendencies and has supplied the right food at the right time. The plant can now take care of itself, find its own food, or be prepared to fast.

Such is the not inapt analogy that we would suggest between the respective developments of that concrete organism called a plant and that abstract organism which is the lexicological stock contained in the brain of a student.

In both cases the development may be carried out by the unaided processes of nature; in both cases this development may conceivably be forced by purely artificial means, and in both cases this development may be brought about by a wise and intense application of natural methods in a semi-artificial manner during a certain period, after which nature unaided accomplishes the rest.

To leave too little to nature and to expect too much from nature are both errors; to determine to what extent conscious intervention and artificial aid may be judicious or essential is an important function both of the gardener and of the language-teacher.

The reader would perhaps wish to push the analogy still farther. He may suggest that the adult plant still requires the attention of the expert gardeners; that there must be pruning and training, constant supervision and ever-present care. He may suggest that the analogy points to similar activities on the part of the teacher even in the third stage.

It is dangerous to push an analogy too far; in this case there is a *différence sensible* between the development of a concrete vegetable organism and an abstract organism which is nothing more nor less than a given quantity of lexicological material in the brain of a language-learner.

(Let it be carefully noted here that we are not forming an analogy between a seed and a person, nor between a seed and a lexicological unit.)

In one case the developed product will be *a concrete mass* of vegetable matter; in the other it will be *the faculty of using* a mass of lexicological or thought-interpreting matter.

The ultimate destiny of the plant is to produce leaves, flowers, fruits, and the seeds of the next generation, whereas in the other case the faculty of using the lexicological units is an end in itself.

We agree that this faculty may also be a means to a further end: the production and appreciation of *literary work*; but this has little or nothing in common with the teaching or learning of a foreign language. The subject of our inquiry and the title of this book is the scientific *study of languages*; we trust that none will expect us to include considerations concerning the scientific production and the scientific appreciation of literature!

The third stage is intended to enable the student to become acquainted with, and eventually to be able to use, the vast mass of the vocabulary. The microcosm is the framework containing innumerable cells called ergonic categories; each of these cells contains a little, and a very little, matter; during the residuary stage these cells will become filled with the rich lexicological matter of the language, new cells will be formed in turn to be filled, and the term *foreign language* will gradually become a misnomer, for it will become transformed into a second native language existing side by side and on intimate terms of amity with the other.

The third stage will give to the student neither a good pronunciation nor fluency, for the obvious reason that long before entering this stage he will possess both. The good pronunciation will have been acquired as early as the first period, and one of the chief objects of the second period was to ensure perfect fluency both of expression and of understanding.

The good habits formed during the first periods should bear

fruit during the whole period of subsequent study. Care, however, must be exercised in order to prevent any relapse or giving way to the vicious tendencies. Should any serious outbreak of these occur, the student must at once be subjected to an intensive special treatment in order to stamp out the incipient pernicious habit. Various ailments and their cures are cited in the part devoted to "Special Programmes" (Section 28).

When necessary, we must inculcate the principles of study, warn the student against an exaggerated use of his synthetic faculties, and drive home the precept that by imitation alone are languages learnt.

Let us occasionally ask the pupil to quote some of the latest acquisitions to his lexicological stock; let him answer the question: "What word or combination of words have you particularly noticed during this last week's work, and which of them have you incorporated into your nucleus of lexicological units?"

Presuming that the student has managed to keep clear of the vicious tendencies, and that quality has been, and is being, maintained, what is solely required during the final period is *quantity*.

To this effect the student must read books and listen to speech in order to enrich his vocabulary, and must speak and write in order to use the material so acquired.

In this connexion let us bear in mind the dictum that "Reading maketh a full man, conference a ready man, and writing an exact man."

The vocabulary of our native language increases by the continual growing of the well-formed nucleus. The microcosm of the second stage forms the nucleus to which the matter of the advanced stage will naturally gravitate and in which it will become absorbed. The symmetrical and continual enlargement of a well-formed nucleus is the formula of the snowball, and also of our 'advanced stage.'

This third stage is *undifferentiated*, if by non-differentiation we mean the simultaneous absorption of all the aspects of each new unit or of groups of new units.

Although undifferentiated, there is no reason why it should not be graduated, especially at the beginning. Not that we would subdivide this stage in a rigid manner into a series of sub-stages each of which is to be preparatory to the next.

What we would imply is that the first texts to be studied and our first conversations should be relatively simple; that now, as before, the more frequent should have a preference over the less frequent units, and that modern colloquial should still preponderate over the archaic and literary forms of expression.

The charm and quaintness of old-fashioned or unusual forms of expression is solely due to the fact that they are not those of current everyday speech, and in order to appreciate the æsthetic value of such forms a sound knowledge of the everyday idiom is essential. Were the language of Gray's *Elegy* the language of everyday speech, and did we express the banalities of daily life by means of lexicological units such as those to be found in Hamlet's Soliloquy, the greater part of their charms would be lost.

When for some cause or other an old-fashioned phrase with a literary flavour comes back from the grave and is used in colloquial and vulgar speech, how rapidly it loses its charm! "What ho, there, ye base varlets!" was once a delightfully old-fashioned gem of diction. Comedians and costermongers have reduced it to the level of a vulgarism.

Thou, *thee*, *thy*, and *thine* are English archaisms; they consequently evoke quaint and pleasing literary emotions. The French *tu*, *te*, *toi*, *ton*, etc., are not archaisms; they consequently evoke no æsthetic emotion whatever. *It is forbidden* has an old-time majestic ring which is not to be found in the semantic equivalent *It is prohibited*; but *Es ist verboten* suggests nothing but unæsthetic severity.

If for no other reason than this, it is essential that the student's first text-books should contain but the plainest and least artistic specimens of the language.

Let us first acquire a perfect knowledge of the commonplace, trivial, and even vulgar expressions of modern inartistic speech, in order to render ourselves capable of appreciating at a later period the æsthetic side of speech.

In this respect, again, the student of the foreign language is, even in the advanced stages, not in the same position as the native. The native, being perfectly familiar with the colloquial language in all its banality, appreciates fully the beauty, the glamour, the delicacy, the majesty, the severity, the tenderness, the asceticism, and the humour to be found in the higher regions of linguistic expression.

The first texts should be prepared carefully in accordance with the principle of gradation. They should contain from 90 per cent. to 95 per cent. of the matter of the microcosm. As time goes on, this percentage may be decreased, but will probably never fall below 65 per cent. or 70 per cent.

The best type of text will consist of short anecdotes, humorous stories, and interesting items of general information selected from current periodicals and carefully edited and simplified. The colloquial and simple explanatory styles should be used; both slang and archaisms should be avoided.

The easiest and most natural texts are those which constitute the most faithful reflection of the language as it is truly spoken by all sorts and conditions of native speakers without the intervention of the descriptive or explanatory styles.

But mere reproductions of street-corner conversations concerning the weather or the current political situation will not suffice. In addition to its simplicity and fidelity to real speech, the subject-matter must have an intrinsic interest. The dramatic or the humorous elements must be present. For adult pupils the only reading matter fulfilling these conditions would appear to be modern comedies by such authors as Pinero or H. A. Jones and their foreign equivalents.

Reading may be intensive and extensive. In the former case each sentence is subjected to a careful scrutiny, and the more interesting may be paraphrased, translated, or learnt by heart. In the latter case book after book will be read through without giving more than a superficial and passing attention to the lexicological units of which it is composed.

All the usual expedients may be utilized to make conversation, to stimulate composition, and to cause the student to exercise his perceptive and imitative faculties. Exercises and tests of the most varied nature may be given in order to ensure a sound and proportionate attention to all the aspects of the matter studied.

The student will read aloud, will listen to the reading of the teacher, will summarize the contents of a chapter. There will be dictation, both phonetic and orthographic; the pupil will convert phonetic passages into the orthographic form, and *vice versa*; he will give answers to a *questionnaire* that must ever be kept up to date by his teacher.

There will be recapitulations in which the newer will be correlated with the older matter. Semantic groups will be formed and new ergonic families will be formulated. The student will learn to use a note-book, or, better still, the loose-leaf book, or, best of all, the card index.

As time goes on the texts will become more and more rich in new material; from the everyday colloquial we pass through various types of style; the simple explanatory style as employed by writers on popular science and current events, the simple descriptive style as found in books of adventure and travel, then the more florid varieties of the explanatory and descriptive styles, and finally into the realms of the classical literature modern and ancient.

Mechanical exercises are replaced to an ever-increasing extent by freer and more ambitious types of work. The linguistic material already acquired has taken deep root and is sending out stout branches, and the quasi-organism can grow and develop by purely natural means.

At the moment when, according to old-fashioned ideas, the systematic study of theory should commence, our pupils under the ideal conditions of to-morrow will dispense with it, for it will have served its purpose.

Practice will now be the order of the day; practice in speaking, in reading, in composing, yes, and practice in translating.

After from one to two years of practice in the advanced stage, speaking, understanding, reading, and writing, not the broken Anglo-French which it was formerly the habit to inculcate, but the real French of France, our pupils will be promoted to the higher forms, and pass from the hands of the language-teacher into the hands of those who are entrusted with the teaching of that branch of art known as French literature. The work of the language-teacher is over.

Section 25.—We may append here a comprehensive and descriptive list of most of the types of exercises which will be found of use during the three stages. While many of them are suitable for work in the class-room, they will generally be utilized as material for homework and for private study.

No serious attempt has been made to classify the following list of exercises; indeed so many of them are designed to fulfil more than one purpose that it would be difficult, if not impossible, to classify them in any precise or satisfactory manner.

Certain types of exercises have been so fully treated in sub-sections 22 and 23 that it is unnecessary that they should figure in the present list.

For the sake of conciseness the instructions for the performance of these exercises have been worded in terms perfectly comprehensible to the reader of the present work, but of too abstract a nature for the use of school-children. In the actual French method, examples will be given in most of the cases in order to show exactly what the pupil is required to do.

Our object in supplying specimens has been to illustrate by more or less typical examples the nature of each of the exercises proposed; consequently no consistent attempt has been made to graduate them nor apply them to particular problems. The object of our present inquiry is to suggest the lines on which French might be taught, but not to furnish the method itself.

(*A*) Mechanical Exercises

Serving to inculcate Primary Matter

1. Copying out matter in the phonetic transcript. (This exercise is characteristic of the elementary stage.)

The object of this exercise is to familiarize the pupil with the forms of the symbols and to make him proficient in tracing them. If the matter so given coincides with the sentences and polylogs to be catenized, this exercise will be an auxiliary to the operation of catenizing.

The text serving as model should be printed in distinct and fairly large type.

While some teachers advocate the use of script characters, others prefer the pupils to ‘ print ’ them. A pupil who has been in the habit of ‘ printing ’ the characters will be less likely to confuse the phonetic and orthographic scripts, and for this reason the latter course is to be recommended.

The pupil should pronounce each letter as he traces it, and pronounce each unit as completed.

2. Copying out matter in orthographic form. (For use during the intermediate stage.)

This form of exercise will be useful as one of the means to teach the orthographic forms of units hitherto met with only in their phonetic form. The pupil should pronounce every word as it is completed.

3. Reading aloud from phonetic transcription. (Characteristic of the elementary and intermediate stages.)

A valuable auxiliary to catenizing, serving to connect the ear and eye memories, and to ensure their correlation.

4. Reading aloud from the orthographic transcription. (Characteristic of the later intermediate and advanced stages.)

This should only be resorted to in the microcosmic stage, when the student is perfectly well acquainted with the pronunciation of the units contained in the reading matter. During the advanced period the reading aloud of an orthographic text will constitute a most valuable form of subconscious assimilation.

5. Phonetic dictation (including nonsense dictation). (Elementary and intermediate stages.)

A useful auxiliary to catenizing and the natural sequence to Exercises 1 and 3.

6. Orthographic dictation. (Intermediate and advanced stages.)

Complementary to Exercises 2 and 4. Of value for orthoepic work (the study of relations between sounds and their conventional representation).

Nos. 3, 4, 5, 6 obviously to be used in the class-room.

7. Transcribing in phonetic form matter supplied in orthographic form. (Intermediate and advanced stages.)

This may be called visual phonetic dictation. It enables the pupil to make progress in pronunciation, orthoepy, and orthography without the presence of the teacher. Especially valuable at the moment of the introduction of the orthographic script.

8. Transcribing in orthographic script matter supplied in phonetic form. (Intermediate and advanced stages.)

Complementary to Exercises 2, 6, and 7.

9. Repeating substitution tables after the teacher. (Intermediate stage.)

The teacher pronounces the model sentence previously catenized by the pupil; the pupil repeats it after him. The teacher pronounces the sentence modified successively by the substitutive elements of the various columns. Each sentence pronounced is immediately repeated by the pupil. This exercise should be constantly performed after the pupil has acquired an adequate stock of model sentences.

10. Reading substitution tables. (Intermediate stage.)

Complementary to and the natural sequence of 9.

11. Copying out substitution tables. (Intermediate stage.)

Complementary to 1 and 9.

(*B*) Semi-Mechanical and 'Intellectual' Exercises

Serving to inculcate primary matter and to develop the pupil's capacity of producing correct secondary matter.

12. Repeating substitution tables, the substitutive elements of which are suggested by the teacher in English. (Intermediate stage.)

Example:

Teacher. Je ne peux pas venir ici demain.
Pupil. Je ne peux pas venir ici demain.
T. Next week.
P. Je ne peux pas venir ici la semaine prochaine.
T. On Monday.
P. Je ne peux pas venir ici lundi.
T. Next month.
P. Je ne peux pas venir ici le mois prochain.
T. At two o'clock.
P. Je ne peux pas venir ici à deux heures. Etc., etc.

One of the most productive forms of work ensuring rapid results on absolutely sound lines. The integral translation does not prevent the pupil from 'thinking in French.'

13. Giving integral English equivalent of French ergonic units previously memorized. (Intermediate stage.)

Example:

Teacher	*Pupil*
La semaine prochaine.	Next week.
La fenêtre.	The window
Regardez le livre.	Look at the book.
Je voudrais.	I would like to.
Faut-il ?	Shall I ?
Deux ou trois.	Two or three.
Encore un peu.	A little more.
Il ne faut pas.	You mustn't.
En France.	In France.
Je ne sais pas.	I don't know.
Je vais.	I am going.
Etc.	Etc.

All matter given in this form of exercise is presumed to have been previously learnt by the pupil in the form of integral equivalents. The introduction of unseen sentences or polylogs would convert this exercise into a type of synthetic translation, a form of work exemplified in Exercise 41.

14. Giving the integral French equivalent of English ergonic units. (Intermediate stage.)

Example:

Teacher	*Pupil*
Come here.	Venez ici.
I don't understand.	Je ne comprends pas.
It's no use coming.	C'est inutile de venir.
I'd rather see it.	J'aimerais mieux le voir.
Is there ?	Y a-t-il ?
I am not reading.	Je ne lis pas.
Give me.	Donnez-moi.
Wait for me.	Attendez-moi.

This exercise, complementary to 13, must be severely restricted to approved and previously assimilated bilingual equivalents. On no account should units be given which have not previously been seen and studied. The English unit must be the exterior cue, suggesting the whole of the French equivalent unit. The non-observance of this principle converts this exercise into that difficult and advanced form of work exemplified by Exercise 42.

15. Giving known French equivalents of certain units of other languages than English—*e.g.* German or Latin. (Intermediate and advanced stages.)

Example:

Teacher	*Pupil*
Heute.	Aujourd'hui.
Schön.	Beau.
Ich bin gekommen.	Je suis venu.
Ich weiss nicht.	Je ne sais pas.
Es ist nicht.	Ce n'est pas.

An interesting variation of 14, strengthening and confirming the semantic associations. In view of the fact that French is (generally) the first foreign language studied in English schools this type of exercise will be of comparatively rare occurrence in the teaching of French. It will probably be found more effective as a feature of the German and Latin courses.

16. The teacher to pronounce various sounds; the pupil to call out their respective numbers as he does so. (Elementary stage.)

Example:

Teacher	*Pupil*
[e]	French, No. 2.
[ɛɪ]	English, No. 13.
[ɑ̃]	French, No. 14.
Etc.	Etc.

A very practical and effective method for developing the auditive perception.

17. The teacher to pronounce various sounds; the pupil to point out each one on the phonetic chart as he does so. (Elementary stage.)

A variation of 16. Calculated to co-ordinate the pupil's auditive and visual perceptions by utilizing the principle of spatialization.

18. Converting foreign units into another etymological form. (Intermediate and advanced stages.)

Example:

Convert the following past participles into the corresponding infinitives: *allé, eu, ouvert, reçu, donné, descendu, fini, mis, compris, su.*

Convert the following singulars into their corresponding plurals: *le crayon, mon livre, la fenêtre, le livre noir, son cahier, leur nom, une plume, une grande chambre, votre devoir.*

Convert the following adjectives into adverbs: *facile, lent, bon, convenable, mauvais, difficile.*

Convert the following examples of the present tense into the past indefinite tense: *je prends, je vois, je reçois, je suis, je viens, il marche, il écoute, il met, vous sortez, vous allez.*

One of the best manners of inculcating the principles of etymology. A favourite exercise of many modern methods. The above examples are shown in orthographic script, but this type of exercise should first be presented in phonetic form. The same remark applies to most of the following exercises.

19. Replacing dashes by words. (Intermediate and advanced stages.)

Example :

Replace each dash by an appropriate word :

Venez —.
— est-il allé.
Dites — de — —.
Il va souvent — France.
Je ne — pas demain.
Je ne le lui ai pas —.

An interesting exercise capable of almost infinite gradation from the easiest to the most difficult degrees. If so designed that the completed sentences are identical with models previously catenized, the exercise will be of the mechanical order, and will serve to inculcate still further the primary matter of the microcosm. If, on the other hand, the resultant sentences constitute original unseens, the exercise will serve as a means of producing secondary matter.

Exercises of this type may be differentiated and specialized by confining each to some particular point of semantic or ergonic importance.

20. Completing unfinished sentences. (Intermediate and advanced stages.)

Example :

Complete the following sentences :

Il m'est impossible . . .
Pourquoi n'avez vous . . .
Donnez m'en . . .
Je les ai vus . . .
Je l'aurai . . .

Je suis ici depuis . . .
. . . parce que la porte est ouverte.
. . . resté chez moi.
. . . n'est pas venue.
. . . si vous l'aimez, oui ou non.
. . . qui est venu ici.
. . . que j'ai mis ici.

A type of exercise similar to 19, but leaving greater scope to the ingenuity of the pupil. If the completed sentences constitute matter of the secondary order, this work may be considered as Limited Composition and will pave the way to Free Composition. The remarks made concerning Exercise 19 are here of equal application.

21. Simplification of developed sentences. (Intermediate and advanced stages.)

Example:

Strike out all the units in the following sentences which are not essential to ergonic completeness:

Les autres sont venus tout de suite.
Le livre rouge est sur l'autre table.
Vous en trouverez plusieurs dans le premier tiroir.
La lettre que j'ai reçue hier m'a été envoyée par un ami.
C'est trop grand et pas du tout beau.

An exercise in disintegration serving among other things to call the pupil's attention to the semantic and ergonic values of various units.

22. Composing simple substitution tables. (Intermediate and advanced stages.)

Example:

Develop each of these sentences into a simple substitution table by replacing the unit enclosed between the vertical lines by appropriate ergonic equivalents:

Je le | donne | à mon ami.
Je | suis ici | depuis trois jours.

Ils | venaient ici | tous les jours.
Je | peux | venir ici.
Où avez-vous | vu | mon livre ?

One of the soundest and simplest methods of converting primary into secondary matter.

23. Composing compound substitution tables. (Intermediate and advanced stages.)

Example :

Develop each of these sentences into a compound substitution table by replacing the units enclosed between vertical lines by appropriate ergonic equivalents. The resultant sentences need not be of ideal semantic value. If it is found that a given unit cannot be replaced by any other, the unit may be underlined and left.

| Je ne peux pas | venir ici | demain.
| J'ai vu | trois | livres | sur | la table.
| Je suis | ici | depuis trois | jours.
| Il | me | l' | a | donné.

This is a developed form of Exercise 22, and will give play to the pupil's ingenuity and power of research and adaptation.

24. Composing ergonic (or complex substitution) tables. (Intermediate and advanced stages.)

Example :

Form a table showing the ergonic relations of the units contained in the following sentences :

Il prend le livre.
Il le prend.
Il prendra la plume.
Quelqu'un la prendra.
Elle ne prenait pas les livres.
Il peut prendre quelque chose.
Il ne doit pas prendre cela.
Elle a pris son parapluie.

Il aura pris sa lettre.
Il ne veut pas les prendre.
Mon ami ne doit pas la prendre.

The exercise may be performed by the use of the ergonic chart, using slips and pins, or may be worked out at home on paper.

25. Finding French synonyms of French units. (Intermediate and advanced stages.)

Example :

Find units (monologs or polylogs) having the same or nearly the same semantic value as the following :

Il faut ; dois-je ; joli ; obscur ; gens ; erreur ; je voudrais ; sous ; sur le plancher ; penser que ; essayer de ; de nouveau ; quelque chose d'autre ; tant soit peu ; complètement ; quoique ; se rappeler.

A useful variety of recapitulation work for the more advanced stages.

26. Expressing the sense of a given sentence in other words. (Advanced stage.)

Example :

Express in other words the meaning conveyed in each of the following sentences :

Veuillez entrer. Je suis ici depuis trois jours. A qui est ce livre? Ça ne me fait rien. Il me faut de l'argent. Cela ne vous ferait-il rien de venir ici? Je tiens particulièrement à le faire. Je me vois obligé de l'accepter.

Similar to Exercise 25, but of a more advanced type.

27. Classifying units according to their ergonic value. (Intermediate and advanced stages.)

Example :

Classify the following units according to the ergonic categories to which they belong :

Aujourd'hui. Je. Venir. Sur la table. Parlerais. Pendant quinze jours. Recevoir. Lentement. Verra. Pendant les vacances. Il. Demain. A Londres. Viendrai. Trop grand. Pris. Souvent. Le semaine prochaine. D'une autre manière. Ce que je veux.

This is a form of analysis perfectly correlated to the various other forms of ergonic work suggested in these pages.

28. Conjugating verbs. (Intermediate and advanced stages.)

Example:

Conjugate the following verbs in all their moods, tenses, and persons:

Donner, finir, recevoir, vendre, être, avoir, venir, aller, se lever.

A classical but none the less useful form of work especially during the later stages.

29. Declining pronouns. (Intermediate stage.)

Example:

Decline the following pronouns according to their case:

Je, tu, il, elle, nous, vous, ils, elles.

An etymological exercise limited (in French) to the above examples.

30. Answering questions. (Intermediate and advanced stages.)

Example:

Answer the following questions:

En quoi est faite une table ?
Quelle heure est-il maintenant ?
Êtes-vous allé faire une promenade hier ?
Avec quoi coupe-t-on ?
Quelle distance y a-t-il d'ici à la gare ?
Quel est le nom de la ville que vous habitez ?
Quelle langue parle-t-on en Espagne ?

Another example of limited composition in a very easy form. The student should recognize the fact that the question itself supplies most of the units required in the answer.

31. Forming suitable questions for given answers. (Intermediate stage.)

Example:

Form questions to which the following sentences are answers:

Je suis venu à deux heures.
Il est allé à Londres.
C'est un livre rouge.
Oui, il est grand.
J'y suis resté pendant deux heures.
Avec un couteau on coupe.

Complementary to Exercise 30.

32. Converting affirmative sentences into the negative form. (Intermediate stage.)

Example:

Convert the following sentences into the negative:

Je lis.
J'écris la lettre.
J'ai vu mon ami.
Je suis allé à la gare.
Je peux venir ici.
Venez ici.
Prenez-le.

A simple method of deriving secondary matter. This exercise may be preceded in the early portion of the intermediate stage by one in which negative sentences are converted into affirmatives.

33. Converting positive sentences into their interrogative form. (Intermediate stage.)

Example:

Convert the following sentences into the interrogative, avoiding as far as possible the use of *est-ce que*:

C'est un livre.
Vous parlez français.

Il comprenait.
Vous le lui avez donné.
Je le prends.
Mon frère est ici.
Le plafond est blanc.

A very necessary exercise for students of French and English, in which the formation of the interrogative presents a certain degree of difficulty.

34. Converting positive sentences into the interrogative-negative form. (Intermediate stage.)

Example:

Convert the following sentences into their interrogative-negative form:

Vous l'aimez.
Il est venu.
Vous l'avez fait.
Mon frère est allé à Paris.
Vous viendrez plus tôt.
Les autres ne les prennent pas.

An extension of Exercises 32 and 33.

35. Converting direct into indirect questions. (Intermediate stage.)

Example:

Convert the following direct into indirect questions:

Vient-il ?
Êtes-vous prêt ?
Où allez-vous ?
Que dit-il ?
Quand viendra-t-il ?
Combien en avez-vous pris ?
Qui est-ce qui a fait ça ?

A practical manner of showing the connexion between the interrogatives and connectives.

36. Replacing nouns by pronouns. (Intermediate stage.)

Example:

Replace the words printed in italics by appropriate pronouns.

Je prends *le livre.*
Je vois *la plume.*
Il écrit *la lettre.*
Il boit *du café.*
Je donne *le livre à mon frère.*
Mon frère me donne *des livres.*
MM. A et *B.* envoient *les lettres à mes amis.*

A very necessary exercise in word-order.

37. Supplying verbs either in the indicative or subjunctive moods. (Intermediate and advanced stages.)

Example:

Replace the dashes by a verb in the indicative or in the subjunctive moods as the case may be:

Il pense que je —.
Il faut que je —.
Je crois qu'il —.
Je ne crois pas qu'il —
Il est dommage qu'il —.
Je veux que vous —.
J'espère que vous —.
Je le ferai à moins qu'il ne —.

A practical method of inculcating the use of the subjunctive mood.

38. Classifying previously seen monosyllabic words on a phonetic basis. (Intermediate stage.)

Example:

Classify the following words into sixteen classes according to the phonetic vowel contained in each:

Main, veux, une, bout, neuf, plein, vieux, clef, mal, autre, eu, un, fais, rose, comme, bon, si, elle, place, beau, me, vent, mais, bonne, pas, tôt, œufs, vin, gai, poche, bas, ne, venu, blanc, jouer, laid, vie, bras, œil, bain, oui, nez, chose, brun, livre, où, table, homme, soif, prêt, crois, train, âge, en, chez, jaune, sain, qui, rue, long, pomme, le, mieux, pris, très, feuille, ouest, double, haut, ton, quinze, cent, que, ville, vous, deux, jeune, douze, plume.

A form of exercise to be used a short time after the introduction of the orthographic script. If the list is sufficiently long this will be an excellent method of teaching orthoepy.

39. Composing matter in French in the form of a conversation with the teacher. (Advanced stage.)

This starts as an oral variant of Exercise 30, but develops gradually into a fluent use of the spoken language.

40. Composing matter in the foreign language in order to illustrate the ergonic and semantic functions of various units. (Intermediate and advanced stages.)

Example:

Compose sentences in order to demonstrate the ergonic and semantic functions of the following units:

D'autre, fasse, il y a, si, lorsque, faut-il, celui, plus, encore, mercredi, laisse, souvent, seul, comme, eux, mon, jusqu'à ce que.

This may be differentiated into two separate types of exercise, one treating the purely ergonic and the other the semantic functions of units. In the former case the sentence will show whether the student understands the formal function of the unit; in the latter whether he appreciates the meanings. In the latter case especially, this exercise is a rather advanced stage of composition.

41. Expressing in English ideas supplied by a French text. (Intermediate and advanced stages.)

Example:

Express the following sentences by more or less approximate English equivalents:

Je n'en suis pas partisan.
Je sais pertinemment qu'il est venu.

Je n'y tiens pas beaucoup.
Je tiens particulièrement à le faire.
Quand même il serait venu, je ne l'aurais pas vu.
De quoi vous occupez-vous ?
Cela ne vous ferait-il rien d'ouvrir la porte ?
Je ne vous en prive pas ?

The above examples are only suitable for the advanced stage. This type of exercise, however, may be graduated from the easiest to the most difficult degrees. Among other qualities it constitutes a sound reagent against habits of so-called 'literal translation' and semantic imprecision in general.

42. Expressing in French ideas suggested by an English text. (Intermediate and advanced stages.)

Example :

Express the following ideas more or less approximately in French :

For some reason or other.
That's one for you !
I have often wondered.
I haven't been there for three years.
I'm particularly anxious to know.

As in the case of Exercise 41, we have only given examples of the most advanced order.

43. Subconscious comprehension. (Elementary, intermediate, and advanced stages.)

Detailed examples of this type of exercise have already been given in Section 23.

44. Free composition. (Advanced stage.)

Example :

Write a description (not exceeding 250 words in length) of the town in which you live.

It cannot too often be repeated that free composition in the foreign language is the worst possible method for acquiring fresh material. The sole object of this form of exercise should be to utilize previously assimilated primary matter and the secondary matter which can be legitimately derived from it. If certain ideas cannot be expressed in French without inventing unseen forms, such ideas must not be expressed at all; they should be abandoned, or replaced by ideas which can be expressed by means of known and authentic units.

45. Answering (in English) questions based on the lexicological theories. (Elementary, intermediate, and advanced stages.)

Mixed examples of such questions:

Describe the sound [ə].

What sort of sound is represented by *a* in *lady*?

Explain the mistakes generally made by a Frenchman in pronouncing the word *worthy*.

By what letter or letters do we generally represent in our ordinary spelling the English sounds [ɛ], [ɛɪ], [ɔː], [z]?

What sound-values are generally given to the following letters or combinations of letters in English orthography: *a, alk, er, th, igh, ea*?

What orthographic modification is made to the verb in order to form the regular preterite?

Draw up a list of the semantic varieties of the verb *get*.

What is the place in the sentence of the adverb *always*?

46. Re-translation. (Advanced stage.)

The student will choose, or the teacher will choose for him, a short passage from an authentic French text. He will translate it into English to the best of his ability; the teacher will read the result and suggest corrections and modifications. The next day the student will translate the passage back into French. On its completion he will compare the result with the original, make the necessary corrections, and repeat the operation until the re-translation is word perfect.

47. The missing-word exercise. (Advanced stage.)

As a modification of the preceding exercise and with a view to facilitating it, the student, after translating the text into English, will make a fresh copy of the French original, replacing, however, a certain number of units by blank spaces. The next day, instead of retranslating the English text back into French as suggested in the preceding exercise, he will merely fill in to the best of his ability the blank spaces. After two or three efforts he will be prepared to perform Exercise 46 in its integrity.

PART VI

SPECIAL PROGRAMMES

Section 26.—In that part of this book devoted to the Preliminary Factors of Linguistic Pedagogy, we have seen that no one programme can possibly be ideally suitable for all classes of students; hence, in addition to the Standard Programme that we have just described, we must be prepared to draw up Special Programmes. Limited Programmes of various types are designed to meet the special requirements of those whose aim is less than the four aspects of a given language.

Limited Programmes

The *Ideal Standard Programme* assumes the pupils to be school-children without any previous knowledge of the foreign language.

All important variations from this may be considered as *Special Programmes*. The most suitable variations to meet special cases can only be determined by a reference to the preliminary factors of linguistic pedagogy outlined in Part III.

We may first consider programmes suitable for students whose ultimate aim is less than the four aspects of a given language (*i.e.* the active and passive uses of both the oral and written forms).

In this respect twelve classes of aims are conceivable. All but two of these (Nos. 7 and 8) are more or less of the freak order and hardly worthy of any consideration from those whose endeavours are to place the study of language on a scientific basis. We will nevertheless examine the special requirements of the twelve classes of students and append a few comments.

1. *Those whose sole aim is to understand the language when written.* Under this heading come those students who study the language in order to be able to acquaint themselves with the contents of their foreign correspondence or to read foreign

books of literary or of scientific value of which no translation exists.

The elementary stage will be confined to the theories of etymology, semantics, and ergonics. No phonetic instruction whatever will be given. The second stage will consist of the study of the microcosm. All the exercises will be based on the passive aspect of the language and will be confined to translating into English isolated units and texts.

The third stage will be characterized by the same features. The end will be considered achieved when proficiency has been attained in the comprehension of foreign texts.

2. *Those whose sole aim is to understand the language when spoken.* It is just conceivable that some persons may be so exceptionally placed that such knowledge will meet the particular end they have in view. It will at least enable them to become auditors of lectures, speeches, and dramatic performances.

The entire programme may consist almost exclusively of a course of exercises in subconscious comprehension.

3. *Those whose sole aim is to speak the language.* The only conceivable case would be that of the traveller or tourist desirous of expressing his more immediate wants when visiting the foreign country.

The programme would consist of causing the student to learn by heart the necessarily limited number of useful sentences and minor units requisite for his wants.

4. *Those whose sole aim is to write the language.* The only conceivable case would be that of a person obliged to communicate with foreign correspondents ignorant of his language. In order to attain the desired limited end, the student, needless to say, will be obliged to acquire the capacity which is the aim of class 1. The programme will therefore be a mere extension of that outlined for class 1, but will at the same time embrace the active aspect of written work. Oral memorizing will be replaced by graphic memorizing. The student instead of *repeating* will *write* a given sentence the given number of times on a given number of separate occasions.

5. *Those whose aims are to understand the language when spoken and written.* Such cases will merely be the combination of the requirements of classes 2 and 4.

6. *Those whose aims are to speak and to write the language.* Such cases will merely be the combination of classes 3 and 4.

7. *Those whose aims are to read and write the language.* This is a case of far more frequent occurrence. Few students of Latin or Greek have any other aims than these. From their very nature, the dead languages are of literary and not of colloquial interest. In the case of living languages we may cite the case of correspondence clerks whose sole aim is generally to understand and to answer letters received from foreign correspondents.

The programme will be essentially that of the Standard Programme, except that little or no attention will be paid to the oral aspect of language. The student will either not pronounce any units at all or will use a fancy pronunciation of his own.

No economy of time will be effected by the exclusion of the oral form ; on the contrary, the student will voluntarily deprive himself of that most powerful instrument of study—viz. his power of auditive perception and association. As a matter of fact, those teachers and students who are loudest in their depreciation of the phonetic aspect of language will never consent to forgo the use of the spoken word.

8. *Those whose aim is to speak the language and to understand the spoken language.* This combination of classes 2 and 3 is of most frequent occurrence. Probably the majority of those who study Oriental languages have no further aim in view ; indeed in the case of many of such languages the colloquial and literary forms differ to such an extent that they must be considered as entirely different languages the simultaneous study of which would entail needless confusion and difficulty.

If the student is illiterate he will have to forgo all the advantages of script forms ; if he is not, the programme to be adopted will be identical with the Standard Programme, except for the exclusion of the traditional form of spelling. The spoken language will be represented graphically by means of a suitable phonetic alphabet without any subsequent reduction to classical writing.

9. *Those whose aim embraces all but the understanding of the written language.*

10. *Those whose aim embraces all but the understanding of the spoken language.* Both classes 9 and 10 are almost inconceivable cases and we may dismiss them from our attention.

11. *Those whose aim embraces all but the speaking of the language.*

12. *Those whose aim embraces all but the writing of the language.* Classes 11 and 12 are rare but conceivable cases. For the sake of economy of effort and of time the student should include the fourth aspect, and then work according to the Standard Programme.

Section 27.—A Documentary Programme is designed to meet the special requirements of those whose aim is not the assimilation of a language in any or all of its aspects, but a documentary knowledge only.

We must provide for students who are desirous not of assimilating the units of the language with a view to making any natural or direct use of them, but of gaining a thorough theoretical knowledge of its mechanism, morphological, ergonic, and semantic.

Their incentive may be one of pure curiosity; they are interested in a given language and want to look into it to see how it works.

Or they may have a more definite end in view. Students of lexicology in the abstract require a sufficient knowledge of some dozen languages in order to obtain the documentation necessary for them to pursue their studies or researches.

Few students of phonetics would wish to limit themselves to the study of the sounds of their own language; their aim is to master as many sounds as possible in order to be able to compare them and discover the laws that determine their relations. There are certain aspects of the science of phonetics bound up with the ergonic and semantic aspects of language; if the phonetician keep himself strictly within the limits of his particular science, many facts of the utmost importance will escape his attention, ignorance of which facts will perhaps lead him to false conclusions. The student of phonetics must have access to a number of languages and acquire a knowledge, if only superficial, of their mechanism.

The student of semantics must also have a certain knowledge of a number of languages; indeed this branch of knowledge from its very character is a multilingual study. He cannot spare the time to assimilate from one to a dozen foreign languages; what he requires is an adequate documentation concerning them.

The student of ergonics is in precisely the same situation. He cannot determine, except by guesswork, the varied phenomena of function until he has examined at first hand examples culled from dozens of languages and dialects. Life is too short to attempt to assimilate all these; it is sufficient to acquire for each language which may be of utility a certain set of data with which to work.

Our Standard Programme must be considerably modified to suit the needs of such students as these. From the very fact that they are students and research workers in the field of theoretical lexicology, we must conclude that they require no preparatory training; for them there need be no preliminary stage.

The all-important stage will be the microcosmic, and the all-important process of study will be mere cognition. The seeker of documentation need neither catenize nor spend his time in assimilating semantic values. All that he asks for is the requisite number of ergonic lists and tables, including the ergonic chart of the language, adequate English translations of each unit, and a concise list of 'directions for use.'

The lessons we give him will consist of explanations; the exercises he writes out will merely serve to show whether he has understood our explanations and is able to apply them.

A documentary course may often profitably serve as an introduction to the assimilatory course. Adult pupils for whom the study of language for its own sake has a certain fascination are justified in considering a thorough documentary knowledge of its microcosm as a necessary preliminary stage of their study.

With their curiosity satisfied as to the number and nature of the sounds, the nature of its ergonic categories and their place on the chart, and the semantic peculiarities of its etymons, they would be prepared by means of the forty odd types of exercises suggested in these pages to convert such documentary knowledge into assimilated knowledge.

Section 28.—Corrective Programmes are designed to meet the special requirements of those who have previously studied the language in so disproportionate a manner that one or more of the four aspects has, or have been, totally or partially neglected, or of those who have previously studied the language in so defective a manner that the unsound knowledge so acquired will have to be converted into sound knowledge.

We now have to meet the case of students who have previously acquired certain notions of the foreign language and who are desirous either of increasing their limited stock of knowledge or of ridding themselves of vicious habits due to defective or disproportionate study.

If the student frankly recognizes the fact that his previous study has been conducted on a defective basis, if he is conscious of his failings, and sees clearly what is lacking, it will be relatively easy to deal with him.

If, on the other hand, he is very satisfied with himself, is not prepared to acknowledge any other defects than that of a limited vocabulary, and is unwilling that we should extirpate the grave flaws which stand as a barrier between his present attainments and the perfection toward which it is his aim to rise, then our task will be an almost impossible one. This type of student is by no means uncommon.

We can only strive to change his views concerning himself and prove to him with all the data at our disposal that with regard to certain fundamentals he is in a state of absolute ignorance, that he must set out to develop his faculties of study, and possibly also unlearn and forget much that he has learnt.

If he is unwilling to be convinced, scientific methods of study are not for him, and the conscientious teacher, if he can afford it, must refer the recalcitrant pupil to some language quack who will teach the pupil not what he *ought* to learn, but what he *wants* to learn.

We shall revert to this aspect of the question in the section entitled "The Student."

Just as there are twelve categories of students whose aims fall short of the complete course for which the Standard Programme is designed, so we find twelve similar categories of students whose previous study has been defective.

There are those who can understand what they read but not what they hear; those who can speak but not write; others who understand what they hear but cannot speak; others who can understand the written and spoken language but who can make no active use of either, etc., etc.

The most frequent case, indeed the only one of which we propose to treat, is that in which the student has already attained considerable proficiency in reading. His written work is very defective, his speech far worse, and he is incapable of understanding anything we say to him unless we deliver ourselves monolog by monolog with a pronunciation distorted so as to conform itself to his foreign ear.

Let us note, by the way, that unless we perform this act of linguistic sacrilege, he will accuse us of speaking our own language badly, and will protest against our abnormally rapid and indistinct enunciation of our native tongue.

Presuming, however, a willing pupil, we may take him in hand firmly and with authority, and treat him to a special corrective programme in order to convert his bad habits into good ones and his defective units into sound ones.

We must start by submitting him to a searching and comprehensive examination in order to see how much he knows, to what extent his lexicological knowledge is superficial or defective.

We shall present him with a list of some hundreds of questions and shall request him to answer them in writing.

The following rough list will show the most useful types of question to be asked of the French student of English. We will add in each case the sort of answers which must, alas, often be expected.

Phonetics

Questions	*Possible Answers*
1. Comment prononce-t-on la voyelle dans *cut* ?	1. A peu près comme *eu*.
2. —et la voyelle dans *leave* ?	2. Comme *i* en français.
3. —et la voyelle dans *man* ?	3. Comme *a* en français.
4. Comment prononce-t-on les mots *take* et *home* ?	4. Comme ték et hôm.
5. Quelle est la prononciation usuelle de *will* et de *can* ?	5. Comme *ouile* et *canne*.
6. Quelle est la différence entre l'*r* français et l'*r* anglais ?	6. L'*r* anglais doit être roulé très fortement.
7. Décrivez le son de *th* dans *thin*.	7. C'est un son qui ressemble à *s* ou à *t* fortement aspiré.
8. Quelle est la différence entre le mot anglais *fort* et le mot français *fort* an point de vue de la prononciation ?	8. En anglais on prononce le *t* ; en français on ne le prononce pas.

Etymology

1. Comment forme-t-on dans la langue parlée le participe passé des verbes réguliers ?	1. En y ajoutant *d* ou *ed*. Quand le mot finit par *y*, on prononce *ied*.
2. Comment forme-t-on dans la langue parlée le pluriel des substantifs réguliers ?	2. En y ajoutant *s* on *es*. Quand le mot finit par *y*, on prononce *ies*.

Semantics and Ergonics

Traduire en anglais :

1. Vient-il ?	1. Comes he ? Do he comes ?
2. Je l'ai vu hier.	2. I have seen him yesterday.

3. Il ira à Londres.	3. He shall go in London.
4. Je le verrai quand il viendra.	4. I shall see him when he shall come.
5. Dites à votre ami qu'il vienne.	5. Say (*ou* Tell to) your friend that he comes.
6. Prenez son crayon et sa plume.	6. Take his pencil and her pen.
7. Je ne m'en souviens pas.	7. I remember not me of it.
8. Qui voyez-vous ? Qui est-ce qui vous voit ?	8. Whom see you ? Who sees you ?
9. Sans rien faire.	9. Without to do nothing.
10. Quelqu'un est venu.	10. Anybody is come.
11. Il veut le faire.	11. He will make it.
12. Votre ami ne l'a-t-il pas ?	12. Has not your friend it ?
13. Je me réjouis.	13. I rejoice.
14. Je vais chercher mon chapeau.	14. I go to search (*or* seek) my hat.
15. Bonjour, monsieur, comment allez-vous ?	15. Good-day, sir, how do you do ?
16. Je me demande ce que c'est.	16. I ask me what is it.
17. Il m'est impossible de l'attendre.	17. It is to me impossible to wait him.
18. Je suis ici depuis quinze jours.	18. I am here since fifteen days.

Repondre aux questions suivantes :

19. Comment doit-on rendre en français le mot *will* ?	19. Par *vouloir*.
20. Comment rend-on en anglais l'*imparfait* français ?	20. Par *l'imparfait* anglais.
21. Comment exprime-t-on le pronom indéfini *on* ?	21. Par *one*.
22. Quelle est la différence essentielle entre *some* et *any* ?	22. *Some* s'emploie dans les phrases affirmatives et *any* dans tous les autres cas.
23. Quelle est la fonction du participe présent anglais ?	23. Pour exprimer qu'on fait quelque chose maintenant.

24. Quand doit-on employer le prétérit anglais (I came, I gave, etc.) ?	24. Pour rendre le passé défini ou l'imparfait.
25. Comment dirait-on en anglais *encore un peu* ?	25. On dirait *still a little* ou (dans les phrases négatives) *yet a little.*

Lest it be thought that the 'possible answers' suggested above constitute a gross exaggeration of the case, the writer here affirms that the above are typical of the answers he has received from a majority of adult French students during a period of sixteen years.

Obviously we do not suggest that *every* student who has previously studied English on defective lines will invariably commit every one of the absurdities quoted above. According to the number and the nature of the errors, the teacher must determine the degree and extent of the corrective course.

In order that the pupil may focus his entire attention on one thing at a time, each of the parts of which the course is made up must be segregated from the others. A sound, even if superficial, knowledge of the laws of lexicology will be essential. To this end the student must be provided with an adequate quantity of literature on the subject, written in his own language. The style should be simple and chatty, accompanied by a number of the most characteristic and striking examples. To each section and chapter should be appended a long *questionnaire* to ensure the perfect assimilation of the matter so read. Indeed the corrective course may well take the form of a long series of concise questions with their appropriate answers, conceived somewhat on the lines of the test questions given above. The student should read each question carefully and compare it with the answer. At the end of each page he should go over the list again, both to make sure that he has understood and to give himself a further opportunity of assimilating the facts stated therein.

He should then endeavour to reproduce the answers in writing, comparing the result with the matter given in his book. By learning and assimilating the correct answers to, say, twenty-five questions per day, with a daily recapitulation of all the previous work, the student in the course of a few weeks will have converted the greater part of his unsound into sound knowledge. This work can, of course, be performed at home; to a large extent the teacher will be replaced by the book. The function of the teacher will be to supplement the information given by the book and to furnish additional examples where necessary.

Furthermore, the teacher having, by means of the answers to the tests, ascertained the student's weaker points, he will give special attention to these, and will successively explain in a clear manner and illustrate by striking examples the various lexicological theories. If the pupil's weak point is pronunciation he must take a course of systematic pronunciation exercises and work intensively at phonetic transcription. If the pupil's weak point is semantics he must take a course of systematic semantic exercises. If his weak point is ergonics, a special course of ergonics, including constant use of the ergonic chart, will eventually enable him to overcome his difficulties.

Most of the exercises enumerated in the previous section will be of great utility; the teacher in face of so extensive a choice of instruments must select those which are the most likely to bring about the required reforms.

Never during the corrective course should the student be encouraged or even allowed to speak his own broken jargon. He will probably want to do so, and may urge that 'practice makes perfect,' etc., etc. The teacher may reply that practice *in broken English* indeed does result in perfect *broken English*, and that as the aim of the student is precisely to eradicate it, and not to foster and to encourage it, he must do his best to let it become atrophied by disuse. It will be time to talk about conversing in English when the student has acquired a sufficient stock of healthy units to enable him to do so without recourse to the broken dialect which it is their joint aim to extirpate.

Nor should the student be encouraged to do any free written composition; in short, all the forms of exercise appertaining to the advanced stage of the Standard Programme should be shunned during the corrective course.

While the proportion of mistakes exceeds 10 per cent. no good purpose can be served by giving the student opportunities of perpetrating blunders or 'abnormalities' on this scale.

A mistake is always 'abnormal,' and always tends to show that there has been a fault in method. To say that a given student makes a number of mistakes in his work is equivalent to saying that his work is too difficult for him and that he is being crammed. The object of the correction course is not to reduce the element of error successively from 50 per cent. to 40 per cent. to 30 per cent. and so on, but so to work during a given period that the student shall have formed an entirely new conception of language and its study based, not on eventual fluency and eventual freedom from error, but on the principle of perfect correctness and perfect fluency from the start.

One of the points on which we must be the most insistent is the necessity for *simple expression.* The average adult student imagines that his first foreign compositions will have all the richness of expression that characterizes his compositions in his native tongue. Forgetting that his proficiency in casting his thoughts in the mould of his own language is the result of years of daily practice, he thinks to express these same complex and highly developed concepts in a language the lexicological material of which he has not yet succeeded in assimilating a fraction per cent.

He must be given to understand in the clearest and most categoric of terms that he must perfectly assimilate a simple and limited vocabulary in order to express *simple thoughts,* that in proportion as his lexicological nucleus grows, so will he be able to express more complex and more subtle phases of thought. His first compositions must be couched in the language of the simplest minds; he can no more aspire toward style and beauty of expression than he can hope to express the complex facts of the higher mathematics without any notions of elementary algebra.

As the art student must learn to use the pencil before attempting the use of the brush, as the student of mathematics grapples with simple equations before aspiring toward the calculus, in short, as we all learn to walk before learning to run or to perform gyrations on the tight rope, so also must the student of language content himself during the early stages with the expression of simple thoughts before attempting to vie with the masters of foreign literature.

PART VII

THE FUNCTIONS OF THE TEACHER

Section 29.—The first qualifications of the expert teacher are a knowledge of the foreign language and of the student's native tongue, and the ability to organize the programme, to choose the appropriate material and the most appropriate means of conveying and of inculcating it.

The first and most important qualification of the ideal teacher is a thorough knowledge of both the foreign language and the student's native tongue. We say the 'ideal' teacher—that is to say, one who is prepared to conduct the pupil from his starting-point through the two preparatory stages and deep into the third stage, treating all the aspects of the language *en route*.

We must not, however, lose sight of the possibilities of limited programmes and of the help that may be afforded on special points by teachers whose knowledge of the language is limited to one or more of its aspects. Competent teachers exist who only profess to give lessons in one particular aspect; they have specialized on this one aspect in connexion with many languages, and being deeply specialized, the help that they can afford is necessarily superior to that given by the 'general practitioner.'

The expert phonetician, with little or no lexicological knowledge other than that which comes immediately within his special scope, is more qualified to teach the pronunciation of Russian, Urdu, or Arabic than native teachers of these languages without such expert knowledge.

It is possible and perfectly feasible to learn the ergonic system of a given language from one who is unversed in its phonetics or semantics.

The qualification of the 'ideal' teacher is not necessarily the *sine qua non* of all teachers. It would be truer to say that all teachers should possess in a perfect degree such qualifications as enable them to teach the branch or aspect that they profess to teach. We may have persons with special qualifications for dealing with pupils in the preliminary stage; others who are in every way fitted to inculcate the microcosm of the second stage; others again who have specialized themselves for work connected with the third stage.

As time goes on, and methods become more and more perfect, we shall probably witness a tendency toward specialization, just as we have seen the advent of specialists in other professions than that of pedagogy.

In the absence of any text-books or manuals setting forth any consistent schemes of programmes suitable for various types of students and their varied requirements, it is the teacher himself who has to consider what course will have to be pursued in different cases and to organize the programme best adapted to each particular end.

A programme can only be carried out with success if it is conceived in advance on systematic and proportional lines and thoroughly organized in accordance with consistent principles. The vocabulary must be chosen carefully, unit by unit; there must be a reason governing the selection of each and a reason for presenting it at a given moment and not at another.

To the trained or expert teacher falls in most cases the responsibility of selecting from among the thousands of monologs and the hundreds of thousands of polylogs those which are best calculated to form the microcosm which will represent the nucleus of the pupil's studies.

The haphazard principle of the 'sack' will not do.

Many methods appear to have been composed on the 'sack' principle. The author takes a sack and fills it with thousands of slips of paper on each of which is inscribed a unit of the vocabulary of the language he is going to teach. The sack is well shaken up in order to prevent any possible chance of gradation or logical succession. He then plunges his arm into the sack and withdraws a handful of slips; this handful constitutes the first chapter of the book and is entitled "First Lesson."

The process is repeated until the book is full, the remaining nine-tenths of the slips are thrown away, and the sack is put on one side against the day when the author will make up his mind to apply the ' sack ' method to another language.

It is ridiculously obvious that the sack method of choosing the matter is the wrong method, and yet time after time we see method-writers making themselves obviously ridiculous by adopting it. When the only qualification of an instructor is a mere knowledge of the language that he proposes to teach, the method of presenting the matter must necessarily be unsystematic. Such methods may possibly lead to eventual success on the part of the student, but such success cannot be attributed to the instruction, but is attained in spite of him at the cost of a terrible amount of wasted effort and misdirected energy.

The presentation of matter can only be considered systematic when a definite selection is made in advance, when the instructor is able to furnish a synopsis of the course of lessons he is about to give, and moreover to adduce a reason why each unit of the vocabulary should be presented at a given moment and not at another.

Systematically presented matter and properly graduated matter are convertible terms, for one implies the other.

There will be found to be five bases of gradation—that is to say, five different considerations governing the choice of matter and the order of presenting it. These, as we have seen, are:

(*a*) Frequency.
(*b*) Ergonic combination.
(*c*) Concreteness.
(*d*) Proportion.
(*e*) General Expediency.

The most difficult task of the method-maker is precisely the choosing and graduating of the vocabulary in strict accordance with these five considerations. The frequency principle, fascinating as it is, must often be subordinated to the claims of ergonic combination. Those two in their turn may have to be subordinated to the pressing claims of concreteness, and even when the best compromise has been made to satisfy the claims of these three principles, we are still faced with the claims of proportion and general expediency.

The normal programme should contain evenly distributed portions of phonetics, ergonics, semantics, and orthography. The only one of these aspects that must suffer if time is limited is the last-named, for orthography, after all, is but the artificial aspect of language. Some instructors teach so disproportionately that they insist on perfection in the pronunciation of a group of words—and then forget to give the meaning of them. Another will spend hours in demonstrating the semantic or ergonic peculiarities of a group of verb forms—and forget to tell the student how to pronounce them.

In the case of Special Programmes the principle of proportion is, however, entirely subordinated to other considerations. The veteran who knows the language from end to end—without being able to produce a single sound in it correctly!—must be treated to phonetics in the strongest possible doses, to the total exclusion of every other aspect.

Proportion also must be observed in the active and passive aspects of study. A course of lessons may be given of which the result is to enable the student to understand the language at sight or at hearing, but without advancing him one iota in the extremely useful art of making himself understood. The treatment should be proportioned to the requirement; the general practitioner in the teaching profession, as in the medical profession, should make it his business to diagnose before treating.

The teacher who is particularly competent in one special kind of teaching must not necessarily follow his accustomed methods under all circumstances. He must adapt them to the special needs of his pupils.

Instructors, like all other mortals, may suffer from absent-mindedness; it may be true—or it may not—that a learned professor once wrote a grammar of the Katanga literary dialect and forgot to inform his readers whether it contained any nouns. It is certainly true that many writers of modern-language manuals frequently forget to inform their readers whether the language it purports to teach contains any sounds!

Neglect of the phonetic aspect of words, as the neglect of the semantic or any other aspect of words, must result in disproportionate work. If the object of the author is to produce a specialized work on one particular aspect of the language, all well and good, but more often than not we find serious omissions arising, not out of design, but from sheer neglect and the ignoring of the principle of proportion.

The most general omission is that of the phonetic aspect; the veteran student who declares, with a tone savouring of pride and disdain, that the sounds of the language have no interest for him, who skips every chapter on pronunciation, and who cannot tell the difference between a high front vowel and the glottal stop, will blush with shame if he so much as omits to dot an *i* when writing the language of which he claims to be a master. He is like a musician who knows everything about music except the notes.

Not only does the expert teacher who is the architect of his own method select the material that will go to make up the microcosm, but to him often falls the duty of determining the appropriate means by which each item is to be cognized by the pupil and subsequently inculcated. He has to decide at each turn whether a given unit or group of units is to be semanticized by material association, by translation, by definition, or whether the meaning is to be gathered from the context.

He has to decide which units are to be treated as primary and which as secondary matter.

His judgment must determine at what moments quantity is to be sacrificed to quality, and *vice versa*. He has to deal with the difficult problems entailed by a class containing pupils of all degrees of intelligence, capacity, good will, and slackness. He must so direct the various forms of mechanical drill that interest is maintained; in order to avoid monotony, and to prevent such mechanical work from becoming tedious, he must devise a constant series of new types of exercise, sacrificing no important principle and never losing sight of the immediate and ultimate end of any particular phase of work.

He has to determine the relative proportions of class teaching and individual teaching. In order that a given lesson may bear the maximum of fruit he must reinforce it and drive home its conclusions by means of well-chosen homework. He must at all times consider the good and evil results of contiguity and other forms of association; he must come to feel intuitively at what moments two subjects of study should be segregated in order to avoid confusion, or be associated in order that each may be contrasted with the other to their mutual advantage.

Moreover, it depends to a large extent on the teacher to make the lessons represent an ever-changing source of interest and novelty, of which each phase will contribute in the progressive and sound building up, strengthening, and developing of the nucleus.

Section 30.—Another function of the teacher is to furnish explanations.

In addition to the choosing and presenting of matter, it comes within the functions of the instructor to furnish explanations concerning it. Without explanation the pupil can do little or nothing; a list of the most useful words and sentences, however well chosen and graduated, is but the groundwork of the teaching. In itself it is but a mass of matter without signification, incapable of being assimilated until put into combination, and supplemented by information respecting it.

The writer possesses rather a good book the object of which is to teach Chinese. There is a large quantity of valuable material in it; there is reason to suppose that it is more or less graduated. He is, however, unable to make the slightest use of it, because, as far as he can see, there are no explanations in it. If there are any, they are in Chinese, and as he does not understand that language he is not able to decipher them.

Many instructors either give no explanations at all, or else give them in the very language of which the student is presumed to be ignorant.

Their object in so doing is to react against some of the vicious tendencies, more especially those relating to bilingual consciousness and illegitimate importation.

It may be said that the child learns his mother tongue without any explanations, and that in order to follow the natural method he and the adult must follow the same plan and dispense with explanatory matter. This is, however, hardly a true statement of the case; for we shall see as a matter of fact that the child does receive explanations during the process of learning his own language. If these explanations do not take the form of rules, equations, diagrams, and general advice, they are none the less present in the form of object and context-lessons, in which the meaning and the use of words are demonstrated by gestures and association of ideas. The meaning of the word *dog* is explained to him when we point to the animal in question and pronounce the word *dog*.

Be it as it may, the adult requires explanations of some sort or other, and we must recognize that he has a right to them and that the withholding of them will retard his progress by many months.

In order to distinguish clearly the difference between the matter of the language itself and the explanations which may accompany it in order to render possible its assimilation, we shall speak of the former as the *concrete* and the latter as the *explanatory* matter.

Some adults maintain that the concrete matter is sufficient for them and that they prefer to discover for themselves the explanation of the phenomena contained in it. You will hear people recommend the plan of taking an easy novel in, let us say, Italian, of starting at the first chapter, and forcing ourselves to understand it. They say that the first pages will give us a vague idea of what it is about, and that as we continue the matter will become less and less vague; we shall guess with more and more success, and before we have reached the end of the book it will be as easy to read as our own language.

They say that this process will enable us to dispense with dictionary, grammar-book, and all other sources of information.

The best refutation of this theory is to hand such a person an easy book written in Russian or Arabic and to ask him to demonstrate the method. He will at once confess his inability to do so, saying that he must first learn the alphabet. But the learning of the alphabet necessitates explanation! Even the child learning his mother tongue cannot learn the alphabet without explanatory matter.

Our friend will concede that the learning of an alphabet indeed requires explanatory matter, but will hold this to be an exceptional case, and will maintain that, apart from this, the non-explanatory principle still holds good. We may then give him a book written in Hungarian; here at least he will be able to contemplate his own Latin characters. If he succeeds, by dint of efforts worthy of Sherlock Holmes, in deciphering a word here or there, that will represent his limit; there will be no progression from the unknown to the known; he will have to give it up.

The fact of the matter is that the method of immediate comprehension of written matter *ab ovo* is only possible when the language is cognate with our own, or with one already learnt. A Frenchman or any one knowing French can easily become acquainted with Italian by the process of guessing the meaning of the words which are already half familiar.

Not long ago an acquaintance of the writer's declared to him that if he were furnished with explanations concerning the mechanism of a given language he would lose all interest in it. For him the charm lay in discovering the key to the various problems without any outside aid. The fallacy (for this is obviously a fallacy) consists in placing linguistic work on the same footing as mathematics, chess, patience, jig-saw puzzles, acrostics, or any other sort of intellectual problem-solving game. Obviously all such amusements would lose their charm if somebody were by our side and insisted on furnishing us with ready-made solutions, for their sole interest lies in overcoming the problems by our own unaided efforts.

But the normal study of language has nothing in common with guessing competitions, however intellectual their nature. To be perfectly consistent, such a person when travelling should shun time-tables, maps, and signposts on the grounds that these things furnish ready-made solutions to problems that he would rather solve unaided.

"I have to go to Glasgow," he would say. "This presents a number of interesting problems which I intend to solve by the method of discovery. Time-tables exist, also maps, but I will have none of them, nor will I follow the man from Cook's. I have a pocket compass to guide me, and by its aid and that of the sun and stars I ought to steer my course with sufficient accuracy."

This method of discovery is the only one available when the country is unmapped and the railway line non-existent; it is the only method when the language is one of those remote tongues of which neither dictionary nor grammar has ever been written. The study of French, however, like the journey to Glasgow, is not an occasion to exercise one's faculties of ingenious guessing, but one where the practical man should profit by all the information which experts are only too ready to place at his disposal.

The practical study of languages in the early stages has nothing in common with chess problems. Rather should it be placed in the same category as geography or history. A foreign language is one of those things of which the 'directions for use' should be carefully read and frequently consulted; the ideal programme of language-study is that which enables us to assimilate in the shortest possible time with the least effort the greatest quantity of the most important matter. The method of discovery is in flat contradiction to this principle, and he who would use such a method may be likened to a deaf and dumb man trying to find his way about the streets of a strange town.

This is no imaginary case. Very many language students, especially those who are engaged at the same time in other studies of a real problem-solving nature, think it a necessary part of their work to discover what has already been discovered, to explore regions that need no exploration.

Explanatory matter is, or ought to be, in the nature of information the object of which is to facilitate our efforts to imitate the models which are set before us.

Its nature may be morphological, ergonic, or semantic—that is to say, it may deal specifically with *form*, *function*, or *meaning*.

Explanations may be of the descriptive or of the historical order. In the practical study of language the descriptive aspect alone is of any real value, for when we are learning a given language we wish to know what its characteristics *are* and not how they have become what they are.

As we have just mentioned, the function of explanation is to facilitate the efforts of the student to imitate and to develop with success the models which are set before him.

We must give him a great deal of phonetic information. His auditive faculties have become so atrophied by disuse and by the associations of the sounds of his own language that he will be unable even to hear the sounds of the foreign language. An Englishman to whom we pronounce the French [y] may possibly think that he hears his familiar English sound [u]; the Frenchman to whom we pronounce the English sound [θ] will be under the impression that he hears [s] or [t]. We must open his ears by means of phonetic explanations. The imitative faculties of the average student are also in a state of atrophy; in his infancy he could pick up new sounds by mere imitation; he can no longer do so, and as a result he produces sounds which are vastly different from those which are required of him. We must make him conscious of his organs of speech by means of phonetic explanations.

It is generally not necessary to give much information concerning orthography. Experience proves that the adult, at any rate, picks up this branch with extraordinary rapidity and accuracy. This is probably due to the great respect in which he holds the traditional spelling and the intensive development of his visual perceptive faculties. If the language (unlike English or French) possesses a rational spelling system, a short series of orthoepic explanations will be useful to him. We may tell him that *ei* in German corresponds to the sounds [ai], that *gy* in Hungarian invariably represents the sound [ɟ], that the Welsh *ll* is the traditional way of expressing [l̥], etc.

Information concerning inflexions and other forms of morphological change will be very useful at a certain moment. There is no reason whatever for withholding the general laws concerning the formation of the plural of regular English nouns or of the English present or past participles. The student of French (like the Frenchman himself) must be informed concerning the nature of the modification which various classes of words undergo in order to change their ergonic values. What has been taught for centuries under the name of *accidence* (declension and conjugation) may still be taught, although more in conformity with the principle of proportion.

It is of distinct utility to explain to the student the laws of ergonics as applied to the language he is learning, to show in what circumstances the subjunctive replaces the indicative, or when the dative replace the accusative pronouns. By dint of prolonged and totally unnecessary efforts, a good problem-solver may discover the key to the ergonic mystery surrounding the use of the twenty-four 'verbal particles' in English; a few pages devoted to the rational explanation of these phenomena will bring about the same result with a vast economy of time, and the days and weeks gained thereby may be devoted to the real business of language learning.

The explanations concerning the semantic aspect of words are of enormous importance for time-saving purposes. Such explanations constitute the chief *raison d'être* of the bilingual dictionary. As a general rule it is profitable to explain to the pupil the meaning or rather the meanings of each word that he learns. If they are not explained, he will have to pick them up himself, and experience proves that the foreigner is not an adept at discovering the meanings of words by his own unaided efforts, especially during the first stages of his study.

If we withhold information on this subject, the student, more often than not will be content to associate the foreign word with a word in his own language, and thenceforth consider the two as identical in semantic nature. So important indeed is this subject that we have devoted a special place to its consideration, and have examined the processes by which the meanings may be attached to the various morphological units that the student has memorized.

The chief *raison d'être* then for clear and abundant explanations is to react against certain of the vicious tendencies of which the student is so frequently a victim.

On the other hand, an excess of explanatory matter will defeat its own ends and lead to other vicious tendencies. In order that the student may not import his own ergonics into the foreign language, we teach him systematically by means of explanatory matter the true ergonic values of the words he learns, and by so doing we may induce him to give way to over-analysis. In order that he may not import his own semantic values into the words he learns, we give him information concerning the real semantic values of these words by means of true equivalents, but by so doing we may encourage the tendency toward an excess of bilingual consciousness.

We shall find a way out of this dilemma if we always make explanation subsidiary to assimilation. Let our ergonic explanations follow and not precede the memorizing of the examples. Let us reserve our explanation of the function of the English preterite until our pupil has already learnt by heart a large number of sentences, such as *I saw him yesterday*, *I came here just now*, or *Why did you do it last night?*

Let us explain to him the semantic value of the different varieties of *get* after he has memorized a stock of sentences containing them.

Explanation is only a vicious process when given in excess of the assimilatory processes. Explanatory matter is only harmful when given out of proportion to the concrete matter.

Let us remember above all that we must do nothing which will have the effect of deadening the student's faculties of auditive perception and imitation. These must not be replaced by explanatory matter, but, on the contrary, quickened by it.

Section 31.—The vehicular language for all explanatory matter should be that which is best known by the student.

While the concrete matter (that is to say, the speech material itself) must necessarily be of the language which is the subject of instruction, it by no means follows that the *explanatory matter* should also be given in this same language. On the contrary, it is difficult at first sight to see on what grounds such a procedure can be justified.

We have already alluded to a certain book which is full of valuable information concerning the Chinese language and to the fact that the average English student is totally unable to make any use of it owing to the fact that it is written entirely in Chinese. Strange to say, methods exist the object of which is to teach the most elementary vocabulary of a foreign language, and in which the 'directions for use' are given in precisely the language of which the student is presumed to be ignorant.

There are three justifications for this seemingly absurd procedure, two of which are based on considerations of expediency and the other on pedagogic grounds.

It is urged that a teacher may be perfectly competent to write a method or to give lessons, but at the same time be ignorant of the language of his reader or pupil. In reply to this we must firmly insist such a teacher is *not* perfectly competent. One of the qualifications for the teacher of the elementary language to those who are unacquainted with it is a sufficient knowledge of the pupil's language to enable him to use it for vehicular purposes. If the teacher is a method-writer, the least he can do is to take the necessary steps to have his explanatory matter translated into the language of the pupil, even though it should increase the expenses of the undertaking.

But it may further be urged that when a class contains pupils of many different nationalities it is obviously impossible to use as many languages for vehicular purposes. This objection is indeed the only one with any claims to respect. We can only say in answer that if a class of beginners is composed of such heterogeneous members, it is impossible to cause them to "assimilate in the shortest possible time with the least effort the greatest quantity of the most important matter." In other terms our teaching in such cases cannot be strictly scientific, but a *pis aller*; it must be conducted in accordance with principles of mere expediency. We shall have to omit explanations altogether, or else give them in the form of diagrams and gestures. But let us recognize that this course is dictated from pure necessity, and, instead of making a virtue of this necessity, let us rather express our regret that circumstances force us to diverge from the principle which serves as the point of departure in our inquiry.

But as a compensation for our inability to speak to all our pupils in their own language we should at least be able to provide each one with a book in which he will be able to read the explanations which we are unable to provide orally. Lest it be said that such a procedure would be too costly, we will observe that the general adoption of one standard system of teaching, recognized as scientific in the best sense of the term, would render superfluous that amazing multiplicity of books which is the cause of so much needless expense at the present day.

This leads us to the second alleged justification of the procedure that we are criticizing. A book designed to teach the elements of some lesser known language lying outside the beaten track, or one written with the object of teaching some special aspect of one of the primary languages, can only command a limited circle of readers. If the explanatory matter is written in Russian, the *clientèle* will be confined to Russia; if written in Dutch the book will only find a sale in Holland, and so on. But when the book is composed according to the principle that a language should be taught without the aid of any outside vehicular language, there is the possibility of finding a sale for it in every country of the world.

The third alleged justification of the principle, strangely enough, professes to be based on pedagogic considerations. It is frequently urged that the use of the mother tongue during the lesson is a dangerous proceeding, and one to be avoided in the largest possible measure. As we have already dealt with this point in that part of our inquiry entitled "The Principles of Linguistic Pedagogy," we will not go over the ground afresh; it will suffice to refer our readers to the various arguments adduced therein, which show with cumulative force that the exclusion of the mother tongue is generally, if not always, a vicious procedure productive of most harmful results.

Section 32.—The teacher should foster and encourage the pupils' capacities of visualization by adopting for explanatory purposes the principle of visual correlation.

Visual correlation is the term that we shall use to express what the Germans call *Uebersichtlichkeit* or 'Synopticity.' It denotes the arrangement of matter on a page or a series of pages in such a manner that the faculties of understanding are assisted by the mere contemplation of it. This is the graphic method, perhaps the most important of the mnemonic devices, including as it does the principles of localization (or spatialization), visualization, association, and separation.

Understanding, classification, and division are almost synonymous terms. No subject is understood until it has been divided up into its component parts. In the Japanese language the root of the verb *understand* (*wakaru*) also means *be divided.* Thus instead of vaguely suggesting, as in English, *standing under*, or *taking with*, as in French, the Japanese expression in accordance with true psychology suggests, *It is to me divided.* Nothing could better express the idea of understanding. Nearly all explanations are prefaced by saying *we must divide our subject into two parts*, and the subject under examination is developed further by processes entailing constant repetition of sentences such as, *There are three aspects of this question*, or *This particular subject must be considered under six headings.*

Our inquiry itself consists of dividing up into parts and of further subdividing the whole question of language-study.

Many subjects are taught almost exclusively by means of diagrams; other subjects can only be learnt successfully by their help. It is virtually impossible to learn geography without maps, geometry without diagrams, genealogy without trees, architecture and mechanics without drawings and plans. With the improvement of pedagogic methods the system of diagrams is coming more and more into vogue; it is being applied to the study of history, statistics, and a host of other subjects. There are indeed few branches of knowledge the study of which is not facilitated by some form of graphic illustration.

This is only right and natural, considering that the faculty of understanding, consciously or unconsciously, works by the mnemonic process of spatial correlation. We listen to a descriptive explanation of some knotty problem; as the speaker introduces his points, establishes differences and identities, we form a mental picture of the subject in which we locate the various factors. The mental graph that we form enables us to grasp the problem, to comprehend it, and to survey it in its different aspects. Those who do not form mental images are probably incapable of understanding. The difference between so-called intelligent and unintelligent pupils consists in their respective ability or inability to form these mental images. The chief function of all ' memory systems ' good or bad is to encourage and help the student to arrange his thoughts spatially or diagrammatically.

It is worth while to try the following experiment. Take a list of twenty names; these may be names of people, places, plants, animals, books, plays, foreign or technical words—in short, any terms whatever. Try to learn them so that you may repeat them off in their order without any mental confusion. After ten minutes your efforts may be successful—or they may not. Take a second group of names and dispose them in some spatial form.

A simple method is to utilize the parts of the room in which you happen to be. Go to the door, and while contemplating it, repeat one of the words slowly and write it in your imagination on one of the panels. Move to the object nearest the door; it may be a corner, a picture, or a piece of furniture; there repeat the second word and trace its graphic form on the object in front of which you stand. Then move on a foot or so and ' localize ' the next word, and go on until the list is exhausted. This process need not take more than five minutes, at the conclusion of which you will probably reel off the twenty names in their correct order with hardly any hesitation or mental effort.

This experiment is not designed to prove that the royal road to language-learning consists of learning lists of words; far from it. What it does demonstrate is the fact that the physical separation of the units of a problem will go far to facilitate its mastery; instead of being superposed, as it were, on one spot of what we may call the receptive surface of the brain, each unit has its own place and acquires an identity of its own.

But these considerations may lead us into the depths of psychology and mnemonics; we must content ourselves at present with stating that when a problem is separated into its component parts and when these are disposed according to their agreements and disagreements either in a real spatial relation or the mental conception of one, that problem becomes 'understood,' we become masters of it, and are able to reproduce the diagram at will.

Probably most of us use this faculty of image-making, but do it with such perfect unconsciousness that we are unaware of it. We are sometimes just conscious enough to note that a particular lesson or lecture was more deeply engraved on our memory because it was given in new or unaccustomed surroundings. Many of us can recall the particular spot in which we learnt a certain word or expression. When turning into the Charing Cross Road from Trafalgar Square, Monsieur X, who is talking French to us, uses some French expression which strikes us as being new material for our vocabulary. It is almost certain that when we use this expression for the first time our thoughts will go out in a flash to the corner of Charing Cross Road, the geographical spot which has served to fix the expression in our memory and to prevent it from being confused with a few hundred others.

Apart from geographical or spatial considerations, however, all good learners form arbitrary mental images corresponding to the factors of the problems they are learning. We describe to a foreigner the phenomena connected with the relative pronoun in English. We say: "The relative pronoun is expressed by *who* (for person), and *which* (for objects)." Our pupil shuts his eyes or gazes into vacuity for an instant, while he places *who* to the left and *which* to the right of the blank surface he has conjured up before himself. "When expressing the objective relation, *who* is replaced by *whom*, but *which* remains invariable."

Our pupil immediately conceives the word *whom* as occupying its space a little distance below *who*, and places a second *which* on the same latitude as *whom* and the same longitude as the first *which*.

"These four words may be replaced by *that*, which performs the same function as each of the four."

The mental image has now become:

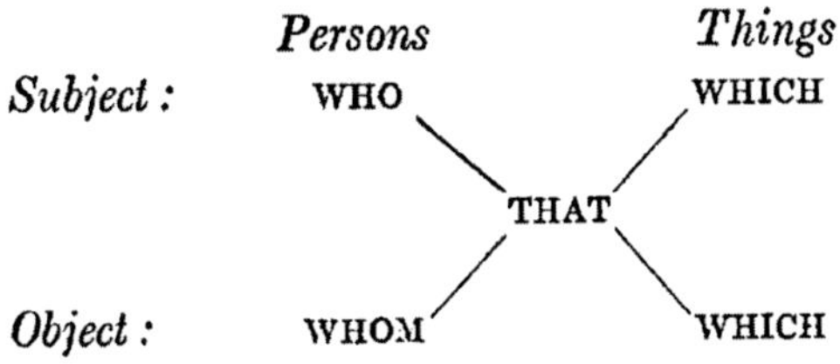

"When used in the objective relation, *that* may be suppressed."

The mental image of our pupil develops into its final form:

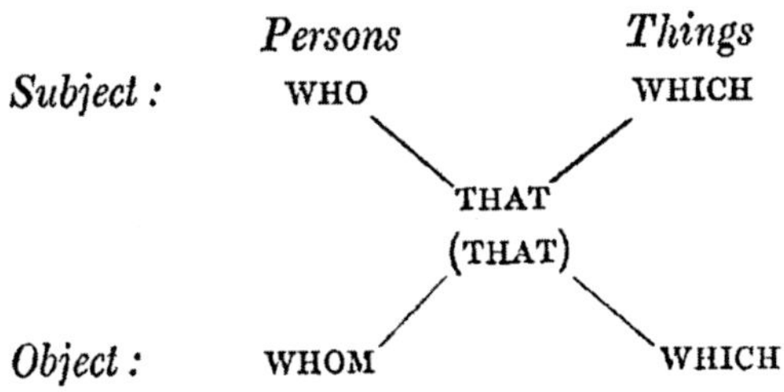

When we come to test his knowledge he will evoke his mental image and read it off to us without hesitation, error, or effort, and we call him an intelligent pupil. And the strange part of it is that our pupil is quite unconscious that he composed a diagram and wrote it down on the tablets of his mind, and that he read off what he had written when called upon to repeat his lesson.

His companion has never developed this visualizing habit. Our remarks were superposed one on the other, each obliterating the preceding one. No wonder that he calls the English language difficult and the problem of the relative pronoun insoluble—and no wonder we call him an unintelligent pupil!

One of the functions of the teacher is to foster the visualizing habit; to aid the visualizer by providing him with ready-made diagrams in order to prevent him from creating them in a less practical form and from having to efface a part or the whole of an inadequate one. We must also strive by concrete devices to develop the latent powers of the so-called 'unintelligent' pupil. If he cannot form his own diagrams we must form them for him. By demonstrating problems before him with constant reference to a wall-chart or a diagram chalked on the blackboard, always with the same disposition of parts, he cannot fail to receive the graphic impressions that we are forcing on his consciousness.

It must not be forgotten that first impressions are the most lasting; the first visualization generally forms the basis for all subsequent knowledge and constitutes the nucleus to which all further acquired matter will be attracted. It is therefore of great importance that each diagram should be drawn up in accordance with sound and consistent principles in order to avoid a subsequent change of form which will shock the pupil's graphic sense and lead to painful mental confusion. We may decide to use the following scheme to show the declension of the German definite article:

	Masculine	*Feminine*	*Neuter*	*Plural*
Nominative	der	die	das	die
Genitive	des	der	des	der
Dative	dem	der	dem	den
Accusative	den	die	das	die

But, if we do so, subsequent considerations must not tempt us to alter it to, let us say:

	Masculine	*Neuter*	*Feminine*	*Plural*
Nominative	der	das	die	die
Accusative	den	das	die	die
Dative	dem	dem	der	den
Genitive	des	des	der	der

for by so doing the sense of visual correlation developed by the former will be thrown into confusion by the second, even though the latter should prove the more practical of the two.

The writer's first impressions of the French conjugation were gained by studying a paradigm in which the infinitive, participles, present, and past indefinite tenses were disposed toward the bottom of a left-hand page; the right-hand page started with the imperfect and was followed by the pluperfect, preterite, past anterior, future, and future anterior; on the next page were the remainder of the tenses. From that day to this he has always visualized the tenses in this relation; for him the conditional is still the over-the-page tense, and a mention of the future anterior always carries his eye in imagination to the bottom of a right-hand page. The writer has taught French for many years and has always used a far more rational disposition, but has never been able to visualize it on account of the depth of the original impression.

The two following schemes are each perfect in their way, but one only should be chosen and used with any particular pupil:

(1)

je	me	me	moi
tu	te	te	toi
il	le	lui	lui
elle	la	lui	elle
nous	nous	nous	nous
vous	vous	vous	vous
ils	les	leur	eux
elles	les	leur	elles

(2)

je	tu	il	elle	nous	vous	ils	elles
me	te	le	la	,,	,,	les	les
me	te	lui	lui	,,	,,	leur	leur
moi	toi	lui	elle	,,	,,	eux	elles

If we decide on using the following visual presentation of certain English prepositions, we must hold to it; the square must not be transformed into a triangle, nor should the positions of each preposition be changed.

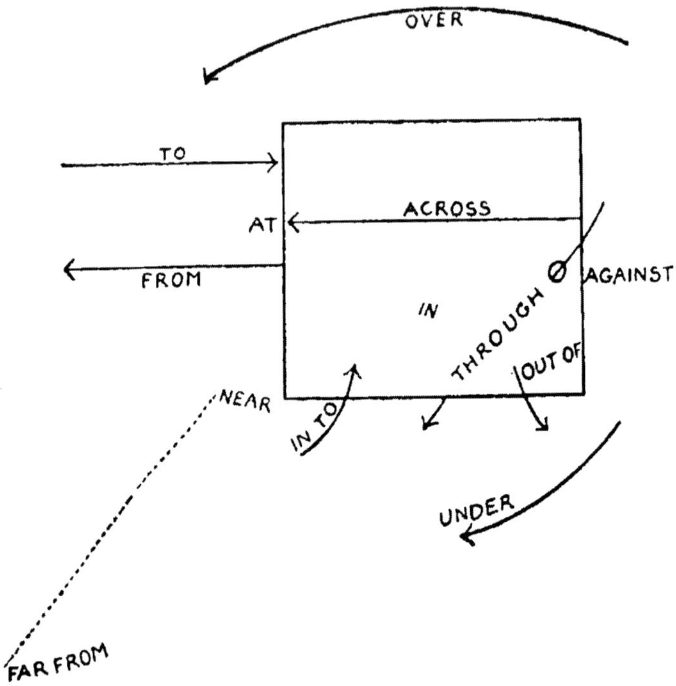

If you have learnt phonetics from a diagram which places the lips on the left-hand side, avoid those which picture them on the right.

The principle of Visual Correlation has been applied to problems of declension and conjugation from time immemorial. Paradigms showing in vertical and lateral columns the relations of gender, number, and case are among the most familiar features of grammar-books. But such graphic methods are generally limited to the classical problems which we have just quoted; it is hardly realized that a principle which has been applied with success to certain special subjects may be applied with equal success to others.

Let us suppose that we teach a foreigner the laws governing the respective uses of the English simple and compound present and preterite. They may be expressed in the following manner:

"The English present and preterite tenses may be simple or compound; the compound tenses are made up of the auxiliary *do* and the infinitive of the verb. When simple, the verb itself undergoes modification; when compound, the auxiliary *do* is modified in place of the verb. The simple form is the more generally used of the two, the compound form generally being reserved for use in cases of inversion, when modified by *not* or in cases of special or emphatic affirmation. The reason that the compound form is used in connection with inversion is because it is contrary to modern usage to invert the subject with the verb unless the latter forms part of a group of twenty-four anomalous verbal units of which *do* and its modified forms are members. Alone these twenty-four particles may be modified by the negative adverb *not*. As each of those twenty-four particles and no other verbal forms have the power of expressing emphatic or special affirmation, we must have recourse to the auxiliary *do* each time that such affirmation becomes necessary."

This is almost an ideal example of how *not* to present matter. The adult student, let alone the child, may be heartily congratulated on his visualizing capacities if he is able from the above involved statement to gain any precise notion of the relative functions of the simple and compound tenses in question. This series of laws may easily be presented in graphic form by means of the diagram on p. 260.

One of the main objects of the ergonic chart is precisely to foster habits of visual correlation and diagrammatic concretization by showing in one comprehensive scheme the sum of all the ergonic lists and substitution tables which have been the object of the pupil's previous study.

Whether in guise of ergonic chart, substitution table, mnemonic diagram, concretized formula, or practical scheme of analysis, the object of each of these graphic representations is identical: *the development and encouragement of the faculty of visualizing.*

The enthusiastic teacher who may be inspired to make graphic representation the beginning and the end of his pedagogic efforts should not lose sight of the fact that this sort of work is of the documentary and not of the assimilative order.

A complete collection of the most perfect and ingenious diagrams will not teach a single student how to speak and understand the language when spoken. They are of immense service for explanatory purposes and will be of the greatest assistance to the student who wishes to utilize to the fullest extent the sentences that he has memorized; but they will

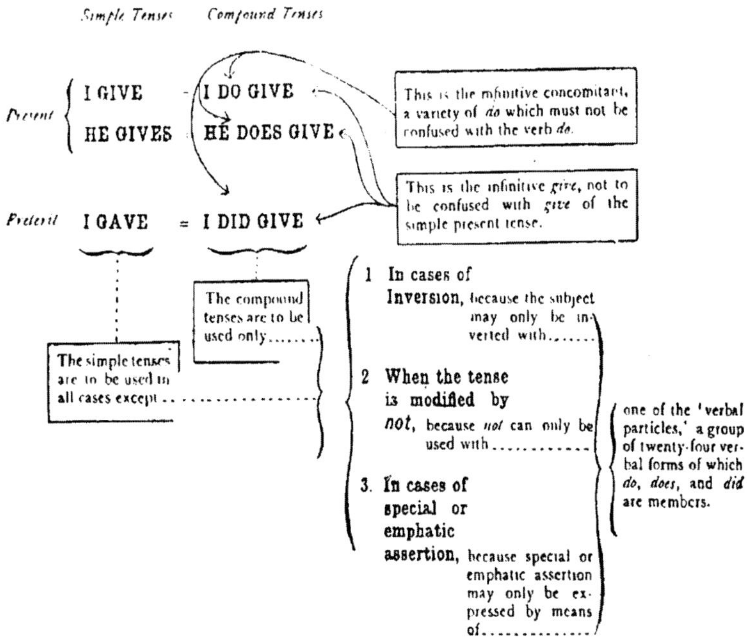

not replace fluency practice, memorizing, and subconscious comprehension.

The use of graphic demonstration at the expense of oral repetition and catenizing work is an obvious abuse of the principle, and will surely tempt the student into many of the habits described under the heading of "Vicious Tendencies," more especially those relating to over-reliance on the visual memory and over-analysis.

It is for the teacher to judge at what moment to have recourse to this auxiliary and in what doses to administer it.

Section 33.—Further functions of the teacher are :

(*a*) To cause or to stimulate the pupil to work.

(*b*) To give the pupil opportunities of hearing the language spoken, and to act the part of second person in a conversation.

(*c*) To act as examiner, to award marks, and to correct errors.

Besides organizing the programme and determining the manner in which the material is to be assimilated by the pupils, the teacher will take all the active measures necessary to stimulate the pupils in their task of assimilation. He must help them to digest the primary matter and must help them to produce the secondary matter. However well organized a programme of study may be, it will be inoperative if the stimulus is not present to act as the mainspring of the perfect mechanism. The teacher will encourage the good pupils by his congratulations and arouse the laggards and slackers by timely applications of the spur.

As every teacher knows, there are always a certain number of pupils, both children and adults, who have not the slightest intention of doing what they are not compelled to do; they will be driven, but not led. In such cases one of the functions of the teacher is to drive. The teacher of real genius may so possess the gift of pedagogy that he will end by convincing the slackers that it will be to their immediate interest and conduce to their immediate well-being to abandon their attitude of driven cattle in favour of the more intelligent and more pleasant *rôle* of interested participators in an interesting game. In every individual there are to be found latent capacities of intense interest and enthusiasm; in the case of children these capacities become active in strange ways, often manifested by the mania of the collector and the curiosity of the investigator.

It is for the teacher to develop these latent capacities, to direct them into useful channels and to utilize them. The schoolboy who becomes an ardent collector of foreign stamps may also become an enthusiastic collector of foreign inflections; those same strange impulses which make of him a veritable encyclopædia of football lore may also make of him a storehouse of phonetic, semantic, or ergonic lore.

The teacher will also constitute an instrument of assimilation. Many adult pupils enlist the services of a teacher solely on this account; he is the indispensable second person in all conversations, he broaches the topic that will bring the conversation into being; he will ask the questions that stimulate replies in the same language; he is the producer of oral material of which the pupil is a passive auditor, or plays the part of passive auditor when the pupil is spokesman. "Je ne veux pas de leçons," says the French adult student (only too often), "ce que je désire, c'est avoir l'occasion de parler et entendre parler, comme ça je me perfectionnerai dans la conversation et j'estime qu'on ne peut faire des progrès qu'en parlant."

If the matter contained in the nucleus is sound, and if the student possesses a well-digested and proportionate microcosm of the language, his procedure is rational, and should be encouraged. It may be noted, however, that no expert teacher is requisite to play this particular *rôle*. Any native speaker of the language will suffice if the pupil's aim does not comprise a constant commentary replete with corrections and suggestions. An economical plan would be for each adult student to engage the services of two teachers, one of these, the expert, will give the necessary information, supply the necessary matter, and make the necessary corrections on a reasoned and systematic basis; the other, the casual or untrained teacher, possessing as his sole qualification a fluent knowledge of his native language, will serve as a mere instrument of conversation, a means by which the student will be enabled to use the material he has assimilated under the guidance and supervision of the other.

We have noted on more than one occasion how important are the services of a 'repeater.' When we hear a foreign sentence repeated many times in a clear voice, with energy and persistency, it will indeed go hard with us if the effect is not lasting and if we are not able to reproduce it with more or less accuracy and fluency.

The teacher is to the oral aspect of language what the book or the text is to its graphic aspect. In this respect the only substitute for a teacher is the phonograph with records which have been made specially with a view to this work of repetition.

Another function of the teacher is to test the pupil's knowledge at any given moment and to award 'marks' in order that the pupil may realize his degree of progress. This in itself is a valuable stimulus to good work, for the competitive instinct is very powerful with most of us. Attempts to break records, to surpass our previous efforts or the efforts made by our fellow-students constitute an incentive not to be despised.

Closely connected with this aspect of the teacher's work is the correcting of mistakes. As we have already seen, the making of mistakes (other than mere slips) on a considerable scale points to a grave flaw in the programme. Whatever mistakes do occur, needless to say, must be corrected at once, and the cause of error ascertained and removed, otherwise the faulty expression will become incorporated into the nucleus and exercise a sinister influence on the sound matter with which it is surrounded.

Section 34.—A very important function of the teacher is to react against the six vicious tendencies to which all students are more or less subject.

All students, especially adults, are more or less subject to a series of what we may term "vicious tendencies." Few are exempt from them, the most experienced language-learners may be their victims, and the vast majority of students are slaves to them.

The most general of these may be grouped under the following six headings:

1. Neglect of the peculiar characteristics of the foreign language.
2. Illegitimate importation of elements from the mother tongue.
3. Artificial separation of monologs (single words), and non-recognition of polylogs (group words).
4. Preference for strong forms.
5. Over-reliance on visual memory.
6. Exaggeration of bilingual consciousness.

It should be made clear at this point that all these tendencies are not wholly bad, nor are they always bad. They bear some similarity to various types of poisons which under certain conditions may be prescribed in small doses as beneficial, but an unrestrained indulgence in which will produce fatal results either immediately or later on as a result of cumulative absorption. Innocuous as they may be when judiciously administered, they are, nevertheless, dangerous instruments. Every one of them is contrary to the natural process by which a child learns to use his mother tongue, and for this reason if for no other it behoves us to exercise the greatest caution when brought face to face with them.

In a general way it is necessary to take a strong line and to react against them ; indeed, it may be said that the first function of the instructor is to help the student to resist them.

In certain cases, however, we shall see that it is possible to mar what would otherwise be an effective system of teaching by an exaggeration of our precautions. To exclude from one end of the programme to the other all graphic forms under the pretext that writing encourages an over-reliance on visual memory would be an exaggeration of the danger, as also would be the total exclusion of translation on the grounds that the pupil must not be encouraged into habits of bilingual consciousness. It is precisely the art of the instructor to determine at what moment a pupil is beneficially or prejudicially affected by a given procedure.

It is precisely in order that these dangerous tendencies may be better resisted and that the pupil may better realize their nature that we have insisted on a course of preliminary work previous to the study proper of a given language. Those who have acquired (or rather reacquired) the faculty of oral imitation, who have a practical knowledge of the nature of language and language-study, and who are acquainted with the leading phenomena of memory are more or less immune. The young child learning his mother tongue is exempt from these tendencies altogether ; his ignorance and inability to abuse his faculties of reason shield him from harm ; he acquires his mother language with no other preparatory course than that of oral imitation. He requires no courses of phonetics, ergonics, semantics, etymology, pedagogy, and mnemonics.

The older student, not enjoying this immunity, does require them.

This indeed is the fundamental difference between the mother tongue and the foreign language.

Section 35.—In order to perform effective work, the teacher (or student) should have at his disposal an adequate number of the right sort of instruments in the form of a practical library for reference and other purposes.

If we wish to make a wooden table, two things are essential: *wood* and *tools*. If we started to convert some rough planks into a table with no other tool than a blunt pocket-knife our work would be laborious and long and the result would be a very indifferent table.

We must have the right sort of material and the right sort of tools. The fact that we cannot make bricks without straw nor make a silk purse out of a sow's ear is proverbial. Experience, moreover, has proved that the best instrument for extracting a cork is a corkscrew, that a hammer is a better tool for driving in a nail than the back of a clothes brush, and that a screw-driver is a poor substitute for a tin-opener.

If we started to learn French with no other material than the average pocket dictionary and no other tool than the average "French Grammar," our work would be in vain. In language-learning, as in table-making, house-building, and machine constructing we must have the right tools and the right material. We must have the instruments which will enable us to overcome with the minimum of effort and of time the obstacles which stand between us and our end, obstacles presented by our ignorance of French phonetics, orthoepy, orthography, etymology, semantics, and ergonics.

Of the 'material' represented by the lexicological units, we have already spoken at length; we will add a few words concerning the instruments.

These will consist chiefly of books, *fiches*, lists, diagrams, and charts containing the units themselves and all the explanatory matter which will help us to understand and to assimilate them.

It is difficult to work with insufficient or inferior material, and it is false economy to study a language without a variety of first-class tools each of which will enable us to learn or to teach something more easily or better.

The following rough list enumerates most of the contents of the library which should be at the disposal of (let us say) English students wishing to learn French.

1. A *French-English dictionary* giving the morphology (orthographic and phonetic), inflexions, ergonic and semantic values, and frequency degree of all the lexicological units contained in the microcosm, accompanied by the most characteristic examples of their regular and irregular uses.

2. A complementary English-French dictionary conceived on the same lines and which might very easily be designed in such a way as to enable an Englishman ignorant of French to compose an almost unlimited number of correct French sentences.

3. A set of Ergonic Lists containing the most important members of the most important ergonic categories, in orthographic and phonetic scripts and with full translations and notes.

4. The large-scale Ergonic Chart of the language, with all the necessary mechanical devices.

5. Limited *relevés* from the Ergonic Chart in the form of a series of graduated substitution tables.

6. A Phonetic Chart of the French sounds.

7. A detailed list of all the French sounds (vowels, consonants, simple and compound), each sound to be described, represented by a diagram showing the position of the organs of speech, and illustrated by a list of some of the more important units (monosyllabic if possible) into the composition of which it enters.

8. Lists of words classified according to their initial and final syllables.

9. Miscellaneous word lists comprising among their features:

(*a*) Words containing only the less difficult sounds.
(*b*) Words having the same spelling in both languages.

10. A series of graduated exercises containing most of those described in connexion with the Standard Programme.

11. A comprehensive set of questions and answers serving to explain the more useful and interesting phenomena of the language in all its lexicological aspects.

12. A supplement to 11 in the form of a series of systematic 'directions for use' of the language in all its lexicological aspects.

13. Easy texts (graduated) containing a high proportion of the units figuring in a given microcosm, with English translation and notes.

14. A *questionnaire* containing some thousand easy questions and their answers. The first part of the book will give these questions and answers in their classified order; the second part will contain the same questions in mixed order.

15. The sentences of most frequent occurrence in everyday speech with indications by which most of them may be converted into simple or compound substitution tables.

16. A series of model letters both of general and special interest.

17. A corrective method designed to cure bad lexicological habits due to previous and defective study.

18. A large bilingual dictionary less precise but more extensive than those described in 1 and 2. Every word should be accompanied by its phonetic transcript and all necessary ergonic and semantic information.

19. An elementary text-book of lexicology, with sections devoted to general phonetics, etymology, semantics, and ergonics.

20. An elementary text-book of linguistics or philology, describing and explaining the phenomena of language in general.

PART VIII

THE STUDENT

Section 36.—There are two categories of students who are necessarily the architects of their own programme or method:

(*a*) Those who are unable to command the services of any teacher whatever.

(*b*) Those to whom the services of casual or non-expert teachers are alone available.

Many students from the force of circumstances are their own teachers. Such must necessarily nearly always be the case when the language is that of a remote people or one of those of which teachers are rare. If the student happens to reside in a village or small town it is rarely possible for him to take lessons. Even in the largest towns it is difficult to find teachers of languages little known and less studied.

In such cases as these the student must perforce be his own teacher and rely on books and phonograph records. Were the language-learner's ideal library an objective fact instead of an abstraction, the student would lose comparatively little by the exchange. As matters stand, however, he must do the best he may by applying to himself advice of the kind that we have suggested in the foregoing sections. He must also to a certain extent be the architect of his own method. Except in rare cases it will be difficult for him at the present day to procure any ready-made ergonic lists, still less an ergonic chart; these he must compose for himself with the help of a large dictionary and a series of 'grammars' and other works presumably written for those who are more or less in his situation.

Those who are unable to avail themselves of expert teachers may as a *pis aller* make use of the help afforded by some one who, without being a teacher, possesses a first-class acquaintance with the foreign language which is possibly his native tongue. If he cannot fulfil all the functions of the teacher he will be able to fulfil a portion of them more or less successfully.

One of the most frequent cases in which the student is thus obliged to engage the services of a casual teacher is that of the traveller, missionary, or trader who goes to some country where the language spoken by the natives is not one of those studied in European schools.

The student must in this case, as before, be the architect of his programme and draw up his own ergonic tables.

The first care of the student working in these unfavourable but interesting conditions is to ascertain which are the sounds of the language in question. He must ask his teacher to pronounce a given unit a number of times. He will then attempt to transcribe what he hears with appropriate symbols. He will also do his best to reproduce orally what he hears and continue to do so until his teacher is fully satisfied. The student will generally have to be more critical than his teacher; too often, unfortunately, the latter is satisfied with mediocre results. It will be permissible for the student wilfully to mispronounce certain sounds in order to ascertain whether his teacher is as strict as he ought to be in correcting everything which is not in order. With patience and perseverance the student should eventually ascertain exactly how many sounds are contained in the language, which they are, and to what extent many of them differ from sounds already known to him. At the same time he will have been careful to note the stress, intonation, and other alogistic features of the language.

When once he is able to write what he hears, his next endeavour will be to draw up the ergonic lists which will serve as material for the chart. His procedure will be somewhat as follows:

"How do you say *I see two men*?"

The answer will be noted and transcribed without any considerations of graphic continuity; it will be written as one word. The English translation will be written on the opposite page.

"How do you say *I see three men*?"

The answer will be carefully noted and transcribed; there

will be a difference between the two sentences, which difference may be taken to represent the change from *two* to *three*. It must then be ascertained how to express *I see four men, I see five men,* etc. The answers will be noted and a simple substitution table will be the result.

It may be asked: "Why not ask the teacher simply to recite the numbers from one upward?"

It would not be a sound proceeding, for there is a strong possibility that the numerals will not have the same form when isolated as when used as modifiers. In French the words corresponding to *five, six, seven, eight, nine,* and *ten* possess two or even three forms, according to their function and position.

We shall then ask how to say *I see one man,* and note the unit corresponding to *one* and also whether the equivalent of *man* differs from that of *men*; if so this sentence will not form part of our table; it can be set on one side for future reference.

We shall then ask how to express *I see two women* and compare this sentence with *I see two men.* We shall note whether the unit corresponding to *two* changes in any way. If not, we shall read the sentences *I see three women, I see four women, I see five women,* etc., in order to be sure that there is neither concord nor assimilation on the part of the numerals. This point being established, we shall replace *women* by *trees, houses, horses,* etc., etc., and note the units corresponding to each of these simple concepts. Our table has now become a compound substitution table. We shall next ask how to say *I hear two men.* The difference between this and the first sentence will correspond to the difference between *see* and *hear*. Other simple verbs, such as *know, meet, wait for, follow,* etc., will successively replace the verbs *see* and *hear*. Care will be taken at each step to pronounce all the new combinations to make sure that they are ergonically sound.

On semantic grounds our teacher will probably protest. If, in making our ergonic combinations, oblivious of all except ergonic considerations, we happen to pronounce the foreign equivalent of *I follow two trees,* we shall at once be informed that it is a sentence not in use among the natives. In all such cases we must calm our teacher as best we can; we may perhaps tell him that we are going to form the sentence *It is impossible to say "I follow two trees,"* or *Only a madman would say "I follow two trees"*; we shall be forgiven and our ergonic study will proceed.

Whenever our teacher is inclined to interrupt our trend of work by considerations of a purely semantic order, we must explain to the best of our ability that the study of the exact meanings of our units will come later. As we go on, our teacher will begin to grasp that there is method in our madness, and may possibly be able to contribute not only a number of appropriate units but certain valuable hints which will enable us to accelerate our pace. In order to bring about this desirable result we first work at the more accessible ergonic lists, such as the one already described. Before venturing on what may prove more difficult ground, considerations of conjugation, declension and other ptosonic features, we may first exhaust the possibilities of the simple and better-known categories. Among these are the complements of place, time, and duration, modifier categories (such as adjectives of colour and dimension), pronouns, etc., etc. For a long time we must never fail to work on the basis of complete sentences, for only those who have had much experience with strange languages know what extraordinary things may happen when an isolated unit finds itself associated with others in a sentence.

The result of the joint labours of student and teacher will be a sufficient number of ergonic lists to form a simple chart; the working of this chart must be controlled and checked in various ways until we are assured of its soundness.

In the meantime, in fact from the moment that the first simple substitution table has been committed to writing, the pupil may start catenizing operations and carry on the work described in the second stage of the Standard Programme.

The semanticizing of the units may be carried out in one or more of the four manners described in the section dealing with this process.

Section 37.—The relations between teacher and student in point of authority can only be determined in accordance with certain delicate factors, among which are the relative degree of expertness possessed or claimed by either, the particular end that the student has in view, and the inducement which the pupil is prepared to offer in order to secure the unconditional and unqualified services of a docile teacher.

The vast majority of students are in the hands of their teachers, just as the teachers are at the mercy of the method-maker. They must generally abide by the decisions of their teacher and be content to follow his programme.

In special cases the student may possess more technical knowledge of language-learning than his teacher; this may result in a mutual state of distrust and passive resistance. In other cases the teacher is the more expert of the two, but the pupil thinks the contrary. In both cases there is distrust, an enormous dispersion of force, and a sad state of friction.

The relationship between a teacher and his pupil may hardly be compared with that subsisting between a doctor and his patient. We go to a doctor prepared to place ourselves unreservedly in his hands, for we recognize him as an expert and we acknowledge our own incompetence.

But in the case of linguistic work the issue is complicated by a cross factor. The teacher works in a double capacity; he is the source from which information touching the language itself is to be derived, and at the same time is presumed to dictate in what manner that information is to be conveyed and assimilated.

To take a concrete example, let us imagine A to be a fairly expert learner with three foreign languages already to his credit. He wishes to study a fourth, and has decided in his own mind exactly how much of that language he wishes to become acquainted with and in precisely what aspect he wishes to specialize. He wishes, let us say, for a thorough documentation on the sounds of the modern colloquial language and no more; he is not interested in its literary form, nor does he wish to study its peculiar spelling system. The language is one of those which is rarely studied; native teachers are difficult to find, few or no books are accessible.

B represents the teacher to whom A has recourse. His principal qualification as teacher is that he is bilingual, knowing both his own language and that of A.

Now B may have peculiar notions of his own as to the method of teaching his language. He may be convinced that all study should be based on the written aspect of its classical form, and that such details as the sounds of the colloquial variety are not worthy of serious consideration.

But A does not go to B in order to learn how or what to study. What he wants is the material itself of which B is the only available source. The obvious consequence is that A and B will both lose a great deal of time and patience, and expend uselessly a great deal of energy.

Or the case may be the contrary. Let us imagine C as a would-be learner with no notions whatever concerning the nature of language, but merely endowed with the usual stock of linguistic illusions.

D will be a teacher well qualified in both of his capacities. He is an efficient source of linguistic information, and has a sound knowledge of the processes of study. He knows far better what C is likely to require than C does himself. Now, unless C places himself unreservedly in the hands of D there will be trouble, misunderstanding will arise, and each will pull in his own direction.

Even the best type of student, who intuitively chooses the right matter and the right path, would derive great benefit and save many months of effort if he recognized what the nature of language really is and what the principles of study are.

A preliminary knowledge of geography always facilitates travel, however well endowed one may be with the bump of locality. Even the most experienced traveller carries with him a time-table and a railway map. But few students possess the faculties of choosing the right material and of following the right paths. The majority of students are bad learners, and one of the aims of the science of language-study should be to convert bad learners into good ones, to point out to them that fully four-fifths of their time, efforts, and money are running to waste so long as they remain bad learners.

Section 38.—The least satisfactory type of student is the one who has neither confidence in the programme suggested by the teacher nor the capacity of working out one of his own. He is the source of constant trouble, and we should do well to advise him to seek another teacher.

Let us distinguish the *bad* learner from the *slow* learner and from the *bad* pupil.

By *bad* pupil we mean the one who will not work; the lazy man or boy; the shirker. The only advice we have to give him is to cease being a *lazy pupil* and to try to become an *energetic student.*

The *slow* student is one who has no natural gift for language, is rather dense, forms conclusions laboriously and often incorrectly.

He is by no means a hopeless case. If he is docile and does what a competent teacher tells him to do, if he works conscientiously and with perseverance, he will eventually learn to use the foreign language in the same way that he has learnt to use his own. He is not a bad learner; merely a slow one.

By *bad* learner we mean the intelligent type of student who either from want of reflection or from ignorance of language and its nature, misdirects all his efforts, does what he ought not to do, and leaves undone all that he ought to do, and finally manages at great expense and a prodigious waste of time to speak broken English (or whatever the language may be), and to compose written matter with an average of ten mistakes to the line.

The more general characteristics of the bad learner are due to:

(*a*) *Thoughtlessness or lack of reflection.* He has no conception whatever of the nature of language or its study.

(*b*) *Mistaken haste.* He is in such a hurry to work that he forgets to buy any tools. Moral: *Festina lente.*

(*c*) *Prejudice.* That is to say, over-confidence in some particular system and too little confidence in others.

(*d*) *Lack of proportionate discernment*, as a result of which he exaggerates or else he unduly belittles difficulties, or forms a mistaken analogy between language-learning and other subjects of study.

(*e*) '*Old fogeyism*'—*i.e.* the incapacity to absorb new ideas, combined with an instinctive fear of the unknown.

There are many types of bad learners, and the mixed and bewildering nature of their vagaries renders these so complex as to defy classification.

In default of this we must draw up a rough and unclassified list of his various shortcomings.

He learns to spell a certain number of words but pays little or no attention to their pronunciation and totally ignores even the existence of such things as weak forms.

He learns to attach to each foreign word an arbitrary and conventional translation, and ignores the self-evident fact that most words have several meanings and translations.

He considers words as mathematical units, and treats them as such. Unfamiliar group-words and word-groups he either avoids or dismisses as unsolvable mysteries.

He neglects all the essential preliminaries. He says that he has no time to waste on phonetics and ergonic charts, and forthwith proceeds to waste precious months in working without those tools which alone ensure rapid and real progress.

He has a passion for creation. He imagines that people speak by rule, that every sentence has its origin in a reasoned calculation.

He avoids the reproduction of models or the rational modification of models previously learnt by heart. He thinks memorizing a vicious process only good for parrots and children. He will not willingly reproduce anything that he has heard, some depraved form of linguistic conscience tells him that this is akin to cheating; he must construct everything in his own way, and that way generally means the way he expresses it in his own language.

He considers a mistake in spelling as a crime, but treats the most flagrant mispronunciations as venial offences.

He learns more or less superficially a number of classical rules of orthographic grammar, but ignores the simple laws underlying them, and is proud to confess to a total ignorance of phonetic grammar.

Not being aware of the distinction between colloquial and literary speech, even in his own language, he conceives the former as being a vulgar, degraded form of what he imagines to be, and terms, 'correct' speech. Never having learnt to distinguish language from literature, he confuses the two subjects, or even denies the existence of a science of language as apart from the art of literature.

Having no precise notion of the number of words that a language may contain, nor any notion whatever of their relative frequency or usefulness, he chooses his vocabulary, or allows it to be chosen for him, on a haphazard method based on the principle that "a word is a word."

His eye-memory being abnormally developed and his ear-memory being proportionately weak, he pays little or no attention to what he hears, or too much attention to what he sees, ignoring the self-evident fact that he learnt his own language by ear long before he ever studied a single word of it by the eye. He maintains with a pathetic insistence that he cannot learn a word until he has seen it written in its conventional orthography. What he really means is that he is too lazy to develop his auditive perceptions or ear-memory, and that he has not enough energy to devote a couple of hours to learning the dozen or so phonetic signs.

It is often to be noticed that those who are the least endowed with the faculty of reason, who are the least capable of learning by logical comparison, are precisely those who proclaim with the greatest insistence that they cannot repeat or use any form until it has been thoroughly explained to them. It is generally the bad pronouncer who shuns phonetics and who refuses to learn a word until he sees it written.

Whatever serious attention he gives to pronunciation is devoted at most to its orthoepic aspect (the study of the orthographic representation of sounds). The study of the sounds themselves he considers either too trivial or too difficult to warrant any serious attention. He is not averse to using or even forging weird systems of imitated pronunciation however complicated and inexact, but shuns a simple phonetic transcription " because it looks so difficult."

He is unable to distinguish between real and fancied difficulties, and consequently will set out light-heartedly to solve the most hopelessly difficult problems, the successful solving of which would not help him an inch on his way. On the other hand, he will studiously avoid the easy and labour-saving devices and the simple (because fundamental) explanations discovered and put at his disposal by modern language specialists.

Cautious as he may be in the pursuit of his own vocation, intelligent as he is in most other branches of study, he is an easy victim to the quack when he takes up the study of language.

His teacher wishes him to acquire the faculty of reproducing orally, rapidly, and by ear-memory, complete sentences. Instead of developing his ear-memory by patient listening and accurate observation, he analyses, isolates the words, and produces, not the sentence, but a mere succession of its individual words.

One type of bad learner has a child-like faith in the efficacy of 'conversation' (he probably means the process of 'spontaneous assimilation') and is willing to spend hours of expensive lessons in order to have the opportunity of speaking broken English (or whatever the language may be) to his teacher.

The bad learner is generally inconsistent. He confesses to a horror of theory of all sorts, more especially of phonetic and grammatical theory. " Practice," says he, " practice is the great thing, theory is a vain thing." He asks his teacher for " conversation," and when he gets it, he interrupts this " conversation " at every moment to ask why such-and-such a form was incorrect, and how such-and-such an idea ought to be expressed, what is the best translation of such-and-such a word; in short, bombarding his teacher with demands for theoretical explanations.

His attention is distracted at every moment. While his teacher by special request is explaining to him why A is A and not B, he wants to know the difference between X and Z. If his teacher is weak enough to drop the subject A-B and turn to X-Z, our student will become inquisitive on the subject of C.

Another type of bad learner pins his faith to theory. He wishes to have the etymology of each word he learns, an 'explanation' of each form. He refuses to learn any verb outside a conjugation table or any noun outside the paradigm of a declension. If he is a Frenchman and his teacher should chance to make use of a few simple sentences in the foreign language, he will meet these with a blank stare and an exasperating: "Qu'est-ce que ça veut dire ?—Dites-le en français."

He cannot conceive the idea of direct comprehension. For him translation is the one and only process of understanding the meaning of foreign words or forms. He imagines that the untranslatable is the unknowable.

When in the more advanced stages of his study he listens to a lecture or a speech in the foreign language, his worried, strained features bear witness to his frantic efforts to translate mentally everything that he hears.

One question is perpetually on his lips and printed on his brain: "Qu'est-ce que ça veut dire en français ? What's that in English ? Wie heisst das auf deutsch ? "

The bad learner has an aversion for any grammatical terms which he has not already learnt in connexion with his own language, and delights in giving familiar names to unfamiliar forms.

Our English preterite the Frenchman will dub *imparfait*; the progressive conjugation of verbs he calls the *participe présent*. He shies at such terms as *causative, frequentative, possessive substantive*, or *proper adjective*. He has never heard of such things in his own native French grammar. If you speak of fricatives, unvoiced consonants, or rounded vowels, he is not certain whether these are mysteries invented to puzzle him, or whether to pass them by as bad jokes.

He diagnoses badly. He learns the spelling and the arbitrary translation of a couple of thousand isolated foreign words, is astonished that this does not enable him to understand the spoken language, and attributes it to a weak vocabulary (" Je ne peux pas comprendre, je ne connais pas assez de mots "), and starts work on the third thousand.

He may recognize that he has acquired bad habits of pronunciation (as a matter of fact he never pronounces a single foreign sound). As a remedy he proposes " plenty of reading " and asserts that in time good pronunciation will come (" On ne peut pas faire tout au début ! ").

The conscientious teacher can never obtain any satisfaction out of a bad learner. The method is always wrong for him. You may run in vain the whole gamut from natural assimilation to abstract theory. What he wants is a little of everything so long as that little is sufficiently superficial and sufficiently scrappy, and then he will lay the blame on the book or on the teacher if he is not able to understand, speak, read, and write after fifty lessons.

We do not maintain that the bad learner commits all the crimes enumerated above. There are various types of bad learners ; some affect one form of aberration, some affect others. In a few instances, however, the writer has met with that extraordinary type which succeeds in combining the sum of all the defects quoted in this enumeration.

Taken in hand firmly at the outset, the bad learner may be transformed into a good one. If, however, his attitude toward language-study has become an ingrained habit, he is a hopeless case. He has so accustomed himself to this caricature of language that he is no longer able to break himself of his habits.

When, conscious of some of these shortcomings, he again applies to a teacher " pour un peu se perfectionner dans la conversation " and when the teacher strives to point out that everything must be relearnt from the start, he is pained and discouraged. When the conscientious teacher suggests a course of elementary phonetics and grammar he is indignant.

In such cases nothing can be done except to hand him over to the mercies of the nearest language quack, who will assure him that his accent is very good, and that with a little time and practice he will use the language like a native.

The object of this severe criticism is to describe with a certain precision exactly what are the obstacles which many otherwise intelligent students create for themselves, and to state in unmistakable terms the nature of their errors in order to be able to correct them better.

It is evident that when the bad learner recognizes himself

to be such, he will immediately strive to become a good learner. If he clearly recognizes that tendencies toward such habits are defects and not qualities, that nobody holding such views has ever learnt a language quickly and well, then he must necessarily make up his mind to make a radical change and become a good learner. If he does not, then we cannot even place him in the category of intelligent learners.

Many may protest that notwithstanding the holding of such views they have successfully mastered the foreign language.

The answer is obvious. If they have arrived at a successful result, it is to their credit that they have done so in spite of their self-created obstacles, and that had they studied on rational lines they would have achieved this result with a tenth of the efforts they have so laboriously expended.

Others may protest that they have been or are the victims of bad methods and of old-fashioned teachers. This is in very many cases true. Circumstances over which they had no control have made bad learners of them, and it is precisely one of the objects of the present work to warn the student against bad methods and to put him on his guard against a continuance of practices and vicious habits of thought such as we have described.

In using the term "bad learner" we have more especially in mind those who, in spite of warnings and in spite of the most evident proofs, persist in their fallacious methods, who persist in imagining that their hastily formed notions and insufficiently pondered theories are profound truths.

Let the student thoroughly understand, let us drill it into his mind insistently and in clear terms, that the good learner can and does perform with success in a few weeks what the bad learner fails to perform in as many months or even years.

Let him understand for his own sake and for the sake of his pocket, if that is of any consideration, that the sooner he begins to learn according to rational principles the sooner he will achieve real results.

He has learnt his own language rationally and with success; let him do the same thing with the foreign language.

CONCLUSION

Section 39.—May all those who have followed us in our inquiry so unite and co-ordinate their efforts that language-teaching and language-study shall be placed once for all on a stable and scientific basis.

In conclusion let us address the following exhortation to critics: if you are not disposed to accept all or certain of the data we have gathered, or if you are not in agreement with all or certain of the conclusions we have derived therefrom, let your indignation not take the form of wild and destructive criticism, for this will not advance the cause in which we are so deeply interested. Rather let your energies be directed into the channels of constructiveness; let your evidence and your matured judgment come to confirm and to reinforce what you may consider as sound, to repair what you may consider as weak, and to supplement what you may consider as incomplete. If you are in agreement with our method of procedure, do not fail to support it; if you hold with us that the future of language-teaching and study should be based on organized and unified thought, then collaborate in the work which so far has barely commenced.

We have avoided in all possible measure any form of dogmatism; if at times our arguments have tended toward destructiveness, it is because our reasoned and matured judgment has convinced us beyond any manner of doubt that they are justified. We have endeavoured throughout these pages to state facts and to form conclusions in absolute conformity with these facts. Our aim has been but to add to the general store of ever-increasing knowledge of the nature of language, and to contribute our share toward ascertaining the principles which will enable us to emancipate language-teaching and language-study from the domain of empiricism, and to place it once for all on a true scientific basis.

APPENDIX I

Shortly after completing the manuscript of this work I was strongly advised by a colleague, who had had occasion to read it through, to append a model of an Ergonic Chart. He urged that this would considerably facilitate and encourage research work, and by so doing would contribute in no small measure to the utility of the book and to the success of the inquiry.

For more than one reason I was reluctant to follow this advice. In the first place, I realized only too well that the perfect Ergonic Chart did not yet exist; the classification of the units, the terminology, and many technical principles were still in an embryonic stage.

In the second place, I doubted whether it was possible to accommodate a chart within the limited dimensions afforded by the pages of a book. To condense it unduly would render it unintelligible; to abridge it unduly would deprive it of its utility.

My colleague pointed out, in reply, that even a rudimentary chart would be better than no chart at all; that the ergonic symbols might be replaced provisionally by an arbitrary system of numbers; that my readers would understand that an appendix is not an exhaustive treatise, and that many of them would probably exercise their ingenuity in constructing large-scale charts from the materials and key plan which I would provide. In short, he overcame my objections and encouraged me to produce the following scheme.

CONDENSED AND ABRIDGED SCHEME FOR A FRENCH ERGONIC CHART

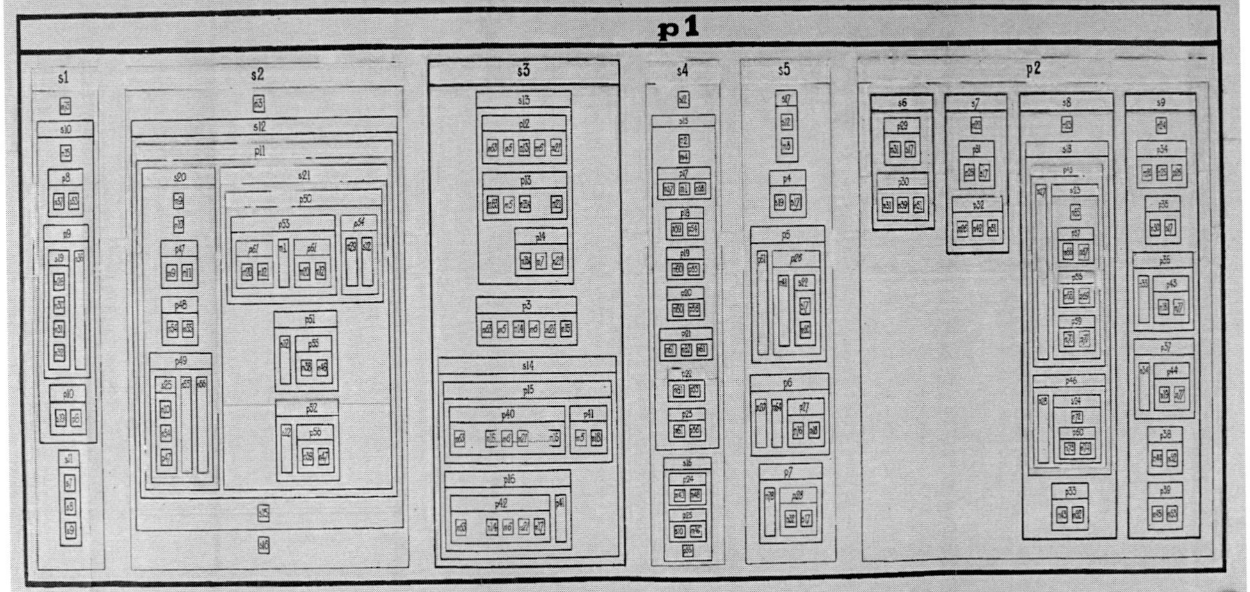

CONDENSED AND ABRIDGED SCHEME FOR A FRENCH ERGONIC CHART

The scheme comprises two parts—the *Catalogue of Units* and the *Chart* itself.

The Catalogue

This contains an infinite number of units, grouped on mathematical grounds into three types.

The first of these consists of groups of *Minimals*—*i.e.* units which it is not possible or not desirable for the purpose of this particular scheme to subject to further analysis.

These we may call the *Minimal groups* (abbreviated to *m*).

> *Example:* m8 = *moi, toi, lui, elle, nous, vous, eux, elles.*
> *Second example*: m22 = *à côté, ailleurs, au coin, au-dessus, au milieu, derrière, devant, ici, là, quelque part, nulle part, là dedans*, etc.

The second type of group consists of two or more lists of units considered collectively. As these groups represent the *sum* of their varieties, we may call them *Sum groups* (abbreviated to *s*).

> *Example:* s19 = m26 + m30 + m31 + m32.

This means that for the sake of conciseness we are using the symbol s19 instead of the cumbrous statement "m26 and m30 and m31 and m32."

> *Second example:* s12 = p11 + s15.

This means that for the sake of conciseness we designate by the symbol s12 the two groups of units p11 (noun compounds) and s15 (a certain category of nouns and pronouns).

The third type of group consists of two or more lists of units used in combination with each other. As these groups consist of the *product* of their components, we may call them *Product groups* (abbreviated to *p*).

Example: p61 = m20 × m12.

This means that p61 stands for all the units contained in list m20 combined with all the units contained in list m12.

m20 will be found to consist of units such as *très*, *trop*, and *assez*; m12 will be found to consist of units such as *beau*, *bon*, and *grand*; hence we have

$$\left.\begin{array}{l}\text{très}\\ \text{trop}\\ \text{assez}\\ \text{etc.}\end{array}\right\} \times \left\{\begin{array}{l}\text{beau}\\ \text{bon}\\ \text{grand}\\ \text{etc.}\end{array}\right.$$

which results in the p61 units *très beau*, *très bon*, *très grand*, *trop beau*, *trop bon*, *trop grand*, *assez beau*, *assez bon*, *assez grand*, etc.

Each of the three types of groups, m, s, and p, have been classified, according to their function, into a series of numbered categories, or lists. Thus we find the series m1 to m78, s1 to s25, and p1 to p61, making in all 164 lists. To combine the elements of each minimal list with other units in such a way as to produce p-units, and to combine successively such p-units with other units until we arrive at an unlimited number of complete sentences constitutes the process of Ergonic Synthesis.

To reduce, by means of symbols and formulæ, complete sentences to their minimal parts constitutes the process of Ergonic Analysis.

Stated concisely, ergonic synthesis, or the systematic composition of sentences, consists of converting m-units into p-units; ergonic analysis consists of converting p-units into m-units. A complete scheme of ergonic analysis consists of reducing the p1 of a given language to its m-values.

The Chart

This key plan or chart bears toward the French language the same relation as a map of the world toward geography.

Just as the map shows us the broad continental masses, the states into which they are divided, the provinces of which these are made up, and the situation of the chief towns contained in each, so does this chart show the main syntactical divisions of the language, the subdivisions of each of these, and their further subdivisions down to the smallest units which can conveniently be shown on a chart of these limited dimensions.[1]

This chart will be found to consist of 238 rectangular panels, each of which is designated by one or other of the 164 ergonic symbols. Each of the panels is assumed to contain that list of units for which its particular symbol stands. The processes of synthesis and analysis described above are therefore shown in spatial form.

The panel serving as a framework for the whole contains the six possible factors of a sentence—viz. s1, s2, s3, s4, s5, and p2. It is therefore a product panel, and is designated by the symbol p1.

Each of the six component panels is built up of smaller panels. Two of these (m75 and m3) contain minimal units only; the others (sum and product panels) are themselves built up of still smaller panels. By this process of dichotomy we arrive ultimately at the last of the minimal panels (which happens to be the components of p61), and thus complete our analytic survey.

The somewhat complicated appearance of the chart is partly due to its extreme condensation; on a background of ampler dimensions the last panel of s2 (viz. s16) would be shown on the more generous scale in which it appears as a component of s4. Similarly the enormous mass of units represented by s12, instead of being condensed into a single panel as in the

[1] Both the geographical and the linguistic charts may be drawn to a large or to a small scale; the advantages and disadvantages of each are similar in both instances. In the case of geography we place at the disposal of the student, not one comprehensive map of the world to answer all purposes, but the *atlas*—*i.e.* a series of geographical charts drawn to various convenient scales, each having its particular use and function and generally accompanied by a gazetteer.

first variety of s4, would be expanded to a scale more worthy of its importance.

The other reason for the complex aspect of this chart is due to the fact that in this concise *exposé* this one chart has to serve all purposes.

Let me add that I *do not* advise any teacher to bewilder and dishearten his young pupils by demonstrating to them the ergonic theory by means of this condensed chart. What I *do* suggest is that the present diagram should serve as a basis for composing an 'Ergonic Atlas,' containing a number of charts drawn to various scales and in various degrees of completeness. Many or most of these would be designed in such a way that each panel would contain a few specimens of the actual units themselves (see pp. 182, 183).

As it hardly comes within the scope of this book to give a more detailed explanation of the ergonic theory and its technique, we must now refer the reader to the chart and the catalogue, and let these speak for themselves.

THE CATALOGUE OF UNITS

I. MINIMAL GROUPS

m1 = nouns normally requiring the antecedency of s20.

si.mas. a. *ami, arbre, bureau, cahier, centime, chapeau, coin, côté, crayon, devoir, élève, exemple, franc, frère, garçon, homme, jardin, journal, livre, morceau, mot, mur, nom, œil, paquet, pays, père, pied, professeur, pupitre, soulier, tableau, timbre, tiroir, verre,* etc.

b. *acier, anglais, argent, bois, fer, français, lait, or, pain, papier, plaisir, verre, vin,* etc.

si.fem. a. *adresse, armoire, boîte, campagne, carte, chaise, chambre, chose, clef, dame, demi-heure, demoiselle, difficulté, douzaine, façon, femme, fenêtre, feuille, fille, fin, fleur, fois, gare, idée, langue, leçon, lettre, main, maison, manière, mère, montre, paire, partie, phrase, place, plume, poche, porte, question, réponse, rue, sœur, table, ville,* etc.

b. *craie, eau, encre, pierre, viande,* etc.

plu.mas. *amis, arbres, bureaux, cahiers, centimes, chapeaux, coins, côtés, crayons, devoirs, élèves, exemples, francs, frères, garçons, hommes, jardins, journaux, livres, morceaux, mots, murs, noms, yeux, pays, paquets, pieds, pupitres, souliers, tableaux, timbres, tiroirs, verres,* etc.

plu.fem. *adresses, armoires, boîtes, cartes, chaises, chambres, choses, clefs, dames, demoiselles, difficultés, douzaines, façons, femmes, fenêtres, feuilles, filles, fleurs, fois, gares, idées, langues, leçons, lettres, mains, maisons, manières, montres, paires, parties, phrases, places, plumes, poches, portes, questions, réponses, rues, sœurs, tables, villes,* etc.

m2 = nouns never or hardly ever requiring s20.

si.mas. a. *Jean, Henri, Charles,* etc., *Monsieur Lebrun,* etc.

b. [le] *Japon,* [*le*] *Danemark,* etc.

c. *Paris, Bruxelles, Genève, Londres,* etc.

si.fem. a. *Marie, Louise, Madeleine,* etc., *Madame Lebrun, Mademoiselle Lebrun,* etc.

b. [*la*] *France,* [*l'*] *Angleterre,* [*la*] *Belgique,* [*la*] *Suisse,* etc.

plu.mas. a. *Jean et Henri, Jean et Marie, Monsieur et Madame Lebrun,* etc.

b. [*les*] *États-Unis,* etc.

plu.fem. *Marie et Louise,* etc.

m3 = personal pronouns, subject.

je, tu, il, elle, on, ce, nous, vous, ils, elles.

m4 = various classes of pronouns.

ça, ceci, cela.
beaucoup, assez, trop, un peu, etc.

si.mas. *celui-ci, celui-là, l'autre, le mien, le tien, le sien, le nôtre, le vôtre, le leur, un, le premier, le dernier, le second, le deuxième,* etc.

si.fem. *celle-ci, celle-là, l'autre, la mienne, la tienne, la sienne, la nôtre, la vôtre, la leur, une, la première, la dernière, la seconde, la deuxième,* etc.

plu.mas. *ceux-ci, ceux-là, les autres, les miens, les tiens, les siens, les nôtres, les vôtres, les leurs, deux, trois, quatre,* etc., *les premiers, les derniers,* etc., *quelques-uns, plusieurs,* etc.

plu.fem. *celles-ci, celles-là, les autres, les miennes, les tiennes, les siennes, les nôtres, les vôtres, les leurs, deux, trois, quatre,* etc., *les premières, les dernières,* etc., *quelques-unes, plusieurs,* etc.

m5 = personal pronouns, non-subject, enclaved in s3.

a. *me, te, le, la, se, nous, vous, les.*
b. *me, te, lui, lui, se, nous, vous, leur.*
c. *y, en.*
d. *me le, me la, me les, m'y, m'en, te le, te la, te les, t'y, t'en, le lui, la lui, les lui, lui en, nous le, nous la, nous les, nous y, nous en, vous le, vous la, vous les, vous y, vous en, le leur, la leur, les leur, leur en, y en.*

m6 = personal pronouns, subject, enclaved in s3.

-je, -tu, [-t]-il, [-t]-elle, [-t]-on, -ce, -nous, -vous, -ils, -elles.

m7 = a certain group of personal pronouns (used only in connexion with the imperative affirmative) enclaved in s3.

a. *-moi, -toi, -le, -la, -nous, -vous, -les.*
b. *-moi, -toi, -lui, -lui, -nous, -vous, -leur.*

c. *-y, -en.*
d. *-le-moi, -la-moi, -les-moi, -m'y, -m'en, -le-toi, -la-toi, -les-toi, -t'y, -t'en, -le-lui, -la-lui, -les-lui,; -l'y, -lui-en, -le-nous, -la-nous, -les-nous, -nous-y, nous-en, le-vous, -la-vous, les-vous, -vous-y, -vous-en, -le-leur, -la-leur, -les-leur, -les-y, -leur-en, -y-en.*

m8 = a certain group of personal pronouns occupying the position shown on chart.

moi, toi, lui, elle, soi, nous, vous, eux, elles.

m9 = a certain group of adjectives (of various classes) constituting the most important member of s20.

si.mas. *le, un, du, ce, chaque, le même, l'autre, mon, ton, son, notre, votre, leur, tout le,* etc.

si.fem. *la, une, de la, cette, chaque, la même, l'autre, ma, ta, sa, notre, votre, leur, toute la,* etc.

plu. *les, des, ces, les mêmes, les autres, mes, tes, ses, nos, vos, leurs, tous les, toutes les, quelques, plusieurs,* etc.

m10 = numeral adjectives.

a. *un, deux, trois, quatre, cinq, six, sept, huit, neuf.*
b. *dix, vingt, trente, quarante, cinquante, soixante, quatre-vingts.*
c. *onze, douze, treize, quatorze, quinze, seize, dix-sept, dix-huit, dix-neuf.*
d. *vingt et un, vingt-deux,* etc.
e. *cent, deux cent(s),* etc., *cent un, cent deux,* etc.
f. *mille, deux mille,* etc., *mille un,* etc.

m11 = ordinal adjectives.

si.mas. *premier, prochain, dernier, second, deuxième, troisième, quatrième,* etc.

si.fem. *première, prochaine, dernière, seconde, deuxième,* etc.

plu.mas. *premiers*, *prochains*, *derniers*, *seconds*, *deuxièmes*, etc.

plu.fem. *premières*, *prochaines*, *dernières*, *secondes*, *deuxièmes*, etc.

m12 = adjectives of quality, and participial adjectives. (Those marked by an asterisk normally precede m1 ; those not so marked normally follow m1.)

si.mas. *anglais*, **beau*, *blanc*, *bleu*, **bon*, *brun*, *cher*, *content*, *court*, *difficile*, *drôle*, *facile*, *fatigué*, *fermé*, *français*, **grand*, *gris*, *important*, *intéressant*, *jaune*, **joli*, *juste*, *libre*, **long*, **mauvais*, *neuf*, *noir*, **nouveau*, *occupé*, *ouvert*, **petit*, *plein*, *prêt*, *propre*, *rouge*, *sale*, *vert*, *vide*, **vieux*, *vrai*, etc.

plu.mas. *anglais*, **beaux*, *blancs*, *bleus*, **bons*, *bruns*, *chers*, *contents*, *courts*, *difficiles*, *drôles*, *faciles*, *fatigués*, *fermés*, *français*, **grands*, *gris*, *importants*, *intéressants*, *jaunes*, **jolis*, *justes*, *libres*, **longs*, **mauvais*, *neufs*, *noirs*, **nouveaux*, *occupés*, *ouverts*, **petits*, *pleins*, *prêts*, *propres*, *rouges*, *sales*, *verts*, *vides*, **vieux*, *vrais*, etc.

si.fem. *anglaise*, **belle*, *blanche*, *bleue*, **bonne*, *brune*, *chère*, *contente*, *courte*, *difficile*, *drôle*, *facile*, *fatiguée*, *fermée*, *française*, **grande*, *grise*, *importante*, *intéressante*, *jaune*, **jolie*, *juste*, *libre*, **longue*, **mauvaise*, *neuve*, *noire*, **nouvelle*, *occupée*, *ouverte*, **petite*, *pleine*, *prête*, *propre*, *rouge*, *sale*, *verte*, *vide*, **vieille*, *vraie*, etc.

plu.fem. *anglaises*, **belles*, *blanches*, *bleues*, **bonnes*, *brunes*, *chères*, *contentes*, *courtes*, *difficiles*, *drôles*, *faciles*, *fatiguées*, *fermées*, *françaises*, **grandes*, *grises*, *importantes*, *intéressantes*, *jaunes*, **jolies*, *libres*, **longues*, **mauvaises*, *neuves*, *noires*, **nouvelles*, *occupées*, *ouvertes*,

**petites*, *pleines*, *prêtes*, *propres*, *rouges*, *sales*, *vertes*, *vides*, **vieilles*, *vraies*, etc.

m13 = simple tenses of verbs. (The eight simple tenses are designated respectively by the symbols a, b, c, d, e, f, g, h. For the sake of completeness, the two archaic tenses *past historic* and *past subjunctive* are included in this list.)

a.	si. 1st pers.	*vais*, *ai*, *dis*, *suis*, *fais*, *parle*, *vois*, etc.
	si. 2nd pers.	*vas*, *as*, *dis*, *es*, *fais*, *parles*, *vois*, etc.
	si. 3rd pers.	*va*, *a*, *dit*, *est*, *fait*, *parle*, *voit*, etc.
	plu. 1st pers.	*allons*, *avons*, *disons*, *sommes*, *faisons*, *parlons*, *voyons*, etc.
	plu. 2nd pers.	*allez*, *avez*, *dites*, *êtes*, *faites*, *parlez*, *voyez*, etc.
	plu. 3rd pers.	*vont*, *ont*, *disent*, *sont*, *font*, *parlent*, *voient*, etc.
b.	si. 1st pers.	*allais*, *avais*, *disais*, *étais*, *faisais*, *parlais*, *voyais*, etc.
	si. 2nd pers.	*allais*, *avais*, *disais*, *étais*, *faisais*, *parlais*, *voyais*, etc.
	si. 3rd pers.	*allait*, *avait*, *disait*, *était*, *faisait*, *parlait*, *voyait*, etc.
	plu. 1st pers.	*allions*, *avions*, *disions*, *étions*, *faisions*, *parlions*, *voyions*, etc.
	plu. 2nd pers.	*alliez*, *aviez*, *disiez*, *étiez*, *faisiez*, *parliez*, *voyiez*, etc.
	plu. 3rd pers.	*allaient*, *avaient*, *disaient*, *étaient*, *faisaient*, *parlaient*, *voyaient*, etc.
c.	si. 1st pers.	*allai*, *eus*, *dis*, *fus*, *fis*, *parlai*, *vis*, etc.
	si. 2nd pers.	*allas*, *eus*, *dis*, *fus*, *fis*, *parlas*, *vis*, etc.
	si. 3rd pers.	*alla*, *eut*, *dit*, *fut*, *fit*, *parla*, *vit*, etc.
	plu. 1st pers.	*allâmes*, *eûmes*, *dîmes*, *fûmes*, *fîmes*, *parlâmes*, *vîmes*, etc.
	plu. 2nd pers.	*allâtes*, *eûtes*, *dîtes*, *fûtes*, *fîtes*, *parlâtes*, *vîtes*, etc.
	plu. 3rd pers.	*allèrent*, *eurent*, *dirent*, *furent*, *firent*, *parlèrent*, *virent*, etc.

d.	si. 1st pers.	*irai, aurai, dirai, serai, ferai, parlerai, verrai*, etc.
	si. 2nd pers.	*iras, auras, diras, seras, feras, parleras, verras*, etc.
	si. 3rd pers.	*ira, aura, dira, sera, fera, parlera, verra*, etc.
	plu. 1st pers.	*irons, aurons, dirons, serons, ferons, parlerons, verrons*, etc.
	plu. 2nd pers.	*irez, aurez, direz, serez, ferez, parlerez, verrez*, etc.
	plu. 3rd pers.	*iront, auront, diront, seront, feront, parleront, verront*, etc.
e.	si. 1st pers.	*irais, aurais, dirais, serais, ferais, parlerais, verrais*, etc.
	si. 2nd pers.	*irais, aurais, dirais, serais, ferais, parlerais, verrais*, etc.
	si. 3rd pers.	*irait, aurait, dirait, serait, ferait, parlerait, verrait*, etc.
	plu. 1st pers.	*irions, aurions, dirions, serions, ferions, parlerions, verrions*, etc.
	plu. 2nd pers.	*iriez, auriez, diriez, seriez, feriez, parleriez, verriez*, etc.
	plu. 3rd pers.	*iraient, auraient, diraient, seraient, feraient, parleraient, verraient*, etc.
f.	si. 1st pers.	*aille, aie, dise, sois, fasse, parle, voie*, etc.
	si. 2nd pers.	*ailles, aies, dises, sois, fasses, parles, voies*, etc.
	si. 3rd pers.	*aille, ait, dise, soit, fasse, parle, voie*, etc.
	plu. 1st pers.	*allions, ayons, disions, soyons, fassions, parlions, voyions*, etc.
	plu. 2nd pers.	*alliez, ayez, disiez, soyez, fassiez, parliez, voyiez*, etc.
	plu. 3rd pers.	*aillent, aient, disent, soient, fassent, parlent, voient*, etc.
g.	si. 1st pers.	*allasse, eusse, disse, fusse, fisse, parlasse, visse*, etc.

si. 2nd pers. *allasses, eusses, disses, fusses, fisses, parlasses, visses,* etc.
si. 3rd pers. *allât, eût, dît, fût, fît, parlât, vît,* etc.
plu. 1st pers. *allassions, eussions, dissions, fussions, fissions, parlassions, vissions,* etc.
plu. 2nd pers. *allassiez, eussiez, dissiez, fussiez, fissiez, parlassiez, vissiez,* etc.
plu. 3rd pers. *allassent, eussent, dissent, fussent, fissent, parlassent, vissent,* etc.

h. si. 2nd pers. *va, aie, dis, sois, fais, parle, vois,* etc.
plu. 1st pers. *allons, ayons, disons, soyons, faisons, parlons, voyons,* etc.
plu. 2nd pers. *allez, ayez, dites, soyez, faites, parlez, voyez,* etc.

m14 = simple tenses of the auxiliary verbs *avoir* and *être*. (For the sake of conciseness, the 3rd person singular only is given.)

a. *a, est.*
b. *avait, était.*
d. *aura, sera.*
e. *aurait, serait.*

m15 = past participles (a = *antecedency of avoir*; b = *antecedency of être*).

a. si.mas. *aimé, attendu, eu, commencé, compris, connu, demandé, dû, dit, donné, écrit, envoyé, espéré, été, fait, fallu, fini, laissé, lu, mis, montré, oublié, parlé, pensé, porté, pu, pris, regardé, rencontré, répondu, su, trouvé, vu, voulu,* etc.
si.fem. *aimée, attendue, eue, commencée, comprise,* etc.
plu.mas. *aimés, attendus, eus, commencés, compris,* etc.
plu.fem. *aimées, attendues, eues, commencées, comprises,* etc.

b. si.mas. *allé, devenu, entré, sorti, venu,* etc.
si.fem. *allée, devenue, entrée, sortie, venue,* etc.
plu.mas. *allés, devenus, entrés, sortis, venus,* etc.
plu.fem. *allées, devenues, entrées, sorties, venues,* etc.

m16 = simple tenses of verbs and verb-compounds constituting the antecedents of the infinitive (m18).

(For the sake of conciseness the 3rd person singular only is given.)

(m6 and m21 may be enclaved at the points marked by the sign ||.)

a. *peut, doit, veut, faut, finit* || *de, commence* || *à, est* || *difficile de, a* || *l'intention de*, etc.

b. *pouvait, devait, voulait, fallait, finissait* || *de, commençait* || *à, était* || *difficile de, avait* || *l'intention de*, etc.

d. *pourra, devra, voudra, faudra, finira* || *de, commencera* || *à, sera* || *difficile de, aura* || *l'intention de*, etc.

e. *pourrait, devrait, voudrait, faudrait, finirait* || *de, commencerait* || *à, serait* || *difficile de, aurait* || *l'intention de*, etc.

m17 = past participles of verbs and verb-compounds of which the simple tenses constitute category m16.

pu, dû, voulu, fallu, fini de, commencé à, été difficile de, eu l'intention de, etc.

m18 = infinitives.

aimer, aller, attendre, avoir, commencer, comprendre, connaître, demander, devenir, devoir, dire, donner, écrire, envoyer, entrer, espérer, être, faire, finir, laisser, lire, mettre, montrer, oublier, parler, penser, porter, prendre, regarder, rencontrer, répondre, rester, savoir, sortir, trouver, venir, voir, vouloir, etc.

m19 = gerunds.

aimant, attendant, ayant, commençant, comprenant, connaissant, demandant, devenant, devant, disant, donnant, écrivant, envoyant, entrant, espérant, étant, faisant, finissant, laissant, lisant, mettant, montrant, oubliant, parlant, pensant, portant, prenant, regardant, rencontrant, répondant, restant, sachant, sortant, trouvant, venant, voyant, voulant, etc.

m20 = adverbs serving to modify m12 and m25.

assez, aussi, bien, exactement, légèrement, parfaitement, plus, beaucoup plus, si, tellement, tout à fait, très, trop, un peu, un peu trop, etc.

m21 = adverbs and adverb-compounds, enclaved normally in s8.

pas, bien, si bien, très bien, cependant, déjà, encore, généralement, justement, mal, très mal, mieux, beaucoup mieux, peut-être, pourtant, quelquefois, rarement, très rarement, seulement, souvent, très souvent, toujours, presque toujours, tout à fait, pas assez, pas bien, pas très bien, pas encore, jamais, presque jamais, pas mal, pas très mal, peut-être pas, plus, que, pas souvent, pas très souvent, pas toujours, pas tout à fait, etc.

m22 = adverbs of place (simple and compound).

à coté, ailleurs, au coin, au-dessus, au milieu, derrière, devant, ici, là, quelque part, nulle part, là dedans, etc.

m23 = adverbs of time.

alors, après, maintenant, plus tard, tout à l'heure, tout de suite, etc.

m24 = adverbs of manner, frequency, etc., never or hardly ever modified by m20.

ainsi, aussi, autrement, ensemble, de temps en temps, tous les jours, chaque fois, chaque année, etc.

m25 = adverbs of manner, etc.

convenablement, difficilement, doucement, facilement, fort, lentement, rapidement, tôt, tard, vite, etc.

m26 = prepositions of place.

à, à coté de, à travers, au bout de, au coin de, au dessus de, au milieu de, autour de, chez, contre, dans, de, derrière, devant, en, en face de, jusqu'à, loin de, par, près de, sous, sur, vers, etc.

m27 = certain prepositions of time (occasional but not necessary antecedents of m65 and m66a; necessary antecedents of m66b, m66c, m68, and m70).

à, à la fin de, à partir de, après, au commencement de, au mois de, avant, depuis, en, jusque, pendant, vers, etc.

m28 = certain prepositions of time and duration.

dans, depuis, il y a, pendant.

m29 = certain prepositions serving as factors of adjective phrases (p54).

à, avec, en, sans, etc.

m30 = certain prepositions serving as factors of phrases of manner, etc. (p35).

à, à cause de, avec, comme, de, en, malgré, par, pour, sans, etc.

m31 = prepositions serving as factors of s6.

à, pour.

m32 = prepositions of the passive voice.

par, de.

m33 = prepositions serving as antecedents of the infinitive.

sans, pour, pour ne pas, afin de, afin de ne pas, etc.

m34 = the preposition *en*, antecedent of the gerund (p44).

m35 = *à quelle heure, combien, comment, depuis quand, lequel, laquelle, lesquels, lesquelles, où, par où, pourquoi, quand, *que, qui,* etc.

*when used as a factor of p25, *que* becomes *ce que.*

m36 = *qui, quoi, lequel, laquelle, lesquels, lesquelles.*

m37 = *quel, quelle, quels, quelles.*

m38 = connectives serving as factors of adjective clauses (p55).

que, dont, à qui, auquel, à laquelle, auxquels, auxquelles, avec qui, avec quoi, avec lequel, chez qui, dans lequel, de qui, duquel, de laquelle, desquels, desquelles, où, pour qui, pour lequel, sur lequel, etc., etc.

m39 = the connective *qui* serving as factor of adjective clauses (p56).

m40 = the connective *que* and *si,* serving as factors of p24.

m41 = the connective of the comparative, *que.*

m42 = the connective of place, *où.*

m43 = connectives of time and duration.

quand, lorsque, pendant que, depuis que.

m44 = certain connectives of cause, purpose, condition, etc.

parce que, puisque, comme, si, etc.

m45 = certain connectives of cause, purpose, condition, concession, etc., requiring a subjunctive sequency.

quoique, bien que, avant que, à moins que, jusqu'à ce que, pour que, etc.

m46 = units which together with the connectives m38 constitute the adjective clauses p55.

il a, il fait, il le fait, il le donne, il me donne, il va, il parle, il me parle, il met, il le met, il voit, il fera, il a vu, il a vue, il a vus, il a fait, il a faite, il a faits, il a faites, etc., etc.

m47 = units which together with the connective *qui* (m39) constitute the adjective clauses p56.

est ici, est sur la table, est à Paris, vient ici, va à Paris, fait ça, le fait, était ici, sera ici, a fait ça, l'a fait, les a faits, doit venir, peut le faire, voulait venir, voulait le faire, est venu, est venue, sont venus, sont venues.

m48 = units which together with the connectives *que* and *si* (m40) constitute the noun clauses p24.

il vient, il viendra, c'est vrai, c'était vrai, ce sera vrai, je suis libre, je suis ici, je suis venu, je peux venir, c'est un livre, etc., etc.

m49 = units which together with the connectives s10 constitute the noun clauses p25.

je veux, vous voulez, je voulais, je voudrais, je peux, il dit, vous dites, vous allez, il vient ici, etc., etc.

m50 = units which together with the connective of the comparative *que* (m41) constitute the clauses p26.

vous ne le croyez, il ne le croit, il ne le dit, etc.

m51 = units serving as factors of clauses p30 (indirect object) and p32 (place).

je veux, je voulais, vous voulez, je peux, vous pouvez, etc.

m52 = units which together with the connectives m58 and m44 constitute respectively clauses p33 and p38.

il est ici, il le fait, il vient, je suis ici, je serai ici, je suis venu, vous voulez, etc.

m53 = units which together with the connectives m45 constitute clauses p39.

il soit ici, je le fasse, il vienne, vous le disiez, il y aille, ce soit bon, etc.

m54 = *beaucoup, assez, tant, autant, trop, plus, moins, peu, un peu*, etc.

m55 = *de* serving as factor of p48 and p49.

m56 = *les, ces, mes, tes, ses, nos, vos, leurs, les autres*, etc.

m57 = *ce, cette, ces.*

m58 = *-ci, -là.*

m59 = *celui, celle, ceux, celles.*

m60 = *celui, celle, ceux, celles, ce, tout ce.*

m61 = *quelque chose, quelqu'un, rien, personne.*

m62 = *de* serving as factor of p21.

m63 = the negative particle *ne.*

m64 = certain adjectives serving as factors of p62.

si.mas.	*beau, bon, difficile, drôle, facile, intéressant, joli, triste*, etc.
si.fem.	*belle, bonne*, etc.
plu.mas.	*beaux, bons*, etc.
plu.fem.	*belles, bonnes*, etc.

m65 = quasi-adverbs of time.

aujourd'hui, hier, demain, avant-hier, après demain, ce matin, cet après-midi, ce soir, hier matin, hier après-midi, hier soir, demain matin, demain après-midi, demain soir, ce mois-ci, cette semaine-ci, cette année-ci, cette fois-ci, le mois dernier, la semaine dernière, l'année dernière, la fois dernière, le mois prochain, la semaine prochaine, l'année prochaine, la fois prochaine, etc.

m66 = the following units :

a. *lundi, mardi, mercredi, jeudi, vendredi, samedi, dimanche.*

b. *janvier, février, mars, avril, mai, juin, juillet, août, septembre, octobre, novembre, décembre.*
c. *printemps, été, automne, hiver.*

m67 = *dernier, prochain.*

m68 = *une heure, deux heures, trois heures*, etc., to *onze heures. midi, minuit.*

m69 = *cinq, dix, et quart, vingt, vingt-cinq, et demie. moins cinq, moins dix, moins un quart, moins vingt, moins vingt-cinq.*

m70 = *dix-neuf cent, dix-huit cent*, etc.

m71 = *un, deux, trois*, etc., to *quatre-vingt-dix-neuf.*

m72 = *longtemps, quelque temps, un mois, un an, une semaine, une heure, un quart d'heure, une demi-heure*, etc.

m73 = *quelques, plusieurs, des, deux, trois, quatre*, etc.

m74 = *moments, instants, secondes, minutes, heures, jours, semaines, mois, ans, siècles.*

m75 = *est-ce que, qu'est-ce que, qui est-ce que, où est-ce que, quand est-ce que*, etc.

Units of the following type might conveniently be added here :

b. *je pense que, je crois que, je suppose que, j'espère que*, etc.
c. *il faut que, je veux que, je crains que, il est nécessaire que*, etc.

m76 = the preposition *à* serving as factor of p27.

m77 = appropriate members of s4, s5, and p2.

s4. *ça, quelque chose, l'autre, le mien, la table*, etc.
s5. *bon, beau, fatigué, fini, commencé*, etc.
p2. *ici, là, sur la table*, etc., *maintenant, aujourd'hui*, etc., *à Jean, à mon ami*, etc., *ensemble, avec moi*, etc.

m78 = past participles of transitive verbs.

si.mas.	*commencé, demandé, donné, écrit, envoyé, fait,* etc.
si.fem.	*commencée, demandée, donnée,* etc.
plu.mas.	*commencés, demandés, donnés,* etc.
plu.fem.	*commencées, demandées, données,* etc.

II. SUM GROUPS

s1 = m75 + s10 + s11.
All units preceding the subject (s2).

s2 = m3 + s12 + s16.
Subject.

s3 = s13 + p3 + s14.
Predicate, but not including the complement (s5) *nor the extensions* (p2).

s4 = s12 + s15 + s16.
Direct object.

s5 = s17 + p4 + p5 + p6 + p7.
Complement (*of verbs of incomplete predication*).

s6 = p29 + p30.
Indirect object.

s7 = m22 + p31 + p32.
Place.

s8 = m23 + s18 + p33.
Time and duration.

s9 = m24 + p34 + p35 + p36 + p37 + p38 + p39.
Various extensions (*or complements*), *including those of manner, cause, result, purpose, frequency, order, condition, concession, hypothesis,* etc.

s10 = m35 + p8 + p9 + p10.
Interrogatives or connectives.

s11 = s7 + s8 + s9.
Complements of place, time, duration, manner, etc., *placed before the subject.*

s12 = p11 + s15.
Nouns and pronouns (excluding personal pronouns) with all their concomitants, adjuncts, modifiers, etc.

s13 = p12 + p13 + p14.
Simple tenses with their modifiers and enclaves.

s14 = p15 + p16.
Infinitive compounds.

s15 = m2 + m4 + p17 + p18 + p19 + p20 + p21 + p22 + p23.
Proper nouns, certain classes of pronouns, and pronoun compounds.

s16 = p24 + p25 + p56.
Noun clauses.

s17 = s12 + m8.
Nouns and various classes of pronouns, with their adjuncts, concomitants, modifiers, etc.

s18 = p45 + p46.
Phrases of time and duration.

s19 = m26 + m30 + m31 + m32.
All prepositions.

s20 = m9 + m10 + p47 + p48 + p49.
Demonstrative, distinguishing, possessive, numeral, ordinal, and fractional adjectives, all necessary concomitants of nouns.

s21 = p50 + p51 + p52.
Nouns and their possible modifiers.

s22 = s17 + m50.
Complement of comparative adjectives and adverbs (not including the connective que).

s23 = m65 + p57 + p58 + p59.
Quasi-adverbs of time.

s24 = m72 + p60.
Quasi-adverbs of time and duration.

s25 = m10 + m54 + p47.
Numeral, ordinal, and fractional adjectives.

III. PRODUCT GROUPS

In the following formulæ all non-essential factors are italicized.

p1 = *s1* × *s2* × s3 × *s4* × *s5* × *p2*.
Complete sentences.

p2 = *s6* × *s7* × *s8* × *s9*.
Various extensions (or complements) of place, time, duration, manner, etc., etc.
The Indirect Object is included for expedient if not for logical reasons.

p3 = *m63* × *m5* × m14 × *m6* × *m21* × m15.
Tenses compounded by auxiliaries and past participles.

p4 = s19 × s17.
Predicative phrases.

p5 = p61 × *p26*.
Predicative adjectives and their modifiers.

p6 = *m20* × m64 × p27.
Certain predicative adjectives and their modifiers, including infinitives preceded by à.

p7 = m78 × *p28*.
Passive past participles with their complementary phrases.

p8 = m37 × p53.
Nouns modified by interrogative adjectives.

p9 = s19 × m36.
Interrogative adverb equivalents.

p10 = s19 × p8.
Interrogative adverb-equivalents containing adjective modifiers (dans quelle rue).

p11 = s20 × s21.
Nouns (with modifiers) and their essential antecedents.

p12 = *m63* × *m5* × m13 × *m6* × *m21.*
Simple tenses (imperative excluded) with their modifiers and enclaves.

p13 = *m63* × *m5* × m13h × *m21.*
Simple imperative negative tenses with modifiers and enclaves.

p14 = m13h × *m7* × *m21.*
Simple imperative affirmative tenses with modifiers and enclaves.

p15 = p40 × p41.
Infinitive compounds in which the antecedents of the infinitive are simple tenses.

p16 = p42 × p41.
Infinitive compounds in which the antecedents of the infinitive are compound tenses.

p17 = m57 × m1 × m58.
Nouns modified by ce—ci, ce—là, etc.

p18 = m59 × p54.
Celui, etc, *modified by phrases.*

p19 = m60 × p55.
Celui, etc., *modified by non-subject clauses.*

p20 = m60 × p56.
Celui, etc., *modified by subject clauses.*

p21 = m61 × m62 × p61.
Quelque chose, etc., *modified by adjectives* (quelque chose de beau).

p22 = m61 × p55.

Quelque chose, etc., *modified by non-subject clauses* (quelque chose que je connais).

p23 = m61 × p56.

Quelque chose, etc., *modified by subject clauses* (quelque chose qui est arrivé).

p24 = m40 × m48.

Noun-clauses with connectives que *and* si (que c'est vrai, si c'est vrai).

p25 = s10 × m49.

Noun-clauses with adverbial connectives (où il va).

p26 = m41 × s22.

Complement of comparative adjectives and adverbs (including the connective que).

p27 = m76 × m18.

Infinitives preceded by à *(corresponding in function with the Latin supine in* -u).

p28 = m32 × m17.

Complementary phrases (in par *and* de) *to passive past participles.*

p29 = m31 × s17.

Phrases expressing the indirect object.

p30 = m31 × m39 × m51.

Phrase-clauses expressing the indirect object.

p31 = m26 × s17.

Clauses expressing place.

p32 = *m26* × m42 × m51.

Clauses and phrase-clauses expressing place.

p33 = m43 × m52.

Clauses expressing time and duration.

(NOTE.—*Clauses of time and duration containing subjunctives are included for reasons of expediency in* p39).

p34 = *m20* × m25 × *p26*.
Adverbs of manner with modifiers.

p35 = m30 × s17.
Clauses expressing manner, cause, purpose, frequency, condition, concession, etc.

p36 = m33 × p43.
Infinitive clauses (expressing manner and purpose).

p37 = m34 × p44.
Gerunds (expressing manner).

p38 = m44 × m52.
Clauses (not containing subjunctives) expressing manner, cause, condition, hypothesis, etc.

p39 = m45 × m53.
Clauses (containing subjunctives) expressing condition, concession, purpose, time, duration, etc.

p40 = *m63* × m16 . . . × *m6* . . . × *m21* + . . . m16.
Simple tenses (together with their modifiers and enclaves) used as antecedents of the infinitive.

p41 = *m63* × m18.
Infinitives together with enclaved pronouns.

p42 = *m63* × m14 × *m6* × *m21* × m17.
Compound tenses (together with their modifiers and enclaves) used as antecedents of the infinitive.

p43 = m18 × *m77*.
Infinitives, together with appropriate objects, complements, extensions, etc.

p44 = m19 × *m77*.
Gerunds (not including en*), together with appropriate objects, complements, extensions*, etc.

p45 = m27 × s23.
Phrases expressing time (hours, days, weeks, months, years, etc.).

p46 = m28 × s24.
Phrases expressing time and duration.

p47 = m9 × m11.
Ordinal adjectives together with their modifiers.

p48 = m54 × m55.
Simple fractionals (or quantitatives) together with de.

p49 = s25 × m55 × m56.
Fractional and ordinal modifiers of nouns, combined, for the sake of expediency, with les, ces, mes, etc.

p50 = p53 × *p54*.
Nouns (already modified by simple adjectives) further modified by adjective phrases.

p51 = s12 × p55.
Nouns (already modified by adjectives and phrases) further modified by non-subject clauses.

p52 = s12 × p56.
Nouns (already modified by adjectives and phrases) further modified by subject clauses.

p53 = *p61* × m1 × *p61*.
Nouns modified (on either side) by adjectives (which themselves are modified by adverbs).

p54 = m29 × s12.
Adjective phrases.

p55 = m38 × m46.
Adjective clauses (non-subject) including connectives.

p56 = m39 × m47.
Adjective clauses (subject) including connectives.

p57 = m66 × *m67*.
Names of days, months, and seasons (with their modifiers).

p58 = m68 × *m69*
Names of hours (with their modifiers).

p59 = m70 × *m71.*
Names of years.

p60 = m73 × m74.
Measures of time.

p61 = m20 × m12.
Adjectives of quality modified by adverbs.

APPENDIX II

GLOSSARY OF TECHNICAL TERMS, WITH THE MEANINGS ATTRIBUTED TO THEM IN THE PAGES OF THIS BOOK

Accidence. That part of etymology which is more especially concerned with the changes of form found in the conjugation of a verb or the declension of a noun, pronoun, or adjective.

Accuracy. The reproducing of a given form in conformity to a given model (not necessarily a classical or traditionally 'correct' model).

Active use of language. Speaking and writing, as opposed to the passive use of language: listening and reading.

Aggregative study. Study in which all the various aspects of lexicology are treated together, instead of being isolated and treated apart as in *Segregative* study.

Alogism. The means of expressing a given concept without the use of any concrete lexicological unit. Alogisms fall into three chief categories: *position, stress and intonation,* and *sous-entendus.* (See p. 41.)

Catenizing. Learning to pronounce accurately and rapidly a given succession of sounds, without conscious calculation, generally apart from all considerations of *meaning.*

A sentence, phrase, or word is said to be 'catenized' when the student can articulate it at a moment's notice with fluency and without conscious effort.

The memorizing or learning by heart of a given unit is only complete when it has been both *catenized* and *semanticized.*

The only sound method of learning the gender of a

French noun is to catenize it to an appropriate adjective (e.g. *le-mur, la-croix, une-belle-promenade*).

[The term *catenating* has been suggested as a more suitable term than the above.]

Cognate. (1) Allied by derivation. (2) A phoneme, a morphon, a language, or a dialect, which is cognate to another or others.

Colloquial. Relating to that style of speech normally used in normal circumstances by the majority of the native speakers of a given language or of a given variety of a given language; as opposed to the classical style of speech based upon literary tradition.

Both the colloquial and classical varieties of speech may be *spoken* and *written.*

The colloquial style may be divided into various ' strata,' according to the social position of the speaker.

Concomitant. Any ergon which is the necessary complement to any other, e.g. *peux, dois, veux, commence à, ai l'intention de,* etc., are concomitants of the infinitive. (See Appendix I, in which p40 and p41 are each concomitant to the other.)

Concretization. A phase of semanticizing. The concrete associating of a given unit of speech with the concept for which it stands (as in ' Material Association '). (See pp. 127, 128.)

Correct. (See *Accuracy.*)

Derivation. That branch of etymology which is more particularly concerned with the deducing of one part of speech from another (*e.g.* the noun *considération* from the verb *considérer*).

As opposed to *inflexion* or *ptosonics,* which is concerned chiefly with conjugation and declension.

Dialect. Variety of a given language (including the classical or standard variety, should such exist).

The popular language of Liége is a Walloon dialect; Walloon is a group of French dialects; French is a group of Neo-Latin dialects; Latin was a group of dialects indigenous to a part of the Italic peninsula.

Direct method. A somewhat vague term loosely denoting a system of language teaching largely based on the doctrine that translation should be excluded in the greatest possible measure.

"The Direct Method expresses neither more nor less than the theory that language should be taught by direct connexion with objects and living ideas."—*Hardress O'Grady.*

Disintegration. (1) The resolving of an integral group of units into its component parts. (2) Learning the meaning of the individual words of which a previously memorized sentence is composed.

Documentary. Relating to knowledge *about* a given subject, as opposed to the assimilation of the subject itself (or *Assimilatory* knowledge).

Ergon. The unit of ergonics. Any speech-unit considered from the point of view of its *function* or powers of combining with other units, as distinct from its *meaning* or *form.*

Ergonics. The science which teaches us (*a*) to classify the units of a given language according to their function in the sentence; (*b*) to build up original (*i.e.* unknown) units from the smaller known units of which they are composed.

Ergonics comprises the whole range of analysis and synthesis from the sentence at one extreme down to the insecables at the other extreme, whereas *Syntax* is only concerned with the reduction of a sentence into Subject, Predicate, and Object, and *vice versa.*

Etymology. (1) The science which teaches us (*a*) to deduce original (*i.e.* unknown) monologs from a given root or cognate (e.g. *journaux* from *journal*, *finissant* from *finir*, *lentement* from *lent*); (*b*) to deduce the meaning of a given unknown word by its morphological relation to its ancestral or other cognates (*e.g.* knowing the meaning of *cadre*, to deduce the meaning of *encadrer*). (2) The science which treats of the history of words in general.

The unit of etymology is the *etymon.*

Most of the phenomena of *inflexion* (*ptosonics* or *accidence*) and *derivation* come into the province of etymology. (See p. 44.)

Etymon. The unit of etymology. Any group of significative speech-units cognate with each other and with their common ancestral form or forms. (See p. 44.)

Graphic continuity. The representation of two or more units of speech by means of one continuous written unit.

Graphic continuity involves the terms *monolog, polylog,* and *miolog.*

Immediate comprehension. (See *Subconscious Comprehension.*)

Immediate (or *non-mediate*) *expression.* The power of expressing a given concept without conscious effort, synthesis, or translation.

Inflexions. (1) Morphological variations of a given etymon consequent on the use of affixes, vowel-change, etc., corresponding to definite etymological or ergonic phenomena. E.g., *looked, gave,* and *them* are the respective inflexions of *look, give,* and *they* (but *a* is not an inflexion of *an,* nor *an* of *a*). (2) The changes undergone by words to express the relations of case, gender, person, tense, etc.

Insecables. The ultimate significative units of speech. They constitute fractions of greater units but cannot themselves be decomposed into lesser units. (See p. 45.)

Integral. Considered as a whole, without analysis, without consideration of the component parts.

Intellectual exercises. Exercises involving the development and use of the *reasoning* powers, as opposed to *mechanical* exercises, which develop the *reflex* powers.

Language. The medium by which thoughts and emotions are expressed and conveyed from one person to another. (See p. 29.)

Language is often confused by the thoughtless with *literature* or *literary variety of language.* (See *Literature.*)

Letter. (1) The ultimate unit of written speech. Any conventional symbol standing for any given phoneme or phonemes. (2) The unit of orthography. Any symbol used in a conventional traditional spelling system; such symbol may or may not correspond to any given phoneme or phonomes.

Lexicological units. (1) Sentences, phrases, clauses, polylogs, monologs, miologs; morphons, etymons, ergons, semanticons. (2) Words, their components and their multiples.

Lexicology. The study of *words* in all their aspects. Phonetics, phonology, orthography, orthoepy, etymology, ergonics, and semantics are branches of lexicology.

Literature. (1) An artificial and æsthetic application of language proper. (2) The application of language to artistic purposes.

Localization. A mnemonic process consisting of forming *place-associations.*

Manifestations. The two mediums by which language is manifested to the perception—viz. speaking and writing.

Material association. A mode of semanticizing in which the unit is associated more or less materially with the object, quality, or action which it denotes.

Mechanical exercises. Exercises involving the use and development of the *reflex* powers, as opposed to *intellectual* exercises which develop the *reasoning* powers.

Memorizing. Learning a given unit by heart. The special variety of memorizing which aims at the correct, fluent, and ready mastery of the succession of sounds contained in the unit is termed *Catenizing.* The special variety of memorizing which aims at the correct and ready association of the unit with its *meaning* is termed *Semanticizing.*

Method. (1) A given means or system of learning or of teaching a language. (2) A given means or system of learning or of teaching a given aspect of language. (3) A book embodying (1) or (2).

Microcosm. A vocabulary of the more important and most characteristic units of a given language, selected by the method-writer or teacher in accordance with and as a compromise between the principles of *frequency, ergonic combination, concreteness, proportion,* and *general expediency.*

Minimals. Units which it is either impossible or inexpedient for a given purpose to submit to further analysis.

Miolog. A significative or functional unit such as an affix; miologs are generally considered as fractions of words. (See p. 40.)

Mnemonics. The science which treats of the systematic and rational cultivation and development of the power of memory.

Monolog. A word considered merely as a conventional unit of vocabulary in virtue of its being (*a*) written all in one piece without any interrupting break or space; (*b*) separated by a break or space from the words with which it may happen to be juxtaposed. (See p. 40.)

Morphology. The science which teaches us the *form* of speech-units, as distinct from their *meaning* and *function.* Phonetics, Phonology, Orthography, and Etymology are special branches of morphology. (See p. 43.)

Morphon. The unit of morphology. Any speech unit considered from the point of view of its *form,* as apart from its *meaning* or *function.*

Orthoepy. The art of deducing a given pronunciation from a given orthographic form.

The various values of *ough* in *plough, cough, ought, thorough, enough* do not constitute a *phonetic* difficulty, but an *orthoepic* difficulty.

Prior to the modern phonetic movement, pronunciation was always studied and taught on an 'orthoepic' basis—that is to say, sounds were considered to be the oral interpretation of the *letters* of a given conventional spelling.

Orthography. The art of writing the right letters in the right places according to a given conventional system of spelling.

The unit of orthography is the *letter*, as that of phonetics is the *sound*, and as that of phonology is the *phoneme*.

Orthography and orthoepy alone constitute the artificial aspect of language.

Passive aspect of language. Listening and reading, as opposed to the active use of language: speaking and writing.

Philology. The science which treats of the history, evolution, and developments of language in general or of a given language or dialect.

Phoneme. The unit of phonology. A sound, an intimate sound combination, a stress or a tone, together with all the variants used by different speakers in the same or in different dialects in the same or in different periods of history.

The phoneme represented by the vowel-letter *o* in the English word *bone* remains the same phoneme whether pronounced [oʊ] (as in the south of England), [əʊ] as in Cockney), [oː] as in Scotland, or [ɑː] as in Early English. (See p. 43.) (See *Phonology.*)

Phonetics. The science which investigates the formation of speech-sounds and the mode of using them in connected speech.

The unit of phonetics proper is the *speech-sound.*

Various aspects of phonetics are associated respectively with acoustics, physiology, lexicology, and philology.

Phonology. That branch of phonetics which is more particularly concerned with the various values of a given phoneme (*a*) during the course of its history, (*b*) according to the dialect in which it is used.

The *phonologist* teaches us that the vowel in *cut* generally has the value of [ʌ] in the south of England, and the value of [u] in certain northern dialects, whereas the *phonetician* teaches us how to pronounce either or both of these sounds, and tells us how they are formed by the organs of speech. (See *Phoneme.*)

Pidgin. Abnormal dialect of a given language as developed and used by speakers of mixed nationalities or races, as the *pidgin English* of the Chinese ports or the *sabir* of the Mediterranean.

Polylog. Unit composed of two or more monologs in juxtaposition but functionally and semantically equal to a *monolog.*

Primary matter. All units learnt by heart integrally (*i.e.* without analysis or synthesis).

Ptosonic. Relating to inflexions as distinct from other derived forms.

Reform method. Generally synonymous with *Direct Method* (*q.v.*).

Secondary matter. All units derived or built up by the pupil from Primary matter (*q.v.*).

Segregation. The principle by which each aspect, phase, or particular difficulty of a language is isolated from the others in order to secure the complete and sole attention of the pupil, thus avoiding confusion or diffusion of thought.

Segregative study. Study in which all the various aspects of lexicology are isolated and treated apart, as when we learn the *pronunciation* of words apart from their *meanings* or *functions* and *vice versa.*

Semantic. Pertaining to meanings.

Semanticizing. (1) Conveying to the pupil (by means of Material Association, Translation, Definition, or Context) the meaning of a given unit. (2) Memorizing the meaning of a given unit, apart from all considerations of correct or fluent articulation.

[The author has not yet succeeded in finding two different terms with which to distinguish these two connotations; he would be glad to receive suggestions in regard to this matter.]

Semanticon. The unit of meaning or of thought. Any group of speech-units each of which expresses the same or nearly the same idea. (Also called a *semantic group.*)

The identification of semanticons in two or more languages constitutes the basis of all rational *translation*. (See pp. 44, 45.)

Semantics. The science which treats of the *meaning* of speech-units, as distinct from their *form* or *function*.

Historical semantics (often called *semasiology*) treats of the changes in meaning of a given etymon during the course of its history and in the range of its geographical distribution.

The unit of semantics is the *semanticon*. (See pp. 44, 45.)

Sound (or *speech-sound*). The unit of phonetics proper. The acoustic effect consequent upon modifying a current of air by the organs of speech.

A speech-sound is a fixed quantity, determined by a given conformation of the organs of speech. A speech-sound may cease to be used, and its place may be taken by some other sound, but a speech-sound proper is not subject to evolution and can therefore have no history. What is generally termed *the history of sounds* is in reality *the history of phonemes*.

Spatialization. The utilization of space with the object of converting the abstract into a semblance of concrete form.

Study. Work performed by anybody in order to get to know something or to get to know how to do something. Study may be conscious or subconscious ; the *extent* of study may be *complete* or *partial* ; the *degree* of study may be *documentary* or *assimilative*.

Subconscious comprehension. The art of understanding connected speech (spoken or written) without conscious effort, analysis, or translation.

The term *immediate* (or *non-mediate*) *comprehension* may be used in the same sense.

Substitution table. A certain arrangement in vertical columns of units having certain powers of combination. (See pp. 180 to 183.)

(Every p-group of an ergonic chart is necessarily a substitution table.)

Synonym. A given unit expressing the same or nearly the same meaning as another given unit.

Synopticity. (See *Uebersichtlichkeit.*)

Syntax. That branch of ergonics which is concerned with the analysis of a sentence into subject, predicate, and object, or the building up of a sentence from these three components.

Transcription. (1) The converting of an orthographic text into a phonetic text or *vice versa.* (2) The result of such conversion.

Translation. (1) The equivalent in a given language of a unit or of a series of units in another language. (2) The process of discovering or the act of expressing such equivalences.

If any given pair of units are cognate in derivation, the result is an *etymological translation*; if they are cognate in meaning, the result is a *semantic translation. Literal translation* is a term which appears to be meaningless.

Uebersichtlichkeit. Visual correlation, 'surveyability,' 'synopticity,' the quality possessed by synoptic tables.

Undifferentiated Programme. A programme which does not observe the principle of *segregation.*

Unit. (See *Lexicological unit.*)

Vehicular language. The language which is used as the medium of explanations.

Visual correlation. (See *Uebersichtlichkeit.*)

Visualization. The power of forming *mental images,* similar to *localization* (*q.v.*).

Word. A loose term without any precise meaning, designating various types of lexicological units, generally monologs.

APPENDIX III

LIST OF PHONETIC SYMBOLS

THE symbols have the values shown by the italic letters in the words given as illustrations.

A. FRENCH AND ENGLISH SOUNDS

Phonetic Symbol	*Value of Symbol when used in French Words*	*Value of Symbol when used in English Words*
VOWELS		
iː	l*i*re	s*ee*
i	s*i*	—
ɪ	—	g*i*ve
e	bl*é*	—
ɛ	b*e*lle	p*e*n (also first vowel element in wh*ere*)
æ	—	c*a*t
a	p*a*tte	(First vowel element in n*ow*)
ʌ	—	c*u*t
uː	j*ou*r	t*oo*
u	t*ou*t	—
ʊ	—	b*oo*k
oː	v*ô*tre	—
o	b*eau*	(First vowel element in g*o*)
ɔː	f*o*rt	*a*ll
ɔ	b*o*nne	st*o*p
ɑː	p*â*te	*a*sk
ɑ	p*a*s	—
əː	—	f*ir*st
ə	p*e*ser	*a*gain
y	l*u*ne	—

Phonetic Symbol	*Value of Symbol when used in French Words*	*Value of Symbol when used in English Words*
VOWELS—*cont.*		
øː	cr*eu*se	—
ø	p*eu*	—
œː	p*eu*r	—
œ	*œu*f	—
ɛ̃	f*in*	—
ɑ̃	t*an*t	—
ɔ̃	b*on*	—
œ̃	br*un*	—
DIPHTHONGS		
ɛɪ	—	l*a*te
aɪ	—	f*i*ve
oʊ	—	g*o*
aʊ	—	n*ow*
ɔɪ	—	b*oy*
ɪə	—	d*ear*
ɛə	—	wh*ere*
ʊə	—	s*ure*
CONSONANTS		
p	*p*as	*p*ut
b	*b*as	*b*e
t	*t*as	*t*ake
d	*d*eux	*d*o
k	*qu*el	*c*ome
g	*g*ant	*g*o
m	*m*a	*m*y
n	*n*on	*n*o
ɲ	ag*n*eau	—
ŋ	—	bri*ng*
ɥ	n*u*it	—
w	*ou*est	*w*ait
f	*f*eu	*f*ive
v	*v*ous	*v*ery
θ	—	*th*in
ð	—	*th*en

Phonetic Symbol	*Value of Symbol when used in French Words*	*Value of Symbol when used in English Words*
CONSONANTS—*cont.*		
ɹ	—	*r*ed
r	*r*at	—
s	*s*i	*s*o
z	dou*z*e	ro*s*e
ʃ	*ch*ou	*sh*ut
ʒ	*j*eu	plea*s*ure
j	*y*eux	*y*es
h	—	*h*at
l	be*ll*e	*l*end
ɫ	—	be*ll* (*final*)
l̥	peup*l*e (*final*)	—

VARIOUS

tʃ = *ch* in *ch*urch.

dʒ = *j* in *j*udge.

ɟ = the Hungarian sound *gy* in ma*gy*ar.

ˈ indicates that the following syllable is stressed.

ː indicates that the vowel to which it is attached is long.

INDEX